BRITISH BUDDHISM

Teachings, practice and development

Robert Bluck

Routledge
Taylor & Francis Group

LONDON AND NEW YORK

First published 2006
by Routledge
2 Park Square, Milton Park, Abingdon, Oxon OX14 4RN

Simultaneously published in the USA and Canada
by Routledge
270 Madison Ave, New York, NY 10016

*Routledge is an imprint of the Taylor & Francis Group,
an informa business*

© 2006 Robert Bluck

Typeset in Times New Roman by
Newgen Imaging Systems (P) Ltd, Chennai, India
Printed and bound in Great Britain by
Biddles Ltd, King's Lynn

British Library Cataloguing in Publication Data
A catalogue record for this book is available
from the British Library

Library of Congress Cataloging in Publication Data
Bluck, Robert, 1947–
British Buddhism: teachings, practice and development / Robert Bluck.
p. cm. – (Routledge critical studies in Buddhism)
Includes bibliographical references and index.
1. Buddhism–Great Britain–History. I. Title. II. Series.

BQ709.G72B58 2006
294.30941–dc22   2005033384

ISBN10: 0–415–39515–1 (hbk)
ISBN10: 0–203–97011–X (ebk)

ISBN13: 978–0–415–39515–1 (hbk)
ISBN13: 978–0–203–97011–9 (ebk)

FOR ALL BUDDHISTS IN BRITAIN

BRITISH BUDDHISM

This book is the first comprehensive account of Buddhism in contemporary Britain. It provides a survey of the seven largest Buddhist organizations, including both traditional schools and more controversial 'new Buddhist movements': the Forest Sangha and the Samatha Trust (Theravāda), Sōtō Zen Serene Reflection Meditation and Sōka Gakkai (Japanese), the Tibetan Karma Kagyu and New Kadampa traditions and the Friends of the Western Buddhist Order. Based on extensive fieldwork, it examines how and to what extent Buddhist traditions in Britain are changing from their Asian roots and whether any forms of 'British Buddhism' are beginning to emerge.

The book covers the full range of teaching and practice in each tradition and includes both an historical overview and new statistical information on British Buddhists. It serves as an important reference point for further studies in this increasingly popular field.

Robert Bluck teaches world religions as an Associate Lecturer at the Open University. He has been a practising Buddhist for over 30 years and has conducted doctoral research into the teaching, practice and development of different forms of Buddhism in Britain.

ROUTLEDGE CRITICAL STUDIES
IN BUDDHISM
General Editors
Charles S. Prebish and Damien Keown

Routledge Critical Studies in Buddhism is a comprehensive study of the Buddhist tradition. The series explores this complex and extensive tradition from a variety of perspectives, using a range of different methodologies.

The series is diverse in its focus, including historical studies, textual translations and commentaries, sociological investigations, bibliographic studies and considerations of religious practice as an expression of Buddhism's integral religiosity. It also presents materials on modern intellectual historical studies, including the role of Buddhist thought and scholarship in a contemporary, critical context and in the light of current social issues. The series is expansive and imaginative in scope, spanning more than two and a half millennia of Buddhist history. It is receptive to all research works that inform and advance our knowledge and understanding of the Buddhist tradition.

A SURVEY OF VINAYA
LITERATURE
Charles S. Prebish

THE REFLEXIVE NATURE OF
AWARENESS
Paul Williams

ALTRUISM AND REALITY
Paul Williams

BUDDHISM AND HUMAN RIGHTS
*Edited by Damien Keown, Charles Prebish
and Wayne Husted*

WOMEN IN THE FOOTSTEPS OF
THE BUDDHA
Kathryn R. Blackstone

THE RESONANCE OF EMPTINESS
Gay Watson

AMERICAN BUDDHISM
*Edited by Duncan Ryuken Williams and
Christopher Queen*

IMAGING WISDOM
Jacob N. Kinnard

PAIN AND ITS ENDING
Carol S. Anderson

EMPTINESS APPRAISED
David F. Burton

THE SOUND OF LIBERATING
TRUTH
*Edited by Sallie B. King and
Paul O. Ingram*

BUDDHIST THEOLOGY
*Edited by Roger R. Jackson and
John J. Makransky*

BUDDHISM, CONFLICT AND
VIOLENCE IN MODERN
SRI LANKA
Edited by Mahinda Deegalle

THERAVĀDA BUDDHISM
AND THE BRITISH
ENCOUNTER
Religious, missionary and
colonial experience in nineteenth
century Sri Lanka
Elizabeth Harris

BEYOND ENLIGHTENMENT
Buddhism, religion, modernity
Richard Cohen

BUDDHISM IN THE
PUBLIC SPHERE
Reorienting global interdependence
Peter D. Hershock

BRITISH BUDDHISM
Teachings, practice and development
Robert Bluck

The following titles are published in association with the
Oxford Centre for Buddhist Studies

 Oxford Centre for Buddhist Studies
a project of The Society for the Wider Understanding of the Buddhist Tradition

The *Oxford Centre for Buddhist Studies* conducts and promotes rigorous teaching and
research into all forms of the Buddhist tradition.

EARLY BUDDHIST METAPHYSICS
Noa Ronkin

MIPHAM'S DIALECTICS AND THE DEBATES ON EMPTINESS
Karma Phuntsho

HOW BUDDHISM BEGAN
The conditioned genesis of the early teachings
Richard F. Gombrich

BUDDHIST MEDITATION
An anthology of texts from the Pāli canon
Sarah Shaw

REMAKING BUDDHISM FOR MEDIEVAL NEPAL
The fifteenth-century reformation of Newar Buddhism
Will Tuladhar-Douglas

CONTENTS

CONTENTS

PREFACE

This study examines the origins, development and characteristics of the seven largest Buddhist organizations in Britain, including both traditional schools and more controversial 'new Buddhist movements', to determine how and to what extent they are changing from their Asian roots and whether any forms of 'British Buddhism' are beginning to emerge. Ninian Smart's dimensional analysis of religions is used as a model, to ensure that the full range of relevant teachings and practices are included. The book is edited and adapted from my doctoral research, *The Dimensions of Buddhism in Britain* (Bluck, 2005): this included extensive fieldwork, with many visits to local groups and national centres and structured interviews with teachers and experienced practitioners in each of the seven traditions.

The Introduction explains the objectives and how the seven traditions were chosen. Chapter 2 gives an historical overview, tracing Buddhism's introduction into Britain, both in general and in terms of its different traditions, particularly during the second half of the twentieth century. New statistical information here shows the number of groups in each tradition, and work on the 2001 UK Census data clarifies the number of individual Buddhists in Britain. Chapters 3 and 4 examine the Forest Sangha and the Samatha Trust from the Theravāda tradition. Chapters 5 and 6 consider Serene Reflection Meditation (Sōtō Zen) and Sōka Gakkai, both originally Japanese. Chapters 7 and 8 look at the Tibetan Karma Kagyu and New Kadampa traditions. Chapter 9 examines Friends of the Western Buddhist Order, a self-consciously westernized tradition. Each of these chapters begins with an historical overview of the tradition and then uses Smart's seven dimensions to build up an overall picture. Chapter 10 summarizes the findings and looks across the seven dimensions thematically before assessing the extent and character of adaptations and presenting conclusions on the common features of British Buddhism.

The study complements contemporary work on American Buddhism and builds on previous work on British Buddhism, describing and analysing a representative sample of the full range of traditions for the first time. It allows similarities and differences to be traced in detail by tradition or by theme and it presents findings in the context of how Buddhism changes when moving to a new country. The rapid growth of Buddhism in Britain during the second half of the twentieth century suggests that its influence is moving beyond that of a fringe religion. I hope that this book will make a contribution to the understanding of religion and social change, and the development of Buddhism in the West, as well as being of interest to students and practitioners of Buddhism in Britain.

ACKNOWLEDGEMENTS

Many British Buddhists have contributed to this book, by welcoming me into their groups and centres, sharing their personal practice in interviews and discussion, and generously offering their time and expertise. I am particularly grateful to Ajahn Sumedho (Forest Sangha), Peter Harvey (Samatha Trust), Rev. Master Daishin Morgan (OBC), Jamie Cresswell (SGI-UK), Lama Yeshe Losal (Karma Kagyu), Kelsang Namgyal (NKT) and Vishvapani (FWBO), as well as all the interviewees from these seven traditions. My thanks also to Christine Blain for transcribing interview tapes, Rev. Dr Ian Duffield for advice on contemporary British Christianity, Jane Moore for obtaining copies of vital research material, the Open University for staff development grants to support the original research and my students for their searching questions on Western Buddhism. I am happy to acknowledge previous research by Sandra Bell, Alison Church, Marilyn Goswell and Philip Mellor and more recent published works by Helen Waterhouse and David Kay. Several people read and commented on draft chapters. I am grateful to Prof. Jan Reed and Trevor Blackwell for advice on research methodology. Ajahn Candasiri, Veronica Voiels, Rev. Master Daishin Morgan, Jamie Cresswell, Ani Lhamo, James Belither and Vishvapani provided valuable feedback on specific chapters, and Helen Waterhouse offered timely and helpful advice on the conclusions. My deepest thanks are due to Prof. Peter Harvey for supervising the research with great understanding, sound advice and meticulous care.

Beyond acknowledgement or thanks, my patient and precious wife Caroline has read and reread the drafts of this work, supporting and encouraging me throughout this lengthy project and throughout our life together.

ABBREVIATIONS

BD   *Buddhist Directory*
Com. Int   Community of Interbeing
EST   English Sangha Trust
FPMT   Foundation for the Preservation of the Mahāyāna Tradition
FWBO   Friends of the Western Buddhist Order
IZA   International Zen Association
J.   Japanese
JOBC   *Journal of the Order of Buddhist Contemplatives*
JTHBA   *Journal of Throssel Hole Buddhist Abbey*
JTHP   *Journal of Throssel Hole Priory*
Liturgy   *The Liturgy of the Order of Buddhist Contemplatives*
            for the Laity
NBO   Network of Buddhist Organisations
NKT   New Kadampa Tradition
NRM   New Religious Movement
OBC   Order of Buddhist Contemplatives
OED   *Oxford English Dictionary*
P.   Pali
RelUK   *Religions in the UK*
SGI   Sōka Gakkai International
SGI-UK   Sōka Gakkai International–UK
Skt   Sanskrit
SRM   Serene Reflection Meditation
Tib.   Tibetan
WBO   Western Buddhist Order
ZMS   Zen Mission Society
ZPCT   Zen Practice Centre Trust

1

INTRODUCTION

At the beginning of the twentieth century, few people in Britain knew anything of Buddhism. A handful of academics were translating ancient Buddhist texts, and some enthusiastic amateurs saw Buddhism mainly as a philosophical hobby rather than a living religion. The small number of practising Buddhists, initially centred mainly on a single group in London, grew slowly during the first half of the century, and expanded significantly during the 1960s. Since then both monastic centres and lay groups have developed, sometimes quite rapidly, and the main Buddhist traditions and sub-traditions are now firmly established in Britain.

Buddhism began of course as a religion of the Indian subcontinent and spread gradually into Sri Lanka, south-east Asia and China during its first 1,000 years, and later into Japan and Tibet. Its teachings and practices slowly adapted to the prevailing cultural, spiritual and psychological backgrounds of the countries involved so that modern Theravāda, Tibetan and Zen Buddhism (while retaining many common elements) sometimes appear quite different to each other.

Although Buddhism is comparatively new in the West, we may at least begin to examine how it is changing in this new context. The Buddhist Society's first president, Christmas Humphreys (1901–83), claimed as early as 1958 that 'a definitely Western form of Buddhism must in time emerge' (Humphreys, 1958: 126); but over 30 years later, while tracing the interaction between Buddhism and Western culture, Stephen Batchelor found no such distinctively Western Buddhism and warned against trying to guess the future. Instead he described a 'spectrum of adaptation', ranging from those holding firmly to a 'pure tradition' (and who only tolerate minimal change to ensure survival) to innovators who wish to abandon *all* previous traditions, which they see as 'weighed down with cultural burdens' (Batchelor, 1994: 337, 379).

This 'spectrum of adaptation' might be seen as applying to Buddhism in Britain. Humphreys suggested in 1956 that 'an English form of Buddhism' was already beginning to appear and later asserted that 'most English Buddhists are frankly eclectic', choosing elements which they found helpful (Humphreys, 1956: 6; 1968: 80). More recently, Helen Waterhouse (1997: 27) has argued that the various Buddhist schools will adapt differently in Britain, since each 'calls on different authority sources to authenticate its practices'; and

1

David Kay (2004: 3) has referred to 'the increasing diversification of the British Buddhist landscape'.

The comments from these four practitioners and academics suggest a series of challenging and loosely related questions about Buddhism in Britain, its character and adaptation, its authority sources and diversity, and its specific teaching and practice. What is the extent and significance of Buddhism in Britain? Why are people attracted to it? What do British Buddhists believe about the Buddha and his teachings? Which forms of spiritual practice have they adopted, and which moral precepts do they follow? How do they organize monastic and lay groups, and what kinds of sacred space and iconography have they created? Beyond these lies a more overarching question: has Buddhism in Britain merely copied the original Asian traditions, or are we able to see new developments, new seeds or shoots that may be growing into distinctive forms of 'British Buddhism'?

These questions will inform much of the work that follows, and we shall return in the final chapter to the four writers quoted above to evaluate their judgements and predictions. The overall aim here is to trace the origins, development and characteristics of the various traditions of Buddhism in Britain, to see how and to what extent their teaching and practice is changing in this new Western context.

Ninian Smart's 'dimensional analysis of worldviews' (Smart, 1996: 8–14) has distinct advantages as an appropriate model of world religions to help structure the investigation. It is sympathetic towards Buddhism, avoids theistic overtones and may legitimately be used to draw comparisons within religious traditions as well as between them. Smart's seven interrelated dimensions have been used to help define more specific objectives. These are as follows: to examine the nature and relative importance of meditation, devotional practice and other activities in different British Buddhist groups (the *Ritual or Practical Dimension*); to examine which teachings are emphasized, downplayed or reinterpreted, and the role of study and teaching (the *Doctrinal or Philosophical Dimension*); to examine how British Buddhists are appropriating, responding to and adding to the stories of their traditions (the *Mythic or Narrative Dimension*); to examine the range of feelings and attitudes fostered by different traditions and their role in attracting followers (the *Experiential or Emotional Dimension*); to examine how traditional moral precepts and monastic codes are related to and utilized (the *Ethical or Legal Dimension*); to examine the organization of various groups and the role of teachers and leaders (the *Organizational or Social Dimension*); and finally to examine the range of buildings, artefacts and artistic expression being developed to support Buddhist practice (the *Material or Artistic Dimension*).

Applying these objectives to the different traditions of Buddhism in Britain will help the construction of an overall picture, showing contrasts and similarities. Of course this is not a static picture: traditions may start in Britain as transplants of their Asian parents – perhaps even copying their internal diversity – but may later develop different characteristics, with variable patterns of adaptation to their new context. Smart's dimensional analysis will be used as a framework rather than a straightjacket and teachings and practice will be dealt with rather differently in each tradition. To avoid constant repetition, the seven dimensions will usually be referred to as the *Practice Dimension*, the *Doctrinal Dimension*, the *Narrative Dimension*, the *Experiential Dimension*, the *Ethical Dimension*, the *Social Dimension* and the *Artistic Dimension*.

A detailed analysis of organizations listed in recent editions of the *Buddhist Directory* (*BD*) (1997, 2000) and *Religions in the UK* (*RelUK*) (1997, 2001) suggests that by the end of the twentieth century there were over 30 different traditions or sub-traditions of Buddhism in Britain with almost 1,000 Buddhist groups and centres in all. It would be impractical to explore every tradition and group fully, and a compromise is needed to ensure both broad representation and a reasonably thorough investigation.

Over three-quarters of the groups and centres listed were associated with seven traditions, either through formal affiliation or more informal support. Sōka Gakkai International UK (SGI-UK), part of a Japanese-based lay movement, claimed 300 groups in Britain (*RelUK*, 2001: 167), though none of these were listed. The New Kadampa Tradition (NKT), a Western development of Tibetan Buddhism, claimed 183 groups and centres (*BD*, 2000: 6), though not all of them were listed. Friends of the Western Buddhist Order (FWBO), a self-consciously westernized movement, had 78 groups and centres listed. The Karma Kagyu tradition had 50 groups and centres, many of them linked to Samye Ling Tibetan Buddhist Centre. The Forest Sangha, a Western branch of a Thai Theravāda monastic tradition, had 4 monasteries and 32 affiliated lay groups, with informal support from other Theravāda groups. The Serene Reflection Meditation tradition (SRM), a Sōtō Zen school centred on the Order of Buddhist Contemplatives (OBC), had 4 monastic centres and 28 affiliated lay groups, and the Samatha Trust, a Western Theravāda lay movement, had 31 groups.

As we shall see, there are also many other smaller traditions; these, however, appear to be the seven largest organizations. Each of them will be examined in a separate chapter, grouped within their four different geographical backgrounds: the 'Southern' or Theravāda Buddhism of south-east Asia (Forest Sangha, Samatha Trust); the 'Eastern' (or more precisely 'East Asian') Buddhism of China and Japan (SRM, SGI-UK); the 'Northern' Buddhism of Tibet (Karma Kagyu, NKT); and the 'Western' Buddhism developed by the FWBO. The focus throughout will be largely on the substantial number of 'convert Buddhists' or 'white Buddhists', rather than the Asian Buddhist community in Britain. Before proceeding to these seven case studies, however, we need to consider more broadly how Buddhism came to Britain, and how its complex pattern developed here during the twentieth century.

2

AN OVERVIEW OF BUDDHISM IN BRITAIN

Scholars and Victorians

The history of Buddhism in Britain sits within the context of Buddhism's changing relationship with the West and the gradual decline of Christianity in Britain. Europeans largely ignored or condemned 'non-Christian' religions until rationalist views began to emerge in the late eighteenth century, according to Batchelor, and during the nineteenth century Buddhism was seen as either 'a field of rational scientific knowledge' or 'an object of romantic fantasy' (Batchelor, 1994: xii). The divisions between Anglicans, Nonconformists and Catholics were compounded by further nineteenth-century splits, and British churches began to lose their authoritative position, as religious belief and practice were increasingly seen as private matters of personal conscience rather than public assertions of the creeds (Ellis, 1988: 49, 55). Harris described the Victorian period as more complex than a progression from initial devotion through anguished doubt towards Edwardian agnosticism, but she concluded that it was 'the diversity and privatisation of religion, rather than unbelief' which eventually led towards a more secular society (Harris, 1994: 150, 179).

There was at least some awareness of Buddhism in Britain before 1800. The *Oxford English Dictionary* (*OED*) gives the earliest recorded usage of 'Buddha' as 1681, long before 'dharma' (1796) or 'Buddhism' and 'Buddhist' (1801). In the early nineteenth century 'other religions' began to be studied in their own right, though still from a rationalist viewpoint. According to Thomas (1988: 74), there was some intellectual appreciation of Hinduism and Buddhism, though they were also condemned for idol-worship. By the 1830s Buddhism attracted closer attention, being seen by some as 'the religious beliefs and practices of most of Asia' (Almond, 1988: 11). Early written attacks on Buddhism by Christian missionaries were often biased and confused; but a few books, such as R. Spence Hardy's *Manual of Budhism* [*sic*] (1853), were more scholarly and 'ironically helped to popularise in England the religion which their authors were working to supplant in the East' (Clausen, 1975: 2).

There was some sympathy towards 'other religions' amongst liberal theologians. F.D. Maurice, for example, looked for good in all of them, and saw in Buddhism 'a profound feeling of reverence for the human spirit' (quoted in Thomas, 1988: 81). Reasons for studying Buddhism included the appeal of an ancient tradition, the desire for intellectual freedom and analogies between Christian and Buddhist ideas (Brear, 1975: 138–9), though such study usually involved Buddhist texts rather than contact with Asian Buddhists. Much confusion remained, with Robert Childers complaining in 1876 that Buddhism was being described as either 'a system of barren metaphysics... [or] sheer mysticism... [or] a code of pure and beautiful morality... [or] a selfish abstraction from the world, a systematic repression of every impulse and emotion' (quoted in Clausen, 1975: 7).

Buddhism was often measured against prevailing British values and applauded for its charity, patience and humility, its fine moral precepts and 'lack of obscenity and vice' compared to Hinduism, but also criticized as lacking 'any sense of sin' and (worse still) 'any sense of duty' (Brear, 1975: 150–1). Almond has neatly called this 'the *creation* of Buddhism' by the Victorians, who saw the East from a viewpoint of confident superiority. Contemporary Asian Buddhism was seen as inferior to the 'ideal textual Buddhism of the past', which had become part of Victorian scholarly culture (Almond, 1988: 12, 40).

Further Buddhist terms came into English usage during the course of the century, with the *OED* listing 'karma' (1827), 'nirvana' (1836) and 'Eightfold Path' (1845); 'bhikkhu' (1846), 'Arahat' (1850) and 'sangha' (1858); and 'Hinayana' (1868), 'Mahayana' (1868) and 'Theravada' (1875). This suggests a progressive recognition of the Buddha, an associated religion, its teachings, its adherents and finally its main schools.

The Buddha was seen as a mythological figure until about 1830, his historicity only being widely accepted during the 1850s: he was sometimes compared to Luther, with Buddhism pictured as a reform movement like the Protestant Reformation (Almond, 1988: 55–6, 73). He was praised for his personal qualities, said to include truthfulness, humility, chastity, patience and self-sacrifice, and 'superior mental endowments... sanctity of character... serene gentleness... wisdom and eloquence... [and above all] compassion and sympathy': we may well conclude with Almond that in English eyes 'the Buddha was an ideal Victorian gentleman' (Almond, 1988: 77–8, 79).

Understanding of Buddhist *teaching* was often confused and inaccurate, concentrating on the supposed pessimism of suffering: rebirth seemed alien to many Victorians, and the notion of *anattā* (not-self) seemed incomprehensible. Some writers praised Buddhism's tolerance and peacefulness, while others condemned these as indifference. Buddhist ethics were often seen as second only to Christianity, though suspicions remained that teachings of atheism, karma and rebirth undermined morality by making it wholly selfish (Almond, 1988: 81ff., 112–15).

Two scholars stand out in the struggle to unravel the truth about Buddhism. Max Müller (1823–1900) spent 50 years at Oxford working on translations of Hindu and Buddhist texts, helping to establish 'Comparative Religion' as an academic discipline rather than an ecclesiastical preserve. As a linguist, however, he tended to rely on scriptural texts as representing the whole tradition of a religion, distrusting evidence from other disciplines (Kitigawa and Strong, 1985: 184, 207). T.W. Rhys Davids (1843–1922) saw Buddhism first-hand while working in

Ceylon (Sri Lanka), founded the Pali Text Society in 1881 and became in 1904 the first professor of Comparative Religion at Manchester University (Thomas, 1988: 93–4). Mostly remembered now for translating Pali texts, his impact on Victorian England was mainly due to his popular *Buddhism*, published by (the) Society for Promoting Christian Knowledge (SPCK) in 1877. Although still working largely from ancient texts rather than contemporary Buddhism, his 'emphasis on moral striving' made Buddhism seem more attractive to a Victorian audience (Clausen, 1975: 12). The concept of Nirvana was particularly confusing for the Victorians, who often saw it as nihilistic, and Rhys Davids made a substantial advance by insisting that Nirvana is not the extinction of the soul, but rather 'the extinction of that grasping condition of mind and heart...a sinless, calm state of mind...perfect peace, goodness, and wisdom' (Davids, 1882: 111–12).

As Pali texts came to be seen as the most authentic, Theravāda Buddhism was assumed to be the original and purest form, with the Mahāyāna often viewed as superstitious idolatry or 'a priestly corruption of the original simplicity' (Clausen, 1975: 7). Buddhist monasticism was widely misunderstood, and superficial resemblances to Catholicism were used to denigrate both traditions. Even Rhys Davids dealt almost exclusively with the Theravāda, and was openly hostile to Tibetan Buddhism, whose priestly hierarchy, worship of saints and 'idols' and elaborate rituals he condemned as having 'a strong resemblance to Romanism' (Davids, 1882: 250).

Well-educated Victorians also read essays on Buddhism in popular journals and found themselves at odds with a Christianity which Almond (1988: 35) described as 'increasingly effete in precept and in practice'. Another important influence was Edwin Arnold's *The Light of Asia*, a long poem on the Buddha's life published in 1879: its huge popularity both exemplified and increased the fascination with Buddhism's romantic background and heroic founder. Clausen (1975: 4–7) argued that Buddhism might well have appealed to disaffected Christians, drawn by its perceived agnosticism, emphasis on self-help and 'an attractive personal founder' who could be accepted without the need for supernatural beliefs.

Despite this considerable interest, there were hardly any Victorian converts to Buddhism. Academic writers rejected personal involvement, and there were no Buddhist organizations. According to Almond, the reticent Victorians felt 'an overt commitment was socially difficult', and even by 1900 the few converts were 'to the somewhat eccentric spiritualistic Esoteric Buddhism of Madame Blavatsky and her Theosophical movement' (Almond, 1988: 36). Although Theosophy was radically different from genuine Buddhist teaching and practice, it acted in some ways as 'a romantic foil to the rationalism of the scholars' (Batchelor, 1994: 270), prefiguring the tension between academics and practitioners in early Buddhist societies.

The beginnings of practice

Western interest in Buddhism gradually began to shift from the academic towards the more personal. Rawlinson (1997: 39) described the period up to the

First World War as 'sowing the seed' for Western teachers, with 'well-meaning but amateurish' Buddhist societies springing up as part of a 'general lay Buddhism' which began to attract interest. Before 1920, interest was almost exclusively in the Theravāda and was mainly 'ethical and intellectual', emphasizing knowledge and personal morality as against 'Christian faith and dogma' (Baumann, 1995: 57). Members of these small societies often saw Buddhism as an intriguing hobby rather than a life-changing spiritual practice.

The Buddhist Society of Great Britain and Ireland was formed in London in 1907 with Rhys Davids as president. Humphreys (1968: 1) described it as a 'somewhat unhappy fusion' between Buddhist scholars and students and those who wished to practise Buddhism. By 1909 there were 150 members, with weekly public meetings for scripture readings, lectures and discussion, and private meetings for an inner group who wished 'to further the teachings, and imitate the life of the Buddha' (Humphreys, 1968: 8), but no mention of meditation. The Society welcomed Ananda Metteyya (Allan Bennett, 1872–1923), one of the first Englishmen to ordain as a Theravāda monk, on his mission to London in 1908. He explained Buddhism as based on reason rather than faith, and criticized the selfishness of Western individualism. However, he was a poor speaker and, hampered by *Vinaya* restrictions on eating, sleeping and handling money, he returned disappointed to Burma after 5 months (Humphreys, 1968: 6–7).

The Christian churches in Britain lost much of their remaining authority in the period between 1914 and 1945. There was a reaction against their uncritical support for the First World War, and increased affluence brought widening leisure interests which competed with church attendance. Church influence was still felt but often only in condemning popular entertainment, alcohol, sexual behaviour and the 'continental Sunday' (Stevenson, 1984: 370).

By the early 1920s the Buddhist Society was ailing, and in 1924 a new 'Buddhist Lodge' of the Theosophical Society was formed, with Humphreys as president. He had joined the Society in 1919, and always saw his role in Buddhism as linked to his Theosophical background. Firmly based on practice rather than scholarship, with a shrine room for meditation, the Lodge was still very much a Society, with its constitution, bylaws proposals and resolutions (Humphreys, 1968: 18ff.). Early editorials in its journal *Buddhism in England* (1926–43) repeatedly attacked Christianity, condemning anti-Buddhist pamphlets as 'further specimens of Roman Catholic mendacity' ('Roman Catholic anti-Buddhism propaganda', 1928: 115) or criticizing church leaders as 'blinded by their egotistical desires to attain their own ends' ('Editorial', 1928: 50). Such hostility is unusual in Buddhist writing in Britain (though we shall see another example much later in the FWBO), and is perhaps the mark of a new movement asserting itself.

Lodge members used Pali to take the Five Precepts at meetings ('On Becoming a Buddhist', 1929: 50), but also produced rites of passage in English. Humphreys wrote his own wedding ceremony (Humphreys, 1968: 29) and a funeral service which included Buddhist scriptures but still sometimes sounded like the

Victorians at prayer: 'Wherefore hearken now, and in the turmoil of the day and in the silence of the night, remember the message of the All-Compassionate One' (Humphreys, 1934: 21).

A Meditation Circle was formed in 1930 for members who wished to continue their spiritual development 'by intensive concerted effort in the inner world of thought' (Humphreys, 1968: 35). This still sounds rather intellectual, and Humphreys (1968: 74) concluded that the 'increasing emphasis on personal spiritual experience' may only have emerged in the Second World War.

Outside the Society, the Sinhalese Buddhist revivalist Anagarika Dharmapala (1864–1933), founder of the Maha Bodhi Society, visited England in 1925; and the influential *Essays in Zen Buddhism* (1927) by D.T. Suzuki (1870–1966) was an introduction to exciting new Mahāyāna ideas which Humphreys (1968: 74) called the 'Himalayas of human thought'. Suzuki visited the Lodge in 1936, and those who met him found that 'an hour with a Zen master was worth weeks of literary study' (Humphreys, 1968: 41). In 1935 Humphreys claimed that Lodge members were only a small proportion of the 'thousands of persons' leading their lives on Buddhist principles (Humphreys, 1935: 160), and a 1937 editorial claimed that Buddhism was 'spreading rapidly', with many students outside Buddhist societies ('Buddhism in the West', 1937: 33), though it is hard to tell if such assertions are accurate.

Buddhism in England continued publication during the Second World War, though the Society's activities were severely curtailed. One editorial suggested that the public still saw the Buddhist as either an idol-worshipper or 'an atheist or crank...a student of comparative religion or a poseur' ('The False and the True', 1940: 149). In 1943 the journal was renamed the *Middle Way*, and the Buddhist Lodge became the Buddhist Society, with new premises, an improved library and more frequent meetings ('The Buddhist Society, London and its New Headquarters', 1943: 25). Humphreys (1943: 28) saw the Society as 'a collective centre for knowledge', which clearly represented Buddhism in Britain: 'by the examples of our members will the Dharma be judged'.

The first half of the twentieth century witnessed a gradual transition from academic interest to personal involvement, though still on a small scale. The Buddha's life and teachings were increasingly seen as examples and principles to follow, and Buddhist rites of passage, together with the interest in meditation, show the beginnings of genuine Buddhist practice.

Postwar revival

The 1950s saw a move in some European countries from a 'general lay Buddhism' towards different schools with Pure Land groups in Britain and Germany, Zen students influenced by D.T. Suzuki and the German-born Lama Anagarika Govinda (1898–1985) founding a Tibetan order in Berlin (Baumann, 1995: 58). In Britain regular church attendance declined to less than 15 per cent, with 40 per cent not attending at all (Marwick, 1996: 106), though many still claimed allegiance. This 'believing without belonging', as Davie (1994: 5) neatly described it, forms part of a complex and changing pattern of religious behaviour in postwar Britain.

Buddhist Society meetings in London were soon taking place several times a week. The Society's 'Twelve Principles of Buddhism' were published in 1945 as 'a clear-cut Western presentation' (Humphreys, 1968: 47), and Humphreys promoted them in several Buddhist countries, commending them in 1952 to the Second World Buddhist Conference in Tokyo as 'a simple creed or set of principles on which the Buddhist world may be united' (Humphreys, 1953: 116). By 1955 he hoped that they might be 'adopted as the basis of World Buddhism', though each tradition would remain 'free to develop in its own particular way' (Humphreys, 1968: 53). He saw neither irony nor cultural imperialism in a Western lawyer advising Asians how to redefine their own Buddhism. The Society celebrated its 25th year in 1949 with an exhibition of Tibetan art, a reception at India House, a new shrine given by the Thai ambassador and the publication of Humphreys' *Zen Buddhism*. He wrote with satisfaction that so many people noticed 'that Buddhism in England was *an established and growing institution*' (Humphreys, 1968: 52). Like the Victorians, the Buddhist Society may have created a form of Buddhism in its own image.

During the 1950s the *Middle Way* began to mention specific traditions with references to Theravāda monks, articles on Zen and suggestions about the future form of Western Buddhism. The Buddhist Society held its first Summer School in 1952, and in the following year speakers included D.T. Suzuki and the scholars and translators Edward Conze (1904–79), I.B. Horner (1896–1981) and Maurice Walshe (1911–98) (Humphreys, 1968: 56). Celebrations in 1954 marked 30 years of the Society, which Humphreys described as 'the oldest, largest and most influential Buddhist organisation in the West', neither proselytizing nor promoting any particular school but acting as 'a collective voice for the growing body of British Buddhism' (Humphreys, 1955: 171, 174). This was a prominent role which the Society would not easily relinquish.

Two books published in 1951 helped to spread the growing interest in Buddhism. Humphreys' popular Penguin volume *Buddhism* sold 110,000 copies in 4 years (and 300,000 by 1967) (Humphreys, 1968: 53, 60), while Conze's *Buddhism: Its Essence and Development* was more scholarly but perhaps equally influential. New Buddhist societies also began to form outside London in several towns and cities.

A wartime *Middle Way* article had suggested that anyone becoming a Buddhist monk in England would be charged with evading taxes, vagrancy and begging, and so 'some more suitable alternative' must be found ('The Sangha in the West', 1944: 123). Yet there remained a strong wish for an ordained Western *saṅgha*. Another attempt was made with the ordination of William Purfurst (1906–71) as Ven. Kapilavaddho in Thailand in 1954 and his return to England the following year (Snelling, 1987: 313). Humphreys (1955: 174–5) hailed the arrival of 'our own bhikkhu' as 'a new chapter in the history of Buddhism in England', but his hopes were premature. Kapilavaddho disrobed due to ill health in 1957, though he helped to found the English Sangha Trust (EST) in 1956, whose efforts finally established a Theravāda *saṅgha* in Britain 20 years later.

The London Buddhist Vihara opened in 1954 with several Sinhalese monks, after discussions supported by the Buddhist Society, and Conze's *Buddhist Texts Through the Ages* was published (Humphreys, 1968: 57). The Society's membership was growing, and there were more frequent meetings, reviews and articles on Buddhism, and broadcast talks. Humphreys (1968: 58) even hoped that one of the visiting Japanese *rōshis* who were 'so impressed with the quality and range of the study of Zen Buddhism which they find in the Society' might soon move to London. The Society saw itself at the centre of this activity, and in 1955 Humphreys claimed that their premises were 'recognised as the headquarters of Buddhism in Europe' (Humphreys, 1968: 56).

By 1958 Humphreys was confident that with Theravāda practitioners and 'Tibetan ritual' in several European countries, and Zen becoming 'so popular that it is in danger of becoming a cult', Buddhism was no longer an unusual minority belief, but had become 'an integral part of Western thought' (Humphreys, 1958: 126). This is clearly overstated, but it shows that followers were increasingly drawn to specific Buddhist traditions, and each of these would soon be developing what Batchelor (1994: xii) calls 'intentional spiritual communities'.

At some point in the 1960s it becomes more appropriate to examine these schools separately, though the diversity did not appear overnight, and each tradition has its own sequence of events. The context here is a rapid change in Western culture, including such diverse elements as greater socio-economic mobility, further decline in church attendance and increased interest in Oriental religions, an information explosion and the expansion of higher education, a new youth culture of rock music, drug-taking and permissive sexual behaviour, the Chinese invasion of Tibet and the American war in Vietnam.

The Buddhist Society began to appear increasingly conservative. In 1967, with anti-war protests sweeping across America and Europe, Humphreys (1968: 82) proclaimed that Buddhist organizations should ignore the fighting, the arguments and 'politics of any kind'. He still saw the Society – with its fine London premises, large library, lectures, classes and dissemination of Buddhist information and literature – as central to (or even synonymous with) Buddhism in England. However, young Britons in the late 1960s were increasingly likely to encounter Buddhism on the hippy trail to Asia or to seek out *bhikkhus* and *lamas* at new monastic centres in Britain, rather than visiting the Buddhist Society's headquarters in Eccleston Square.

The pattern of Buddhism in Britain between 1945 and 1965 is one of gradually increasing complexity, including awareness of a wider range of teaching and practice, early attempts to establish a monastic *saṅgha* and the growth of lay groups. The emergence of separate schools, the possibility of a westernized Buddhism and the tensions between progressive and conservative Buddhists all suggest that the subsequent development of Buddhism in Britain should be traced in a rather different format.

The expansion of Buddhism

Religious belief and practice in Britain has grown much more diverse since the 1960s, partly as a result of Asian immigration. Church membership declined still further and by the 1990s Christianity had become one of many spiritual alternatives, ranging from traditional oriental religions to New Age beliefs and practices (Davie, 1994: 41–2).

New organizations emerging in Europe and America – some of them with Asian roots, such as Hare Krishna and Transcendental Meditation – are often described as New Religious Movements (NRMs). Barker (1999: 20) has pointed out that such movements are so varied in their origins, teaching, practice and organization that the label of NRM is all they have in common, though an active 'anti-cult movement' and the British tabloid press tend to condemn all NRMs together as 'dangerous, manipulative [and] exploitative'. Even popular Buddhist writers sometimes refer to 'cults' in such terms: Christopher Titmuss, for example, warned meditators against 'groups whose primary goals are conversion and empire-building', and which tend to be authoritarian, dogmatic and intolerant, with unquestioning obedience to leaders or writings, and perhaps financial exploitation of members (Titmuss, 1999: 91). From a more scholarly viewpoint, Barker suggested that common features of NRMs often include 'first-generation enthusiasms', clear and firmly held beliefs, an urgent message, commitment to a particular lifestyle, a 'charismatic leadership' and perhaps a firm separation between those inside and outside the movement, though these characteristics may change rapidly as movements grow (Barker, 1999: 20). As the new Buddhist movements we shall be examining are occasionally referred to as 'cults', the distinction between the popular image of such organizations and a more academic approach needs to be borne in mind.

A further context has been the rise of New Age activities, again sometimes with Indian roots. Cush argued that while New Age movements and Buddhism appeared as 'close allies' during the 1960s and 1970s, traditional Buddhists often prefer a more orthodox approach, though there are still overlapping interests in meditation, human potential, rebirth, environmentalism and world peace (Cush, 1996: 195f.). Although Buddhism's analytical approach contrasts with New Age utopian optimism, Cush concluded that there remains 'a close, entangled and ambiguous relationship' between them, with a wide variety of views, 'a common ancestry in Theosophy', and for some 'a positive value in a diversity of paths' (Cush, 1996: 206). In a spiritually diverse Britain, it is sometimes difficult to tell whether New Age ideas are influencing Buddhism or vice versa.

Baumann (1995: 55) has described the expansion of Buddhism in Europe since the 1960s, reporting media claims in the 1990s that Buddhism might become 'the leading religion of the next century'. While this seems unlikely, one reason for Buddhism's growing popularity emerged from the 1992 congress of the European Buddhist Union, which reported a move towards egalitarianism, where the Asian 'hierarchy between ordained and lay people' is fading, and the *sangha* is becoming 're-interpreted as the community of all Buddhists', often including lay teachers (Baumann, 1995: 66).

Gross argued that well-educated and dedicated Western Buddhists may be developing 'a new style of Buddhism', less influenced by 'the dichotomy between monks and laypeople' (Gross, 1994: 24). Coleman went further by describing a 'new Buddhism' in America which may involve Zen, Vajrayāna or *vipassanā* practice, but where the 'fundamental distinction between monk and layperson is swept away' (Coleman, 2001: 13). In Britain, Church had earlier referred to 'the growing role of lay Buddhists, in particular as founders and spiritual directors of Buddhist groups' (Church, 1982: 196). A religion which appears inclusive and democratic might well appeal to Westerners familiar with a hierarchical Christianity, and we will need to judge how far each tradition exemplifies this important development.

By 1966 there were at least 22 lay Buddhist groups, including 4 in London. There may have been others, but the Buddhist Society chose to exclude those 'no longer worthy of the name' from the *Middle Way* (Humphreys, 1966: 81, 84). The character and affiliation of such groups might often change. A 1972 report described how the Midlands Buddhist Society started partly as 'an academic debating society', though members soon began meditating and following 'a Buddhist way of life' ('Buddhism in Birmingham', 1972: 88). Speakers included Sangharakshita (FWBO) and Rōshi Jiyu-Kennett (SRM); regular meetings included silent meditation, chanting and discussion, and several members became committed practitioners in either the Theravāda tradition or the new FWBO.

The founding of important groups and centres such as the FWBO (1967), Kagyu Samye Ling (1967), Throssel Hole Priory (1972), the Samatha Trust (1973) Manjushri Institute (1976) and Ven. Sumedho's arrival at the Hampstead Vihara in 1978 indicate the scale of activity during this period. The Buddhist Society, by contrast, grew much more slowly from 1,000 members in 1964 (Humphreys, 1964: 99), when there were fewer than 20 Buddhist groups, to about 1,600 in 1983 ('The Size of the Society', 1983: 55), when there were well over 100 groups.

Further groups were soon formed, so that there were at least 40 by 1974 and almost 100 by 1978. Church (1982: 60, 65, 102) confirmed this rapid growth by identifying 140 Buddhist groups in Britain in 1981, the majority being Theravāda (41), FWBO (27), Tibetan (24) or Zen (14), with 25 following no specific tradition. She found there were links between individual groups and 'key centres' (such as the EST, the Buddhist Society, Manjushri Institute or Throssel Hole Priory), and sometimes between groups in the same tradition, but relatively little contact between groups from different traditions (Church, 1982: 112–17). This suggests a pattern of increasingly separate development. In 1981 the *Buddhist Directory* (*BD*) listed 95 groups, centres and organizations, the largest numbers being Theravāda (33), Tibetan (22), FWBO (21) and the more diverse 'East Asian' (15) (i.e. Zen and other groups based on Chinese or Japanese Buddhism)

(*BD*, 1981). These figures are lower than those given above by Church, perhaps due to different coverage. In 1991 there were said to be 201 groups, the largest numbers again being Theravāda (56), Tibetan (47), East Asian (45) and FWBO (39) (*BD*, 1991). However, only 2 years later *Religions in the UK* (*RelUK*) (1993) listed 295 groups, including 62 for the emerging New Kadampa Tradition (NKT), not listed in the *BD*. Again coverage seems to vary.

In 2000 *BD* listed 359 groups, centres and organizations, the largest numbers now being East Asian (107), Theravāda (94), Tibetan (71) and FWBO (52) (*BD*, 2000). However, in addition Sōka-Gakkai International UK (SGI-UK) and the NKT claimed 300 and 183 groups respectively. Combined information from *BD* (1997, 2000) and *RelUK* (1997, 2001) gives a more complete picture and suggests that in 2001 there were almost 1,000 Buddhist groups in Britain, the largest numbers being East Asian (454), Tibetan (284), Theravāda (124) and FWBO (78). Unaffiliated groups also expanded, but the 58 listed in 2001 make only 6 per cent of the total. A summary of this picture is given in Table 2.1. The most recent *BD* (2003: v, 10, 14) confirms this picture, listing 437 groups and referring to a further 300 SGI-UK groups and 240 NKT groups. The overall pattern here is a steady expansion of Theravāda and FWBO groups but a spectacular development of East Asian and Tibetan groups, particularly during the 1990s, largely due to SGI-UK and the NKT (see also Bluck, 2005: 424–35).

Identifying such groups, centres and organizations does not answer the deceptively simple question: how many Buddhists are there in Britain? A large centre such as Samye Ling has about a hundred residents, while a local meditation group may have only a handful of members. Each group has its own pattern of regular and occasional attendees, making numbers difficult to determine, and groups are continually forming or disbanding.

More broadly, independent practitioners or 'lone Buddhists' who rarely attend a Buddhist group or centre form an important but shadowy part of the British Buddhist landscape. They may not live near a local group or may practise in a different tradition from it or may simply prefer their own company. The spread of Buddhists throughout the country, the number of different traditions and the independent outlook of many practitioners all suggest that there are substantial numbers of people involved here.

There are also those who have some interest in Buddhism, perhaps combined with teachings and practices from other traditions (such as 'Zen Catholics' or New Age practitioners). They may not see themselves as Buddhists, and both other Buddhists and academic researchers tend to ignore them. Tweed described them as a range of 'sympathizers' who may have 'dual or multiple religious identities' or may practise intermittently or move between different groups (Tweed, 1999: 84). Although he is writing about America, these '*not-just-Buddhists*' or '*Dharma hoppers*' are certainly to be found in Britain, as are those who perhaps read and enjoy the Dalai Lama's books without being drawn into formal Buddhist practice. Again there may be many such people, with no adequate way of investigating their numbers.

Table 2.1 Buddhist groups and centres in Britain in 2001

Main tradition	Sub-tradition	Group affiliations	Total	Totals with NKT/SGI
Theravāda	Forest Sangha	36	124 (18.7%)	124 (12.4%)
	Samatha Trust	31		
	Others	57		
Tibetan	Gelug	11	244 (36.8%)	284 (28.4%)
	Kagyu	50		
	Nyingma	19		
	Sakya	8		
	NKT	143 [183 claimed]		
	Others	13		
East Asian	SRM	32	157 (23.7%)	454 (45.4%)
	Community of Interbeing	28		
	International Zen Association	11		
	Other Sōtō	13		
	Rinzai	4		
	Zen Practice Centre Trust	11		
	Other Zen	12 (Total Zen 111)		
	Ch'an	21		
	Korean	3		
	Pure Land/Shin	5		
	Nichiren	5		
	Shingon	7		
	SGI-UK	3 [300 claimed]		
	Others	2		
Western	FWBO	78	80 (12.1%)	80 (8.0%)
	Others	2		
Others	No affiliation	58	58 (8.7%)	58 (5.8%)
Total affiliations			663 (100%)	1000 (100%)

Sources: BD, 1997, 2000; *RelUK*, 1997, 2001.

Note
There are 645 groups and centres listed (982 including the claimed NKT and SGI groups), though several practise in more than one tradition. There may also be further unrecorded university groups.

There have been several recent published estimates of the numbers of Buddhists in Britain. Weller (*RelUK*, 2001: 33) gave the lowest figure as 30,000, though he added that the ethnic Chinese community might boost the overall figure to as many as 130,000. Baumann (2002: 95–6) suggested that there are 180,000 British Buddhists, with perhaps 130,000 of them coming from Asia (and so about 50,000 'convert Buddhists'), though he warned that giving figures for European countries is 'a risky undertaking, due to methodological uncertainties'. Keown (2003: 42) estimated that there are 'something of the order of 200,000

Buddhists in Britain', most of whom are said to be Caucasian converts rather than Asian immigrants.

The UK 2001 Census seems to offer a definitive answer here by including a question on religion, and the responses gave two important headline figures for Buddhists in Britain. There were said to be 144,453 Buddhists in England and Wales (0.28% of the population of 52,041,916), and 152,000 Buddhists in the United Kingdom as a whole (0.26% of the population of 58,789,000) (www.statistics.gov.uk/census2001; see also Bluck, 2004).

These figures should be treated with caution, for several reasons. Over 4,000,000 people (7.7%) chose not to answer the religion question (and of course their responses might have been different from those who did). The UK total figure given above takes account of this and is only accurate to the nearest thousand. The question was worded differently for those in Scotland and Northern Ireland, which may have had some effect. There will have been both Buddhists who did not declare themselves as such and non-Buddhists who claimed to be Buddhists. Waterhouse (2001: 122) pointed out that even those who call themselves Buddhists will include both those with a 'full-time' commitment, such as monastics and lay community members, and those who occasionally attend Buddhist groups or who only read about Buddhism.

Bearing all these warnings in mind, we can turn to the 'Religion by Ethnic Group' spreadsheet of 2001 Census data, which cross-tabulates the main religions with the main ethnic groups. This is based on the England and Wales figures given above, and is given in percentages, and translated into raw numbers in Table 2.2. Figures for the United Kingdom as a whole may be derived by combining the percentages given above with the overall estimated figure of 152,000: these are translated into numbers in Table 2.3, and rounded to the nearest hundred. These figures may still give a misleading impression of accuracy, but we may reasonably conclude that in 2001 there were roughly 150,000 Buddhists in

Table 2.2 Ethnicity of Buddhists in England and Wales

Ethnicity	Percentage	Numbers
White	38.79	56,033
Mixed	3.22	4,651
Asian or Asian British	9.64	13,925
Black or Black British	1.04	1,502
Chinese	23.75	34,308
Other ethnic group	23.56	34,033
All Buddhists in England and Wales	100.0	144,453

Source: UK 2001 Census Data.

Table 2.3 Ethnicity of Buddhists in the UK

Ethnicity	Percentage	Numbers
White	38.79	59,000
Mixed	3.22	4,900
Asian or Asian British	9.64	14,600
Black or Black British	1.04	1,600
Chinese	23.75	36,100
Other Ethnic Group	23.56	35,800
All Buddhists in UK	100.0	152,000

Source: UK 2001 Census Data.

Britain of whom almost 60,000 were white, about 35,000 were of Chinese origin, nearly 15,000 were Asian, about 5,000 were of mixed ethnicity and fewer than 2,000 were black.

A further 35,000 said that they were from 'Other Ethnic Groups'. This may reflect differing perceptions of the term 'Asian', where sub-categories were given for Indian, Pakistani and Bangladeshi but not for other countries, which were combined as 'Other Asian'. Although nearly 12,000 Buddhists (8.09%) described themselves as 'Other Asian', this seems a very low figure for all the Thai, Sri Lankan and Burmese Buddhists in Britain – not to mention smaller numbers of Koreans, Vietnamese and Tibetans. Perhaps many of these did not find their own ethnicity listed, and ticked 'Other Ethnic Groups' rather than 'Other Asian'.

Much of the research on Buddhism in Britain has focused on those who have been called 'white Buddhists', though we can now see that there are also Buddhists who are neither Asian nor 'white'. A better term might be 'convert Buddhists', though this may become less appropriate as the children of 'white Buddhists' grow up in families where Buddhism is the norm. Whichever term is used, we can at least say with some confidence that there are about 60,000 ethnically European people in Britain who have converted to Buddhism, rather than coming originally from an Asian Buddhist background. This 'top–down' figure from the Census data is very helpful when it is combined with the available 'bottom–up' data from individual Buddhist groups and movements.

The three largest Buddhist groups in Britain – the FWBO, SGI-UK and the NKT – have all been described as controversial movements with an undue influence, but their numbers have to be seen in context. As we shall see, each of these organizations is said to have between 3,000 and 5,000 members or followers. Even if we use the higher figure here, the total of 15,000 is only a quarter of the convert Buddhists in Britain, or only one-tenth of the British Buddhist community as a whole.

There are no comparable figures for the other Buddhist organizations in Britain. As we have seen, there are almost 1,000 Buddhist groups in Britain, including substantial numbers of FWBO, SGI-UK and NKT groups and smaller numbers of Theravāda, Zen, Tibetan and other groups. Many of these are small local groups, and it would be wholly unrealistic to think that they have 60 members on average (bringing the total neatly up to 60,000). This confirms the suggestion that many Buddhists in Britain have little formal contact with Buddhist groups, practising instead on their own, and perhaps visiting Buddhist centres occasionally for festivals or retreats.

We still do not know how many British Buddhists practise in the Theravāda, Tibetan or Zen traditions, or as what might clumsily be termed 'unaffiliated convert Buddhists'. Until the Census offers more detailed questions, or Buddhists keep membership records, such figures will still remain elusively beyond our grasp.

Theravāda Buddhism

As well as the Forest Sangha, the Samatha Trust and independent lay groups, the development of Theravāda Buddhism in Britain has also reflected the needs of Asian Buddhists. The London Buddhist Vihara moved to Chiswick in 1964, and the King and Queen of Thailand opened the Buddhapadipa Vihara in London in 1966 (Robins, 1966: 132). These *sanghas* were supported largely by the Sri Lankan and Thai communities. The Hampstead Buddhist Vihara opened in 1962 as 'the first intended for Western-born monks' (Walshe, 1963: 172), though as we shall see, Sangharakshita's unconventional approach as senior monk there soon polarized traditional Theravāda supporters and those looking for new forms of Buddhism.

There was a lively *Middle Way* correspondence during 1972 on the prospects for a British monastic *sangha*. Hackney (1972: 181–2) complained that attempts to provide monastic training in England had failed, as the EST insisted on 'transplanting the Theravadin Sangha' without adapting it to Western conditions, where an evening meal and agricultural work might be more appropriate. Austin (1972: 90) agreed that we should not 'transplant an Oriental, tropical type of life into Western, temperate countries'. Walpola Rahula, a senior Sri Lankan monk, argued that while a monastic *sangha* is essential for Buddhism to develop in England, the *Vinaya* can and should be changed to suit a Western lifestyle or Buddhism 'will always remain a tropical plant in a hothouse in the West' (Rahula, 1975: 179). He recommended that a council of monastics and lay people be convened to look at solutions.

With the arrival of Ajahn Sumedho and three other Western monks at the Hampstead Vihara in 1978, a British Theravāda *sangha* was at last established. By 1981 there were Forest Sangha monasteries in Sussex and Northumberland and 5 further Theravāda temples or *vihāras* led by Asian monks, including 3 in London (*BD*, 1981), with 30 or 40 Theravāda monastics living at these centres (Church, 1982: 119).

In Wiltshire, the House of Inner Tranquillity opened in 1980 as a lay *vipassanā* meditation centre, but developed into an unusual sub-tradition. The founder, Alan James, had been a Theravādin monk for 3 years but later ordained monks and nuns on his own authority, aiming to develop a Western Theravāda Buddhism, with a monastic order following rules adapted from the original *Vinaya* 'to reflect modern cultural and social conditions' (*BD*, 2000: 72). There was little contact with other Buddhist organizations, and financial support came from a local group of professional people, who regarded James and his wife Jacqui as enlightened beings (Waterhouse, 1997: 75–7, 89).

Currently the Forest Sangha has 4 monasteries, and there are at least another 16 Theravāda *vihāras* in London, Birmingham and other cities (where Asian communities support Thai, Burmese or Sri Lankan monks), and two Ambedkarite *vihāras* in London for Indian neo-Buddhists (*BD*, 2000; *RelUK*, 2001). By 2001 there were 124 Theravāda groups. As well as the Forest Sangha (36) and Samatha Trust (31), there were 57 unaffiliated groups, sometimes with a less formal connection with their local Theravāda monastery.

East Asian Buddhism

The pattern of East Asian Buddhism in Britain is rather more complex. The two largest traditions, SRM and SGI-UK, still attract mainly convert Buddhists, with several smaller groups catering for those from specific Asian countries. However, there are a dozen separate or overlapping sub-traditions here, some with both Asian and convert supporters.

We have seen that Humphreys mentioned Zen's popularity in Europe as early as 1958, but he concluded that 'Western clothing' can and must be made for Zen, and help from Japan will be needed only 'until our own *roshis* have emerged' (Humphreys, 1958: 130). This question of adapting Asian culture will recur in each tradition.

In 1981 there were 15 East Asian groups, 11 of them Zen, including a Rinzai Zen Centre in London with an Asian monk (*BD*, 1981). By 1991 there were 45 East Asian groups, including 39 Zen groups, 22 of which were SRM groups affiliated to Throssel Hole (*BD*, 1991). The current picture is rather different. In 2001 there were 454 East Asian groups, which include 300 SGI-UK groups and 111 Zen groups, the latter including SRM (32) and the Community of Interbeing (28).

The Community of Interbeing is an international Zen movement led by the Vietnamese monk, peace activist and author Thich Nhat Hanh, who has written widely on meditation in daily life, and on Buddhist *sūtras* and the life of the Buddha. With a large centre at Plum village in southern France and well established in other European countries, the UK branch was only founded in 1996 (Bell, 2000: 404), but there were already 31 groups by 2003 (*BD*, 2003). There are plans to establish a Being Peace Centre in Britain, a secluded retreat for 'a four-fold Sangha community of practising monks, nuns, and male and female lay practitioners', which will offer retreats and courses on both 'inner and outer peace', as well as 'support for a growing UK community of practitioners' (www.interbeing.org.uk).

The most prominent Western figure in Rinzai Zen in Britain has been Dr Irmgard Schloegl, who trained in Japan for 10 years, returned to teach at the Buddhist Society, and started the London Zen Centre in Christmas Humphreys' house, which became the Shobo-an Temple in 1984 (Snelling, 1987: 237, 341). She was ordained as Myokyo-ni in 1984 by Rōshi Soko Morinaga (1 of 7 monks flown from Japan for the purpose) at Chithurst Monastery, with Forest Sangha monks as witnesses ('Zen Ordination at Chithurst', 1984: 195). The Fairlight Zen Temple, a branch of Shobo-an, was opened near Luton in 1996, and Myokyo-ni has ordained monks there; but it is Sōtō rather than Rinzai which has become the predominant Zen tradition in Britain.

Smaller Zen sub-traditions include the International Zen Association in the Sōtō tradition, and the Zen Practice Centre Trust, part of the US-based White Plum Sangha, which follows both Sōtō and Rinzai traditions (*BD*, 2000: 4, 10–11; *RelUK*, 2001: 168). The Western Ch'an Fellowship holds introductory courses and 'intensive retreats in orthodox Ch'an (Chinese Zen)' (*BD*, 2000: 10). The Pure Land Buddhist Fellowship includes Shin Buddhism in a network of groups practising in 'the Pure Land or Other-power tradition of Mahayana Buddhism' (*BD*, 2000: 7). The British Shingon Buddhist Association has a temple in London and also supports 'training in healing and remedial sciences according to Buddhist tradition' (*RelUK*, 2001: 159). As well as these specific sub-traditions, there are 39 further Zen groups (13 Sōtō, 4 Rinzai and 12 unaffiliated), 9 unaffiliated Ch'an groups, 3 Nichiren groups and 3 Korean groups (*BD*, 1997, 2000; *RelUK*, 1997, 2001).

Tibetan Buddhism

Following the Chinese occupation of Tibet in 1959, many Tibetans fled across the Himālaya to India and beyond. Monks and teachers soon began to arrive in Britain, and in 1961 the Dalai Lama agreed to become the Patron of the Buddhist Society (Robins, 1961: 125). All four major schools of Tibetan Buddhism – Gelug, Kagyu, Nyingma and Sakya – are now represented here, though they are not always mutually exclusive, with some teachers drawing on more than one school.

In a special Tibetan Edition of the *Middle Way*, Sogyal Rinpoche (1979: 197) suggested that Tibetan Buddhism's popularity with Westerners was due to its flexibility, offering different forms of meditation 'to suit different temperaments, propensities and stages of development'. Baumann (1995: 61) felt that the interest was often due to the 'calm, humorous and unassuming appearance of the lamas': he described the rapid expansion of Tibetan Buddhism in the West in the 1980s, with the Kagyu tradition prominent, followed by the Gelug, and modest support for the Nyingma and Sakya schools. Bishop traced the impact of Tibetan Buddhism on Westerners, arguing that their superficial understanding may ignore cultural and spiritual complexity, though there are 'deeply committed individuals' amongst Western monks and nuns in the Tibetan tradition, and even lay practitioners may 'sustain a high level of spiritual practice' (Bishop, 1993: 98).

The first Tibetan Buddhist centre in Europe was established at Samye Ling in Dumfriesshire in 1967 by Akong Rinpoche and Chögyam Trungpa, followed in 1973 by Kham Tibetan House in Saffron Waldon, led by Lama Chime Rinpoche. These were both from the Kagyu tradition, as was Kagyu Ling, opened in Manchester in 1975 and led by Lama Jampa Thaye (David Stott), one of the few Westerners authorized to teach Tibetan Buddhism ('Kagyu Ling', 1976: 192). His teacher Karma Thinley Rinpoche is recognized in both Kagyu and Sakya schools, and Jampe Thaye himself taught at a Sakya centre in Bristol, confirming that even Western teachers may operate within more than one school. In 1989 he became 'the first Englishman authorised to give Vajrayana initiations' ('Sakya Thinley Rinchen Ling', 1989: 189), and he also founded the Dechen Community, an association of Kagyu and Sakya groups. By 1996 he was teaching at several Dechen centres, concentrating on his own text *Diamond Sky*, composed 'in traditional style [as] a substantial introduction to Tibetan Buddhism' ('News from the Dechen Community', 1996: 138).

In the Gelug tradition, Lama Thubten Yeshe and Lama Zopa taught Westerners in Nepal, visited Europe in 1974 and set up the Foundation for the Preservation of the Mahāyāna Tradition (FPMT) in 1975 to coordinate their emerging groups and centres (with over 80 in 17 countries by 2001 (*BD*, 2003: 7)). The Manjushri Institute in Cumbria was founded in 1976: Geshe Kelsang Gyatso arrived in 1977, and by 1981 there were almost 80 monastics, lay people and children in the community (Church, 1982: 150–1), which later formed the NKT. The Manjushri London Centre also began to offer weekend courses introducing the Gelug tradition, but in 1990 it changed its name to the Jamyang Meditation Centre to emphasize its separateness from the Manjushri Institute, remaining a traditional Gelug centre rather than joining the NKT. Geshe Tashi arrived at Jamyang in 1994 as 'the only resident Gelugpa Geshe living and teaching in London', and new premises opened in the former Kennington Courthouse in Lambeth in 1996 ('Jamyang Meditation Centre', 1990: 179, 1994: 54, 1996: 69). Jamyang has become a leading centre for Tibetan Buddhism in London, hosting visits by both the Dalai Lama and Sakya Trinzin, head of the Sakya School. As well as introductory courses on meditation and various aspects of Tibetan Buddhism and culture, Geshe Tashi has designed a 2-year course on Tibetan Buddhist teaching and practice.

The Longchen Foundation, led by Rigdzin Shikpo (Michael Hookham) and his wife Shenpen Hookham, 'presents the teachings of the Nyingma-Kagyu tradition in a style suited to Western students' (*BD*, 2000: 5), with groups linked to the Awakened Heart Sangha. Their course 'Discovering the Heart of Buddhism' is advertised as offering 'an introduction to the Mahamudra and Dzogchen teachings of the Kagyu and Nyingma traditions' (Awakened Heart Sangha, 2000: n.p.).

Tibetan teachers based in the East have visited Britain, most notably the Dalai Lama, whose teaching tours have become major events and whose books are widely read by Buddhists and others alike. Such visits are often widely advertised, sometimes emphasizing unusually accessible benefits. For example, publicity for both Lama Zopa Rinpoche and Penor Rinpoche (head of the Nyingma school) offered empowerments outside the traditional teacher–pupil relationship ('Lama Zopa Rinpoche', 1995: 24; 'His Holiness Penor Rinpoche', 2003: n.p.), and a White Tara initiation at Jamyang was advertised as 'open to all ... with no stated commitments, vows or prerequisites' (Jamyang Buddhist Centre, 2001). It is difficult to tell whether such events are genuine developments or attempts to satisfy Western expectations.

As well as specific schools and teachers, there are several organizations supporting Tibetan exiles, such as the Tibet Society and the Tibet Foundation, which aims to promote the understanding of Tibetan Buddhism and Tibetan culture, and to publicise the Dalai Lama's peace message.

In 1981 there were at least 22 Tibetan groups in Britain, 5 of which were Kagyu (*BD*, 1981), and about 25 Tibetan monks and nuns, most of them at the Manjushri Institute or Samye Ling (Church, 1982: 119). By 1991 there were 47 Tibetan groups, mostly Gelug (20) or Kagyu (12) (*BD*, 1991). The rise in Gelug groups may reflect the beginning of the NKT, which had 63 groups by 1993 (*RelUK*, 1993). In 2001 there were 284 Tibetan groups, including NKT (183), Kagyu (50), Nyingma (19), Gelug (11) and Sakya (8), with 13 unaffiliated groups. We should also remember the terrible reason for such expansion: Hodge (1999: 123) pointed out that after four decades of Chinese rule 'there are now more Tibetan temples operating in the West than remain standing in Tibet itself'.

'Western' Buddhism

There has been much debate about whether a 'Western' Buddhism is emerging, and what characteristics it might have. Smart, for example, suggested that the West is absorbing Buddhist ideas such as rebirth, non-violence, concern for animals and the environment, and an experiential rather than a dogmatic approach. Western Buddhist scholars, integration between Western and immigrant Buddhists and increased Buddhist–Christian dialogue may all help to establish a uniquely Western form of Buddhism which will have 'the power deeply to affect Western life' (Smart, 1997: 81). Gross pointed out that enthusiastic and gifted Western Buddhist women will no longer accept passive roles in 'Asian maledominated forms of Buddhism', expecting instead to practise as equals and to 'take leadership roles in emerging Western Buddhism' (Gross, 1994: 24). Rawlinson argued that Western Buddhism is starting to become 'a new kind of Buddhism altogether' as Western teachers develop new and varied teachings and practices, sometimes derived from outside Buddhism (Rawlinson, 1997: 13).

Western Buddhism in Britain has sometimes been seen in rather limited terms, particularly in the *Middle Way*. A 1965 editorial questioned whether meditation is a necessary part of the emerging Western Buddhism ('Meditation: Its Place in Western Buddhism', 1965: 97). R. Eaton *et al.* (1975: 42) appealed, rather like Protestant evangelists, for British Buddhists to set aside the variations between schools and to work in unity 'for the sake of propagating the Dhamma'. Basil Cox

(1978: 95) even suggested a tie or lapel badge for (presumably male) British Buddhists, without which 'the reason for their confidence and tranquillity would go unnoticed'. However, there is also a wider view. John Blofield (1987: 153) praised the development of Buddhism in Britain as non-sectarian and tolerant, though sometimes hampered by 'a strong tendency to cling to words'. More broadly, Deirdre Green (1989: 289) warned that the 'skilful means' of adaptation might go too far and become a 'selling out', diluting British Buddhism to such an extent that it becomes unrecognizable.

As well as the FWBO, which will be considered later, there are several other organizations and initiatives which appear specifically Western in their character or scope. The Network of Buddhist Organisations (NBO), formed in 1994, aims to support 'communication and co-operation between the diverse Buddhist organisations', and almost all the main traditions in Britain are represented (*Roots and Branches*, 1994: i, 27–8). According to Waterhouse (2001: 154), the NBO (rather than the Buddhist Society) is now 'the primary inter-Buddhist organization in the UK'. All groups are entitled to join, which can create difficulties: several Tibetan groups left in 1998 when the NKT joined. While the NBO does not claim to speak for Buddhism, their representatives took part in planning the London Millennium Dome's Faith Zone.

The involvement of Buddhists in various forms of social action, typically in small informal groups, has been described as 'engaged Buddhism'. The Network of Engaged Buddhists, started in 1982 by activists in 'the British Green Party and other peace and environmental groups' (Bell, 2000: 403), describes itself as 'both affinity group and pressure group, attempting both personal and social transformation' (*BD*, 2000: 6). According to Ken Jones, engaged Buddhism ranges from the 'soft end' of simple kindness or 'promoting a society based on the principles of the Dharma' to the 'hard end' which asserts that 'governments and other institutions should be included in the active concerns of Buddhist morality' (quoted in Bell, 2000: 405). However, Bell felt that 'the disparate British Buddhist scene' is more complex than this, and she has examined engaged Buddhism in Britain in detail under the headings of psychotherapy, social and environmental projects, and education (Bell, 2000: 407–15).

Psychotherapeutic initiatives include the Karuna Institute in Devon, offering a professional training based on Buddhist psychology, the Amida Trust's psychotherapeutic courses, and the Rokpa Trust's Lothlorien centre in Dumfriesshire, which supports people with mental health problems. In a broader context, Brandon (1976) has considered social work from a Zen perspective, Grimwood and Howes (1983: 12) have used Buddhist ideas to help social workers relate to their clients, and de Silva (1993: 32) found Buddhist 'strategies for behavioural change' appropriate in both counselling and promoting mental health.

Social and environmental projects include the Rigpa Fellowship's courses for the terminally ill and their professional and family carers, based on Sogyal Rinpoche's famous *Tibetan Book of Living and Dying*, and the Buddhist Hospice Trust also aims 'to provide emotional and spiritual support for dying people and those close to them' (*BD*, 2003: 134). In Devon, the Golden Buddha Centre project hopes to provide 'self-contained homes for older Buddhist practitioners', combining sheltered housing with a sense of community (Buddhist Publishing Group, 2003). The Rokpa Trust, founded by Tibetan Buddhists at Samye Ling, has established soup kitchens and other support for homeless people, and Angulimala, the Buddhist Prison Chaplaincy Organization, works to make Buddhist teaching and practice available in prisons, with chaplains from all traditions of Buddhism (*BD*, 2000: 93).

Turning to education, the Dharma School opened in Brighton in 1994 as the first full-time Buddhist school in Britain (Medhina, 1994: 209). While its origins were Forest Sangha family camps, it is 'open to children of all cultural and religious backgrounds' (*BD*, 2000: 95), though it remains fee-paying, and is currently limited to primary school pupils. In adult education, Sharpham College of Buddhist Studies in Devon, founded by Stephen Batchelor, has offered introductory courses on Theravāda, Zen and Tibetan Buddhist practice, and both psychotherapy and Western philosophy, and a 1-year residential course combining Buddhist studies with a 'communal and meditative life' (*BD*, 2000: 99).

Several British writers on engaged Buddhism suggest that our overconsumption of resources will have adverse psychological effects as well as damage the environment, according to Bell. She concluded that most British Buddhists would agree and that a greater willingness to engage with 'social and political realities' showed increasing confidence amongst those working 'to integrate Buddhism further into the mainstream of British society' (Bell, 2000: 418).

Although many British Buddhists have few contacts outside their own tradition, some groups follow more than one school, or join with others for festivals: Edinburgh Buddhists, for example, have celebrated Buddha Day together for several years ('Edinburgh', 1990: 123). Annual summer schools run by both the Buddhist Society and the Buddhist Publishing Group include Theravāda, Tibetan and Zen traditions.

There are considerable resources available to support the practice of British Buddhists, including libraries with substantial Buddhist collections and organizations supplying Buddhist books and other material (*BD*, 2003: 149–68). These range from a small *vihāra* bookstall to Watkins Books in London (with perhaps 1,000 copies of Buddhist books) and the *Wisdom Books Catalogue* (with almost 2,000 titles). Some Buddhist organizations publish their own material, from small presses to substantial businesses such as Windhorse Publications (FWBO) and Tharpa Publications (NKT). There is a growing range of material on Buddhist websites, including those of specific traditions. Finally, there are organizations supplying Buddhist requisites, from meditation cushions to Buddha statues, either made in the West or imported from Asian countries.

* * *

Buddhism in Britain has become much larger and more complex since 1965, within a diverse religious pattern that includes a fragmented Christianity, other major world religions, NRMs and New Age spirituality. There are Theravāda, Tibetan, Zen and FWBO groups in most cities and large towns (with all four present in both Cornwall and the Scottish highlands) (*BD*, 2000; *RelUK*, 2001), and more informal 'engaged Buddhism' activities in several areas of social welfare and education.

Perhaps the most obvious change during this period has been the emergence of Buddhist centres as a focus for activities within each tradition. There are now both large and small Theravāda, Tibetan and Zen monasteries in Britain and further lay centres. Their development raises overlapping questions about adapting monastic life to a British context, flexible approaches for different temperaments, the legitimacy of new movements and the sometimes fuzzy boundaries between Buddhist schools or between Buddhism and New Age spiritualities. We have also seen Buddhist publicity using the language of Western advertising, and public initiations outside the traditional teacher–pupil relationship. An enhanced role for lay people, especially lay women, underlies many of these changes.

A more specific development is the emergence of the FWBO, SGI and NKT as three large organizations which may be seen as 'new Buddhist movements', due to their separation from their Asian traditions. Bell has described them as 'closely bounded, hierarchical organizations with clearly delineated institutional structures and forms of membership and an undisguised commitment to recruitment and expansion' (Bell, 2000: 398). We will need to consider how they have adapted, why they are so popular and whether, as Bell suspects, they point to 'a new direction in British Buddhism'.

The last 40 years have seen an astonishing rise in the number of Buddhist groups, from perhaps a dozen in 1961 to about 1,000 in 2001, with over 30 different sub-traditions and affiliations, and further internal variation in teaching and practice. By 2001 there were about 60,000 convert Buddhists, with an even larger Asian Buddhist community. Bell concluded that while Buddhism in Britain is both 'extremely diverse and prone to sectarianism', some practitioners have gone beyond the establishment of introspective meditation groups, and instead wish 'to reach outward to establish their position within the wider religious landscape' (Bell, 2000: 398, 399).

The question of whether Buddhism in Britain might be diverse without being sectarian, and the extent to which British Buddhists are looking outward rather than inward, will be returned to in Chapter 10. The next seven chapters will each examine a single tradition, using an historical outline and the seven dimensions as a model, and attempting to draw conclusions about its overall character and its adaptation to the British context.

3

THE FOREST SANGHA

Historical background

The Forest Sangha is a Thai Theravāda monastic tradition which appears to have come to Britain with little adaptation. However, it has a wholly changed context here, where Thai traditions may be inappropriate and lay supporters may have different perspectives. Earlier attempts by Western monks to establish a Theravāda monastic *sangha* in Britain were hampered by their lack of experience of monastic life, with its 'training conventions and mendicant relationship with the laity' (Sucitto, 1992a: 16). By contrast, Ajahn Sumedho (b.1934) had spent almost 10 years as a monk in a Thai forest monastery when he met the English Sangha Trust (EST) Chairman George Sharp in London in 1976. His teacher, the Thai meditation master Ajahn Chah, visited England at the EST's invitation in 1977 and left Sumedho and three other Western monks at the Hampstead Vihara, a small house on a noisy street, where they attempted to continue their Thai practice. Bell (1991: 91) pointed out that these four monks were the first group of Western *bhikkhus* 'committed to strictly practising the Vinaya discipline', and Ajahn Sucitto (1992a: 16–17) described their difficulties adjusting to their new environment, with much confusion as to 'how the tradition was to be altered, if at all, to fit English conditions'.

There were soon plans to move from London to 'a place where something approximating to the atmosphere of a Thai forest monastery could be created' (Walshe, 1978: 168), and in 1979 the EST bought Chithurst House, a semi-derelict Victorian mansion in Sussex. The move to Chithurst marked the final success of the EST's attempts to establish 'a viable branch of the Theravada Sangha, composed of Western-born monks' (Walshe, 1979: 135), though the initial emphasis was often on renovation work rather than spiritual training. In 1981 Ajahn Sumedho was authorized to ordain monks and the first *bhikkhu* ordinations were carried out (Anando, 1992: 81–4). Many saw this as the 'true establishment of Buddhism in Britain', according to Bell (1991: 95): the local council granted monastic status, and people could 'ordain and live as monks and nuns in an English environment'.

There was also a small women's community. Ajahn Chah gave permission for Patricia Stoll (Sister Rocana) to live as an *anagārikā* (a female postulant) at Chithurst (Bell, 1991: 274), and soon she, Candasiri, Thanissara and Sundara began living in a small cottage at Chithurst as *anagārikās*, wearing white robes and taking the Eight Precepts of a committed lay person. They subsequently received the same Ten-Precept ordination as *sāmaṇeras* (male novices), wearing dark brown robes and gradually developing their own rules and monastic lifestyle.

The Chithurst community began to expand, with monks giving talks, visiting lay groups and conducting retreats. Small branch vihāras opened at Harnham in Northumberland and Hartridge in Devon, and by 1983 there were 'over thirty *bhikkhus*, nuns and *anagārikās*... with more waiting to ordain' ('Chithurst Newsletter', 1983b: 125–6; 1983a: 222). When Christmas Humphreys died, the Buddhist Society invited Ajahn Sumedho to become their Honorary President, describing his appointment as the end of 'intellectual Buddhism' in Britain and the beginning of a period of 'more serious and committed study and practice' ('Editorial', 1983: 141). The 1984 Wesak celebrations in London were sponsored jointly by the Buddhist Society and Chithurst, with an invitation to 'all members of the Buddhist community' ('Wesak Celebration', 1984: 54). The Forest Sangha was becoming, for many, the monastic wing of official Buddhism in Britain.

The expansion of the monastic *saṅgha* and the rapidly growing interest in Buddhism brought its own challenges at Chithurst, with relatively inexperienced *bhikkhus*, frequent requests for teaching, and crowded accommodation. A larger centre was needed for the nuns' community and to provide 'systematic teaching, retreats and seminars' for lay people ('Chithurst Newsletter', 1983c: 184). In 1984 a former school in Hertfordshire was purchased, and Amaravati was established there as the Forest Sangha's main centre in Britain. By then there were 40 residents in the monastic communities, with monks and nuns giving regular talks to Buddhist groups and schools, and with expanding support from a lay community who had 'growing confidence and understanding of Dhamma' (Sharp, 1984: 100).

Ajahn Sumedho said he was inspired by the unexpected growth of the Forest Sangha in the first 10 years ('Amaravati Sangha Newsletter', 1988: 279), and monks and nuns continued to teach at the Buddhist Society after he stepped down as President in 1988. Although two monks chose to 'disrobe' (i.e. to leave the monastic *saṅgha*), there were further ordinations at both Amaravati and Chithurst ('Amaravati Sangha News', 1988: 172). Tenth anniversary celebrations at Chithurst in 1989 saw 'over 1200 people... [and] over fifty monks, nuns and anagarikas' ('Chithurst', 1989: 188). As well as four busy monasteries, the monastic *saṅgha* were 'also contributing to school education, Dhamma literature and environmental awareness' ('Editorial', 1989: 7).

Plans were begun for a new temple at Amaravati. Ajahn Sumedho explained that this was neither missionary work nor 'spiritual property development' but reflected the need to balance the simple monastic life with providing lay people with 'access to spiritual teachings, and places to learn and practice meditation' (Sumedho, 1995: 2). Donations were invited for parts and materials costing over £700,000, though four-fifths of the overall funding came from Thai supporters (Eden, 1997: 268). The consecration of the temple in 1999 completed substantial building and renovation work at Amaravati, including monastic accommodation, a large retreat centre, a fine library collection and a cottage for Ajahn Sumedho. Some 2,500 lay visitors and '150 monastics of several Buddhist traditions' from many countries witnessed the opening (Eden, 1999: 67). Sharp (1999: 7) commented that after 20 years this 'proper Buddhist temple with traditional English monastic cloisters' showed how the Forest Sangha had 'grown, flourished and taken root in the foreign land'.

By this time there were both nuns and *anagārikās* at Chithurst, Amaravati and Hartridge monastery in Devon, which became 'the first Theravadin community for Western nuns', reflecting the *saṅgha* elders' confidence in their ability 'to live and practise independently' ('From the Nuns' Community', 1998: 17). Some senior monks and nuns also disrobed during the 1990s, bringing a sense of contraction in the monastic community, though in 2002 there were still 60 monastics in Britain and 8 further monastic centres in Australia, New Zealand, North America, Italy and Switzerland.

The number of lay groups supporting the Forest Sangha grew from 4 in 1981 to 24 in 1991 and 36 in 2001. Sayers (1981: 139–42) described a typical early lay Buddhist group in Berkshire, with weekly evening meetings in a private house for chanting, meditation and a talk or discussion, monthly visits from the Chithurst *saṅgha*, guest speakers from other traditions but no lay teacher or leader. There are no figures for individual lay followers, but the *Forest Sangha Newsletter* is sent to 1,500 people, which seems a reasonable estimate of committed supporters. Many will practise alone rather than in affiliated groups, perhaps visiting Amaravati for talks or retreats, and there are further Asian supporters from the Thai and Sri Lankan communities.

Theravāda meditation and devotion

Meditation is usually seen as the most distinctively Buddhist practice, though its forms may vary considerably, and devotional activities, adaptations and differences between monastic and lay practice also need to be considered. With the Forest Sangha there is a particular reason for beginning with *dāna* (Pali (P.) 'giving'), as it underlines the difference between British and Thai culture. Offering food and other necessities to the monastic *saṅgha* is seen as an important devotional act in Thailand, where often 'the giving of dana IS Buddhism' (Goswell, 1988: 2/162). By contrast, Bell (1991: 240) found that British lay people offered *dāna* out of 'gratitude for the teaching and spiritual counselling they receive' from the monastic *saṅgha*, rather than for 'the joy of giving'. Ajahn Sumedho (1992a: 71–2) has encouraged lay people to learn how to practise generosity, giving themselves mindfully to acts of devotion, rather than considering what they stand to gain, but while Thai people often have *puñña* or 'karmic fruitfulness' in mind when they offer *dāna*, British lay followers may see supporting monks and nuns as a more reciprocal arrangement.

Bell (1991: 155) argued that British Theravāda Buddhists see meditation as a highly beneficial practice which also 'defines a person as a Buddhist in Britain'.

The Forest Sangha have consistently emphasized three specific forms: Walshe (1978: 168) described an early retreat where meditation began with 'watching the breath to calm and collect the mind', followed by developing awareness of the present moment and generating 'loving-kindness for oneself and all beings'. Bell (1991: 203) explained how monks 'refer to insight meditation by the compound *samatha-vipassanā*', using both forms together rather than seeing *samatha* as a preparation for *vipassanā*. She also found that the *mettā-bhāvanā* meditation was regularly used at Amaravati to generate 'a more compassionate and caring attitude towards others' (Bell, 1991: 208). These methods were combined in lay retreats of up to 3 weeks, silent apart from questions and private interviews with the retreat leader.

Ajahn Sumedho (1991: 16, 49) described *vipassanā* meditation as a courageous investigation, confronting memories and emotions by simply 'reflecting on "the way it is" in order to see the fears and desires which we create'. Correct practice is about letting go rather than attaining or acquiring anything, so that *ānāpānasati* or 'mindfulness of breathing' is simply observing each breath without 'attaching to any ideas or feelings that arise' (Sumedho, 1991: 78).

Ajahn Sucitto's *Buddhist Meditation* encourages lay people to find 'an experienced and trusted teacher' and to focus in turn on the 'four foundations of mindfulness': the body, the feelings, the state of mind and 'the patterns that the mind goes through' (Sucitto, 1998a: 5, 10). Awareness of the body and breathing calms the mind and allows it to focus. A further practice is 'developing the heart' by contemplating the four *brahma-vihāras* or 'boundless states': loving-kindness (*mettā*), compassion (*karunā*), sympathetic joy (*muditā*) and equanimity (*upekkhā*). This will help to remove the 'five hindrances' of sense-desire, ill will, doubt, restlessness and dullness, and to develop 'skilful mental patterns' including 'mindfulness... investigation... energy... joy... [and] calm' (Sucitto, 1998a: 25, 35).

Mettā practice is seen as particularly beneficial. Ajahn Sumedho (1992a: 100) found at first that English people felt this was 'soppy, wet, foolish' or 'false and superficial', preferring to examine their faults rather than generate loving-kindness towards themselves and others. Properly understood, however, *mettā* includes being kind to your own unpleasant qualities, instead of squashing them (Sumedho, 1996: 45). Encouraging the most helpful practice for an individual's situation is typical of Ajahn Sumedho's pragmatic approach.

At Amaravati there are normally 2 hours of group meditation each day and often further individual practice, including outdoor walking meditation. Ajahn Sumedho (2002) described how the 'structure and discipline' of formal practice is only a beginning for meditation, whose aim is 'to point inwardly to where the liberation can happen'. Those focussing on meditation technique will become frustrated and perhaps give up. Ajahn Candasiri (2002) explained that monastics 'try to make the whole day, the whole of our life, a meditation'. Even formal sessions are unstructured, with individuals using rather different methods as appropriate. Ven. Suvaco (2002) agreed that while the silence of formal meditation is important, it is not 'a sacred or holy moment when I am sitting cross-legged', but part of a fully meditative life.

The distinction between meditation and devotion may only be superficial. As with meditation practice, genuine devotional experience only occurs 'when you're not attached, when your heart is open, receptive and free', according to Ajahn Sumedho (1991: 167). Walshe (1978: 168) recognized that 'endless chanting in Pali' and 'continual prostration before Buddha-images' may seem inappropriate, until one has the humility to appreciate their value. Ajahn Sumedho (1996: 34) described the devotional practice of bowing (regarded with suspicion by some lay Buddhists) as 'putting what we identify with at the feet of the Buddha – offering ourselves to the truth'. Ven. Suvaco (2002) explained how bowing and chanting helped to establish 'a sense of clarity and presence' before meditation, but with deeper involvement they become 'symbolic gestures of going for refuge'.

At Forest Sangha monasteries the morning and evening *pūjās* (ceremonies including bowing, offering incense and chanting) are chanted in Pali or English, offering homage, recollection and praise to the Three Jewels or Refuges (the Buddha, the Dhamma and the Sangha), with further reflections and dedications (*Chanting Book*, 1994). Monastics also have their personal devotions, often with a shrine in their own room. Lay people may make a formal request to receive the Three Refuges and Five Precepts, usually recited in Pali. While Pali chanting is seen as 'the authentic sound of Buddhism' (Bell, 1991: 254), many lay people and some monastics prefer chanting they can understand. Some Asian lay Buddhists chant in their own language, but Asian Theravāda monks chant only in Pali. So English chanting is a significant innovation.

Devotional practices are often combined with other elements. At the major festivals of Wesak (celebrating the Buddha's birth, enlightenment and paranirvana) and Kathina (offering robes and other gifts to the monastics), Western and Asian Buddhist communities join together for a communal meal, chanting and a talk from a senior monk or nun. Other festivals may include a candlelit circumambulation, an overnight vigil or perhaps tree planting, as well as the familiar chanting and Dhamma talk.

There are further adaptations from Thai practice. After initial experiments, the traditional monastic alms-round is rarely practised, though monks and nuns may visit lay people for a meal or sometimes stand in public with their alms bowl, their silent presence inviting people to offer food if they wish (*Opening the Doors to the Deathless*, 1999: 12). While meditation and devotional practice remain firmly Theravāda, there is room for personal experiment with elements from other traditions. The bodhisattva ideal of practising the Dharma for the sake of all beings (more prominent in Mahāyāna Buddhism) is readily accepted, there are pictures of the Tibetan bodhisattva Tārā in the nuns' *vihāra* and devotional mantras are sometimes used. Ajahn Sumedho's broad-minded approach undermines any clinging to a specific outward form: unlike most Asian Theravāda Buddhism, the Forest Sangha is at least open to Mahāyāna ideas and practices.

However, traditional elements are often retained. Each fortnight monks gather to hear the monastic rules chanted in Pali, when individuals acknowledge any offences, and the nuns have a similar practice. Monasteries hold a winter retreat from January to March, keeping silence and reducing activity to a minimum, but they also keep the 3-month 'Rains Retreat' (established to avoid travelling during the monsoon season), which seems curiously inappropriate in the relatively dry British summer. There may be a tension between tradition and pragmatic adaptation here.

Lay meditation and devotion often copies monastic practice. A typical lay retreat weekend at Amaravati will include periods of silent meditation in the shrine room and *pūjās* which include bowing to the Buddha image, offering flowers, incense and candles, and chanting in both English and Pali. Local group meetings usually follow this pattern, perhaps with a reading and discussion, unless a monk is visiting to give a talk. Chanting may be in English rather than Pali, though this varies between groups. Meditation instruction is usually available for newcomers, who may be invited simply to observe the *pūjā* until they feel comfortable joining in. Group members often visit their local monastery for *pūjās*, meditation, talks and retreats.

Lay supporters may ask Forest Sangha monks and nuns to carry out baby blessings, marriage blessings or funerals. These ceremonies reflect what Bell (1991: 251) described as a wish 'to declare their Buddhist identity and to introduce non-Buddhist friends and relatives to the monasteries'. Simpler than Thai ceremonies, they have a similar (though less sacramental) role to Christian rites of passage, marking important changes in the family and the community. There are also activities for children, such as the annual Amaravati Summer Camp.

Forest Sangha monastic practice is clearly based on traditional Thai Theravāda meditation and devotional activity, though individuals may also explore Mahāyāna methods. Lay practice sometimes copies this pattern, though meditation is emphasized rather than generosity and devotion, and family needs included through rites of passage. Monastic practice appears much closer to Thai Buddhism, which may cause tension if lay people expect the tradition to be more fully adapted to British culture.

Theravāda teaching and study

Ajahn Sumedho has found that Buddhism often confuses Westerners 'because it has no doctrinal position...there's just suffering and the end of suffering'. Even the Four Noble Truths are not dogmatic beliefs: *dukkha* needs to be understood, desire to be let go of, cessation to be realized and the Eightfold Path to be practised (Sumedho, 1991: 52, 53–5). If we think of 'teachings' inviting exploration rather than 'doctrines' demanding adherence, this may help in examining how particular teachings are emphasized and recommended by the Forest Sangha and other traditions.

The most substantial collection of Ajahn Sumedho's teachings is *The Mind and the Way* (Sumedho, 1996), which includes discussion of the Four Noble Truths, the Three Refuges, loving-kindness, karma and rebirth, Nirvana, meditation and moral behaviour, and wider issues including family roles, education and society.

An earlier collection, *The Way It Is* (Sumedho, 1991), includes talks on the mind, impermanence, the precepts, patience, and letting go of desire. Taped talks by Ajahn Sumedho and other monastics frequently deal with similar topics, with particular emphasis on meditation, dukkha, Nirvana and the mind, but also on desire, the heart, daily life, mindfulness, impermanence, silence and love.

Ajahn Sumedho often talks about 'the uniquely Buddhist expression of "not-self" (*anattā*)', which he sees as 'the Buddha's way of pointing to the experience of Ultimate Reality that is the goal of many religions' (Sucitto, 1991: 7). He has argued that when we are 'just *aware* of the conditions of the mind', rather than focussing on the need to change ourselves, we begin to see our experience as 'a changing condition and not "self."' This is looking from 'a perspective of being Buddha, rather than doing something in order to become Buddha' (Sumedho, 1991: 25). We shall hear this again in Dōgen's teaching on the Buddha Nature: the British expressions of Theravāda and Zen teachings may be closer than is commonly supposed.

Some traditional teachings tend to be less emphasized. According to Ajahn Jutindharo (2002) mythological or cosmological elements such as the heavenly realms were often included in teachings given in Thailand but are rarely spoken of in Britain. There also seems to be little emphasis on rebirth, though Ajahn Candasiri (2002) does sometimes speak about the continual rebirth of our mental states. This is not an intention to downplay traditional teachings but a recognition that they may need different presentation in a British cultural context – particularly to those with a Christian background – to bring understanding rather than confusion.

Interviewees emphasized 'mindfulness' in daily life as the teaching which distinguishes the Forest Sangha from other traditions. According to Ajahn Candasiri (2002), this involves 'looking very directly at suffering' and how to let go of it, as well as 'using the ordinariness of living in community'. This is neither passive nor fatalistic, as it might appear, but rather an active awareness of one's body, mind and environment, observing what arises and passes away without grasping it or rejecting it.

In Thailand, scriptures may be studied formally in Forest Sangha monasteries and examinations taken, but in Britain this is left mainly to personal choice and may be discouraged if the approach becomes too academic: Ajahn Chah once advised Sumedho to 'lock his book away, as the really important book to study is your own heart' (Suvaco, 2002). Most monks and nuns read English translations of the *suttas*, and some may become proficient in Pali, but there is no pressure to do so. The exception here is the *Vinaya*, or monastic discipline, which is studied during the Rains Retreat, with formal classes and group discussion (Ariyasilo, 2002). The extensive Amaravati library includes material on Zen and Tibetan traditions, which monastics are free to read, and it is quite acceptable for them to study Mahāyāna as well as Theravāda texts if they wish.

Lay people have a wide range of understanding about Theravāda teachings. Newcomers often visit monasteries or lay groups with little or no previous knowledge of Buddhism, while others may have been practising and studying for many years. Teachings are often acquired by reading Ajahn Sumedho's books or hearing talks by senior monastics; both emphasize the *practice* of Buddhism rather than academic learning. Amaravati weekend retreats have included such topics as the *brahma-vihāras*, right livelihood and the three fires (greed, hate and delusion), while study days have examined the Four Noble Truths, the Eightfold Path, meditation, suffering, death and rebirth. These events are again centred on reflection and practice rather than intellectual understanding.

Lay groups are sometimes called 'study groups' and may work through texts together, though they may choose practice-based commentaries rather than scriptures: one group spent several meetings examining Ajahn Sumedho's *Four Noble Truths* (1992b), with discussion informed by personal experience as well as Buddhist teachings. Understanding of such teachings is usually acquired outside group meetings either from talks or tapes by monks and nuns or through personal reading. Some groups offer newcomers the free literature available from Forest Sangha monasteries and may have small libraries of Buddhist books for members to borrow.

Forest Sangha monastic teaching focuses on the traditional Four Noble Truths, emphasizing the practice rather than the study of Buddhism, though lay people may value study more highly. However, the repeated emphasis on mindfulness and the nature of the self, and the downplaying of mythical elements and rebirth, may be a pragmatic adaptation for an ego-obsessed and largely post-Christian society such as Britain.

Ancient and contemporary narratives

Popular Theravāda Buddhism has many stories (often derived from the Pali scriptures) about the life of the Buddha, his disciples, previous Buddhas and other beings in the various realms of Buddhist cosmology. While Forest Sangha monks and nuns in Britain are detached from the oral tradition and do not study the scriptures systematically, interviewees all valued narratives about the Buddha and his disciples, though none expressed an interest in stories of previous Buddhas or heavenly beings in the Pali canon. The Buddha's life story in particular was mentioned as an inspiring and exemplary narrative.

Interviewees also valued stories about contemporary teachers, especially Ajahn Chah, who has a special place as the originator of the tradition in Britain and the teacher of most of the senior monks. Even a decade after his death in 1992, Forest Sangha monasteries in Britain still had a real sense of Ajahn Chah's presence, and he is seen as an exemplar for monastics in training. The Forest Sangha is synonymous with Theravāda Buddhism for many monastics and lay people, who may not distinguish between Theravāda orthodoxy, Thai tradition and Ajahn Chah's style of teaching and practice. Western monks who trained with Ajahn Chah in Thailand might even regard pressure for change in Britain as somehow disloyal to his memory or diluting his monastic practice.

Several interviewees saw a difference between monastics taught directly by Ajahn Chah and those trained in England, as it may be 'difficult to transmit his charisma, his *mettā*, his kindness and compassion' (Candasiri, 2002). Stories from his life and teachings are frequently used in talks, especially by the senior monks who trained with him. More junior monks may look instead to Ajahn Sumedho as their exemplar, and he often uses stories from his own life to illustrate points or explain difficulties. Junior monks and nuns may feel more independent of Thailand and may rely more on scriptural narratives to understand the Four Noble Truths (Ariyasilo, 2002).

Lay supporters tend perhaps to refer more frequently to incidents from the life of the Buddha, and there is a common understanding of well-known stories from the Pali texts, often gleaned from talks by monks and nuns rather than their own reading. Such narratives are repeatedly used to inform discussions at Amaravati retreat weekends, and lay groups often use them in their meetings, either taken directly from the scriptures, from books by Ajahn Sumedho and others or again from talks at local monasteries. In this way narratives about Ajahn Chah or Ajahn Sumedho may also inform lay practice. Stories or teachings from the Zen or Tibetan traditions are also sometimes introduced and there is usually no sense that these are inappropriate in a Theravāda group affiliated to the Forest Sangha.

A relative lack of evidence might suggest that this dimension does not figure prominently in the Forest Sangha tradition. There is no connection with the Asian oral tradition, little systematic study of the Pali scriptures and perhaps little interest in Theravāda cosmology, which may remind followers of the Christianity they have rejected. However, the inspirational use of stories from the life of the Buddha and his early disciples, as well as the life of Ajahn Chah (and even Ajahn Sumedho), suggest that mythic and narrative elements have a significant part to play.

The experience of mindfulness and peace

This is the most personal of the seven dimensions and the most difficult to investigate. The literature has little about feelings, and interviewees may be unwilling or unable to articulate or share them. I am particularly grateful to those in the Forest Sangha and other traditions who have spoken from the heart, and so allowed some common experiences, emotions and attitudes to be discerned.

Goswell (1988: 2/76–80) found several common elements in the motivation and experience of Forest Sangha monks and nuns. They were often drawn to Buddhism due to unhappiness or a need for greater understanding or spiritual development. The wish to ordain might be prompted by reading, the example of monastics, or the attraction of a meditative and disciplined lifestyle, but there was also inspiration, mystical experience and a sense of vocation (Goswell, 1988: 2/123–37). Some had experimented within Buddhism to find a tradition that suited them, and my own interviewees sometimes reported visiting Zen and Tibetan monasteries or practising with the Samatha Trust or the FWBO before coming to the Forest Sangha.

Asked about their personal experience of practising in this tradition, monastics responded in different ways, though there was a common theme of calmness or peacefulness. For Ajahn Candasiri (2002) 'mindfulness or collectedness' was the key to a balanced approach, since 'calmness without energy is just dullness'. Ven. Suvaco (2002) mentioned energy, joy and tranquillity (three of the seven factors of enlightenment) as specific 'fruits of the practice': even pain and restlessness during meditation can focus one's energy and so help to bring insight and peace. Ven. Punnyo (2001) confirmed that the Forest Sangha emphasized serenity and calmness rather than the emotional approach of faith and devotion, their devotion to the Three Jewels being 'a quieter, cooler kind of devotion'.

Positive teachings such as generosity, kindness and compassion are also emphasized. Ajahn Candasiri (2002) often speaks and reflects on kindness and well-being, including 'kindness towards yourself, self-respect', as she senses that Westerners 'need a lot of encouragement'. This again applies traditional teaching to a particular situation, rather than giving lectures on *mettā*.

Monastics were also asked about negative feelings such as anger or unhappiness, and several mentioned the importance of dealing with such emotions honestly. When a negative emotion arises, Ajahn Jutindharo (2002) said it was important to 'recognise it, to feel it and investigate it'. As the senior nun, Ajahn Candasiri (2002) was keen to reassure colleagues that these feelings are quite ordinary and can be acknowledged openly, knowing that they will change. Ajahn Ariyasilo (2002) suggested that hate or anger brings an opportunity to develop loving-kindness, and understanding emotions as impermanent makes them bearable. Ven. Suvaco (2002) spoke of taking responsibility for our own mental states, rather than blaming others for our feelings, patiently bearing with powerful emotions until they subside.

Several senior *sangha* members left in the early 1990s. After almost 20 years, Ajahn Pabhakaro felt he was stagnating, his heart no longer in the monastic practice, and he disrobed in 1991 (Kappel, 1991: 5). He was followed by Ajahn Kittisaro and Sister Thanissara, and suddenly Ajahn Anando (previously abbot of Chithurst) in 1992 ('Amaravati Sangha News', 1992; 189). Ajahn Sucitto (1994: 8) referred to 'a wave of psychic and psychological upheavals at Chithurst in 1991', partly related to Anando's interest in the paranormal, astrology and healing, and his disrobing reinforced opposition to 'New Age' ideas in the monastic *sangha*.

These events were extremely unsettling, but monastics and lay followers were encouraged to accept the uncertainty of things and to appreciate the offerings made by 'our former companions in the spiritual life' ('Amaravati Sangha News', 1992: 189). Almost all of those who left remained committed lay Buddhists and still valued their ordained life. When Ajahn Vipassi disrobed in 2000 he expressed 'a feeling of being too tightly held by the form' of monastic convention: but he also felt he would always be 'an inner monk' through the firm establishment of a contemplative life (Vipassi, 2000).

Ajahn Sumedho (2002) felt that those who ordained to escape from Western individualism or unhappy family backgrounds may long for 'some kind of stable, harmonious community', a perfect environment which the monastic *sangha* cannot provide. He underlined the need for monastics to develop confidence, internalising the tradition rather than simply following the rules. Even in Britain, he suggested, monasteries are viable because the 'goodness of the lifestyle...generates generosity'. This goodness (seen as loving-kindness, compassion and joy) 'reaches out and opens other people to that same experience' (Sumedho, 1991:173). Ajahn Sucitto (1992a: 25) explained that lay people who enjoy giving to monastics – an unusual feeling in our acquisitive society – often experience 'a change of heart' as part of 'a mature and sensitive relationship between Sangha and laity'.

Committed lay practitioners with an established meditation practice, who attend retreats at monasteries, may well have a similar pattern of emotional experience to the monastics. Weekends at Amaravati, for example, often generate a balance between energy and tranquillity, with animated discussion on practice within a peaceful and meditative atmosphere. Longer retreats may generate more intense feelings. Goswell provides a rare personal account of such an experience. During the Pali chanting at the end of a 2-week retreat at Amaravati, she felt

> as though the room was filled with a brilliant light...I was filled, quite suddenly, with the most intense, indescribable joy...In the centre of my chest there was a feeling of warmth, energy and vibration...a stream of energy rose up like a spring of water above my head, then cascaded down around my body like a fountain...it seemed that from high above came a shower of something like petals or small flowers...Tears were pouring through my closed eyelids...and I was trembling, my whole body was shaking. Yet curiously, a part of me watched all this unmoved.
>
> (Goswell, 1988: 4/45)

At a more mundane level, there is often a quiet and reflective atmosphere in lay group meetings. Those who lead busy lives often value the silence of the meditation period. Discussions may deal with personal experience, and members often speak from the heart, expressing their own feelings or difficulties, or perhaps offering support to others, though the focus remains on spiritual practice rather than group therapy.

This is a genuinely problematic dimension. We can see a variety of emotional responses from individuals practising in a particular tradition, rather than any characteristically 'Forest Sangha' emotional pattern. Even the idea of confronting emotional difficulties honestly owes as much to Western psychotherapy as to Buddhism. Certainly the Forest Sangha emphasizes calmness and peacefulness rather than fervent faith and devotion, and so may attract people who relate to the coolness of *samatha-vipassanā* rather than the warmth of *bhakti*, though the joy described by several interviewees seems to spring in equal measure from calmness and devotion.

The monastic *Vinaya* and the Five Precepts

Monastic discipline and conventions are considerably wider than the ethical dimension but will be considered here for convenience. The question of whether and to what extent the *Vinaya* rules should be adapted in Britain is important for both monastics and lay people: it affects the relationship between the two communities, in a situation very different from that in Thailand.

The Forest Sangha is clearly a conservative tradition. Although adapting some monastic rules would make things easier, neither Ajahn Chah nor the British Thai community would agree to this, and the EST were also firmly against adapting Buddhism for the West (Walshe, 1978: 168). According to Bell (1991: 166), this self-conscious location 'within the total Theravada Order' gave the Forest Sangha 'useful credentials in the new Western context', emphasizing their distance from controversial NRMs, particularly those with Western origins. Ajahn Sumedho argued that religious conventions should be used skilfully, without clinging to them or rejecting them. Instead of consciously adapting to English customs, he said, 'I simply brought the tradition and played it by ear... If one trims the tradition down before even planting the seed, one often severs or slightens its whole "spirit"' (Wheeler, 1984a: 41). Sumedho felt that change would come in its own time, and that monastic life demands constant alertness to become firmly established in Britain (Wheeler, 1984b: 82; 1985: 237). However, with experience he also began to see what helped or hindered, 'and how to use the good things about English culture as Dharma rather than always holding up Thai values as the ideal' (Side, 1996: 8). The gradual move from copying a Thai interpretation of the *Vinaya* towards examining what is appropriate in a British context signals a more pragmatic approach to tradition and adaptation.

Theravāda monks observe the 227 *pāṭimokkha* rules, which fall into several categories. Serious offences including theft or murder bring expulsion from the *sangha*: successively less serious breaches merit suspension, forfeiting prohibited articles or merely acknowledgement (Harvey, 1990: 225–7). Some rules reach beyond monastic behaviour: Ajahn Sumedho (1992a: 131) explained that growing food, for example, would undermine the crucial dependence on lay support.

Ven. Tiradhammo (1985: 11) described the *Vinaya* as 'a comprehensive framework for harmonious and wise social and personal conduct', giving detailed guidance without demanding 'blind following of empty rules and rituals'. While the rules themselves appear fixed, the Buddha may have intended them as 'procedures for making decisions', allowing some flexibility of interpretation, according to Ajahn Sumedho (2002). Even he felt 'suffocated' by the detailed rules in Thailand, until he saw that Ajahn Chah was emphasizing mindfulness rather than conformity. Monastic discipline can simplify rather than complicate one's life, if the *Vinaya* rules are seen as 'criteria for reflection... for developing awareness', forming an agreed 'standard of conduct' which can then be adapted as needed for different times and places (Sumedho, 2002). According to Rawlinson (1997: 558), Ajahn Sumedho has defended the *Vinaya* training as the 'solid foundation' without which there can be no lasting change in the Theravāda tradition. Sumedho maintains these firm standards despite monks and nuns who disrobe, challenges to the rules and a growing rejection of 'the orthodox view of women', but it is not yet clear 'whether this rigour can be maintained in the choppy waters of Western culture' (Rawlinson, 1997: 558).

Goswell (1988: 2/177f.) described how postulants found difficulties adjusting to the monastic lifestyle, particularly the precepts concerning right speech or total celibacy and the restrictions on food and sleep. Some of these rules continued to cause problems for some monastics. Not eating after midday caused hunger, chronic fatigue, weight loss, and reduced resistance to illness, while overeating to compensate might cause 'vomiting, stomach pains or constipation' (Goswell, 1988: 3/41). She concluded that this precept – not used in other cold countries – is a serious danger to health, and claimed that many monks and nuns feel it may eventually be modified in the West (Goswell, 1988: 3/42). However, while monks doing physical work in a cold climate are allowed cheese or chocolate as a 'medicine meal', a more digestible meal of soup and bread would bring disapproval from Thai elders as 'outside the boundary', according to Ajahn Sumedho (2002).

Ayya Thanissara pointed out that although the *Vinaya* does not cover 'modern inventions like television and cheques', the Forest Sangha feels their use would undermine the rules on entertainment and handling money (Cush, 1990: 58). However, there are signs of adaptation in Britain. Key changes, introduced gradually, included developing the nuns' order, adapting monastic robes for a colder climate and revising social etiquette, as British lay people are uncomfortable with constant deference to monks (Side, 1996: 8). Initially advice was sought from senior Thai monks to ensure that proposed changes did not conflict with the *Vinaya*, but the Forest Sangha is increasingly trusted by Thai elders to maintain the spirit of the rules without continual consultation (Jutindharo, 2002).

However, the suggestion by Walpola Rahula (1975: 177) for a council of monastics and lay people to examine how the Theravāda *Vinaya* could be adapted to suit a Western lifestyle has still not been taken up. Any change would require the agreement of Theravāda monastic communities throughout Asia, and the *Vinaya* rules deal solely with the conduct of monks: cultural change or lay opinions are simply outside their scope.

Few subjects have aroused more interest than the role of women in the Forest Sangha tradition. Western women are often uncomfortable with monastic rules, which appear to treat them as a threat to the celibate lifestyle (a monk may neither touch a woman nor be alone in private with her). Ajahn Sumedho acknowledged criticism of these *Vinaya* rules, but argued that they protect reputations and avoid emotional entanglement (Wheeler, 1985: 242). He has defended them as protecting women and monks from temptation or gossip, pointing out that celibate monks may still find women attractive (Sumedho, 2002). There seems to be a tension here between traditional practice and the legitimate expectation of gender equality.

In this context, the development of the nun's order was probably the most radical change from Thai practice, where the Ten Precept *mae chi* is not seen as having the same status as male monastics (Harvey, 1990: 222–3). As the Theravāda *bhikkhunī* order has long died out, the nuns were first ordained as

Eight Precept *anagārikās* (involving celibacy and restrictions on food and sleep), and then as Ten Precept nuns or *sīladharas* (where the rule against handling money made them dependent on lay people). Extra rules for women dating from the Buddha's time required that nuns must have monks as preceptors and teachers and that even senior nuns must defer to junior monks. However, Ajahn Sumedho (2002) recognized that attitudes have changed, and so nuns no longer assent to these rules in their ordination ceremony. Ajahn Candasiri (1993: 13) reported that the nuns' community at Chithurst had been given 'a considerable degree of autonomy' over several years, holding *pūjās*, discussions and classes at the nuns' cottage rather than the main house and softening the rule that nuns are junior to monks. She felt that the Forest Sangha hierarchy is 'simply a helpful way of organising things', where one's own position is less important ('Buddhism in Britain: Conference Report', 1987: 184). The nuns themselves are perhaps less concerned about status than lay women.

Bell (1991: 275) found that although the nuns' Ten Precept ordination is 'essentially the same as that for *sāmaneras*' (who were traditionally young boys), their rules were being developed and refined, as the nuns were mature women who may well become teachers. Ajahn Candasiri (2002) confirmed that the nuns' rules are still flexible and evolving. They were developed in consultation with Ajahn Sucitto, refining the Ten Precepts into various offences and a series of observances covering eating, speech and behaviour. Many of them were taken directly from the *Vinaya*, but others have been formulated specifically for Western community life. Unlike the monks' rules, they are 'all relevant, they're all about the kinds of things that we experience in our lives, and they're in English, which makes them very accessible' (Candasiri, 2002).

Ayya Thanissara felt that although the Buddha 'gave full ordination to women and made it clear that enlightenment is available to both sexes', the question of full *bhikkhunī* ordination is less important than the opportunity to develop a monastic lifestyle which 'can be lived according to the principles that the Buddha intended' (Cush, 1990: 60). Rawlinson reported that Ajahn Sumedho would 'support the full ordination of women', though this would need the assent of all Theravāda monastic communities, unless the Forest Sangha was to 'establish its own independent *bhikkhunī* ordination'. As Sumedho says, 'It is more important that women should be able to attain enlightenment than that they should be able to use a particular label' (Rawlinson, 1997: 557). *Opening the Doors to the Deathless* (1995: 5) concludes that the nuns' training is now led by senior nuns who 'occupy a position in the monastic establishment equivalent to that of the bhikkhus'. This is the closest to admitting the equality of women in the Theravāda monastic *saṅgha*.

Ajahn Sumedho is conscious that lay people may feel excluded by the emphasis on monastic life, and he is keen to encourage them to meditate, keep the Five Precepts and 'develop the spiritual path' (Sumedho, 1996: 133). At Amaravati lay guests are expected to 'observe the monastic precepts and conventions' ('Staying at Amaravati', n.d.: n.p.), rising at 4.00 am, attending morning and evening meditation for an hour and not eating after midday. Following the Eight Precepts precludes radios, music and all sexual behaviour. A more relaxed weekend regime in the Amaravati lay retreat house may include rising at 6.00 am and an evening 'medicine meal' of soup, bread and cheese (unless a monastic is leading the retreat). A booklet on *Discipline and Conventions* (n.d.: n.p.) explains how and when to offer food and other requisites to monastics (encouraging the donation of vegetarian food) and explains the rules proscribing physical contact or being alone with a lay person of the opposite sex. However, all this only deals with lay people adapting to a fixed monastic practice: there is no suggestion that monastics adapt *their* behaviour to the needs of lay people in Britain.

Pamutto described a communal experiment at Harlow Buddhist Society, where lay people adapted some of the monastic training for their own use. By 1994 they had taken on training rules based on the Five Precepts, so that the Society 'has evolved ... into a lay Sangha' (Pamutto, 1994: 17). Also in 1994 there was a 'lay people's day' at Amaravati to discuss the possibility of 'a more formalised and supportive training system for committed lay Buddhists' (Amaro, 1994: 15). The outcome here was the idea of an '*upāsikā* training' (borrowing a Pali term for lay followers, and significantly using the female form), with a monastic at each centre providing teaching and guidance.

'The Upasika Training' (1997: n.p.) encouraged *upāsikās* to practice the Five Precepts, visit their local monastery regularly, meditate daily, attend retreats and festivals, learn more about Buddhist teachings and support the monastic *saṅgha*. The aims were to 'support individual practice [and] develop experiential understanding of the Dhamma', to 'encourage more contact with the monastic Sangha and other like-minded people' and to enable lay supporters to 'communicate the teachings with others' ('The Upasika Training', 1997: n.p.). *Upāsikā* weekends at Amaravati include discussion of ethical practice in lay life, such as Right Livelihood: it is not yet clear whether the *upāsikā* training will develop into a kind of 'lay *Vinaya*', copying the monastic model, or into a new form of lay practice more adapted to life in Britain.

Lay group members often take the Five Precepts together at meetings, though they may interpret them differently, some becoming vegetarian and teetotal while others continue to eat meat and drink alcohol. Although the Five Precepts are traditionally phrased negatively, as refraining from harming living beings, taking what is not given, sexual misconduct, false speech and drink or drugs which cloud the mind, lay people often emphasize the positive aspects of compassion for others, generosity, self-restraint, truthful and kind speech, and insight or awareness.

Attitudes towards ethical rules or guidelines exemplify differing monastic and lay perspectives within the Forest Sangha. Ajahn Sumedho rightly sees the *Vinaya* rules as guiding monastic life, but lay people (particularly women) may also see them as restricting the development of Buddhism in a British context. The divergent perspectives of traditional monasticism and contemporary lay practice may also reflect reactive and proactive attitudes to change. There is a danger of polarization here, especially if lay people are seen primarily as *supporters* of a monastic community rather than genuine *members* of the Forest Sangha tradition.

Monastic and lay social organization

This is perhaps the most complex and diffuse of the seven dimensions, where examining the Forest Sangha involves a wide variety of monastic and lay roles. These often interact with each other, but will be separated for convenience here. We will look first at the monastic *sangha* and its teachers, the nuns' order and the role of women, contact with other traditions and society as a whole, social action and finance, and then at the wider 'fourfold *sangha*' of monastics and lay people, and at specifically lay organization.

The Buddhist monastic *sangha* is probably the world's oldest surviving institution and appears to be organized on hierarchical lines, with length of ordination bringing seniority. It is dedicated to pursuing the goal of enlightenment, with material support traditionally provided by a lay community seeking karmic fruitfulness from their generosity rather than rapid spiritual progress in this lifetime. Monastics might find this bald summary unfair, seeing the hierarchy as for convenience rather than power, and the relationship with lay people as mutually supportive, the monastery providing spiritual inspiration and guidance. However, the monastic *sangha* may appear undemocratic and elitist from a Western viewpoint where egalitarianism and ego-obsession are difficult to distinguish.

According to Goswell, both lay people and ex-monastics have expressed doubts about whether Buddhist monasticism is appropriate in Britain, accusing it of being anachronistic, divisive and sexist. She felt instead that its commitment to a spiritual world view gives monasticism a 'timelessness' at odds with contemporary society, only divisive if it 'creates a sense of first and second class citizens' (Goswell, 1988: 3/286–7). However, while monasticism avoids distraction and supports concentrated practice, it also denies Theravāda monastics 'many life experiences which would be conducive to the increase of wisdom and compassion' (Goswell, 1988: 3/289), unlike modern Zen or Tibetan monks and nuns who can engage more fully with the secular world. One crucial adaptation in Britain is developing the *anagārika* or postulant role to include cooking for monastics and liaising with lay people over monastic conventions and donations. They spend up to 2 years in this kind of 'liminal state' between monastic and lay life, and Bell (1991: 249, 105) argued that this has 'contributed significantly to the growth of the Sangha in Britain', by preparing candidates for ordination and reducing the difficulties faced in a new 'host culture'.

The teacher's role is not strongly emphasized in Theravāda Buddhism, which invites followers to respect the Three Jewels rather than 'a particular personality or guru', according to Ajahn Sumedho (1992a: 127). He warns against becoming attached to a single teacher, particularly one whose sectarian approach insists that students learn from nobody else. Rawlinson (1997: 556) underlines that the Forest Sangha is '*sangha*-based rather than teacher-based', in that 'teachers arise within the *sangha*; a *sangha* does not develop around a teacher'.

However, British monastics and lay people certainly regard the teacher's role as important. Ajahn Sumedho is seen more as 'a senior spiritual friend' than an autocratic leader, and decisions are usually taken by consensus (Jutindharo, 2002). While he is always available to support monks or lay people, experienced monks may practise more independently, and interviews with him are optional, unlike the formal interviews in the Zen tradition (Ariyasilo, 2002). Ajahn Candasiri (2002) describes her role in similar terms as 'an older sister...a sort of spiritual companion' for the other nuns. They meet regularly as a group, learning from each other and making decisions together, and again individuals are encouraged to speak with senior nuns whenever they wish. The teacher–pupil relationship may vary between monasteries, depending on the style of the senior monastic, and is less formal than in Thailand. One monk saw his abbot as a friend and mentor rather than a teacher and there is encouragement to be self-sufficient: monastic training often involves learning informally from each other, rather than being taught by a single figure.

Monastics may be asked to teach after 5 years, at first leading meditation classes or short retreats, though a flexible approach avoids pressurizing individuals unready for such responsibilities. Even those who give talks to lay groups may not view themselves as teachers, partly to guard against becoming 'carried away and inflated' by the admiration of lay people (Punnyo, 2001).

Ajahn Sumedho confirmed that with no precedent in Thailand, establishing the nuns' order in Britain was 'quite a daring thing to have done...I was sticking my neck out'. However, after consulting with Thai monks, he went ahead, and the move has not been criticized: perhaps the nuns in Britain are even 'setting a standard that may be copied in Thailand in years to come' (Sumedho, 2002). Goswell found that although the introduction of a nuns' order brought some new tensions into a previously male-only community, there was widespread agreement from monastics and lay people about the benefits: 'the balancing effect of the female energy' has encouraged the Buddhist qualities of 'patience, tolerance and gentleness' (Goswell, 1988: 3/307). Although the nuns' order began as 'a small subsidiary' of the *bhikkhu saṅgha* and some women later disrobed, the nuns were gradually recognized and trusted 'to take responsibility for their own training and community leadership' ('From the Nuns' Community', 1998: 17). Ajahn Sucitto (1996: xxi) felt that the nuns' order gives women 'the practical opportunities to teach and help direct monasteries', in line with Ajahn Chah's pragmatic approach to change.

As nuns began to lead retreats and become teachers, some lay people felt they would gradually achieve parity with monks, while others argued that their unequal status should be addressed without delay. Bell (1991: 286) suggested that the establishment of the Forest Sangha would have failed without the nuns' order, as many lay supporters are articulate women unwilling 'to support an institution that forbade women active involvement'. Although the situation is changing, the tension between the traditional male-dominated monastic *saṅgha*, linked to Thailand and Thai culture, and the spiritual aspirations of lay women in Britain has still not been resolved in this tradition.

The Forest Sangha has established links with other traditions both within and beyond Buddhism, including interfaith conferences and peace vigils.

The Amaravati Wesak celebrations in 1986 included 'Tibetan, Western Buddhist Order, Japanese and Theravadin Sanghas', with many of the 600 visitors deliberately 'joining a different tradition from their own' at the *pūjās* and meditation ('Buddha Day at Amaravati', 1986: 121–2). Speakers from all four *saṅghas* addressed the assembly, each stressing that honouring the Buddha was more important than specific traditions.

Ajahn Candasiri has argued that there is 'no need for a consensus within British Buddhism; for people are suited to different ways' ('Buddhism in Britain: Conference Report', 1987: 184). Tibetan or Japanese monks and nuns still sometimes stay at Amaravati or visit for festivals. She said how much she enjoyed receiving and visiting these monastics, with whom she has developed 'a close friendship...like cousins really, like brothers and sisters'. She also has contacts with Christian groups, leading several Christian–Buddhist retreats, and gradually developing 'quite a strong connection with several Christian orders' (Candasiri, 2002).

Rawlinson (1997: 556) pointed out that while 'a traditional core' does not preclude innovation, Ajahn Sumedho's encouragement of 'an exploration of other traditions' is unusual in the Theravāda school. Sumedho himself does not claim the Theravāda as 'the best or only way', as this would encourage attachment, and attachment even to Buddhism only makes you 'a sectarian Buddhist'. Instead, he argues, Buddhists and others can 'work towards a common truth among all religions', rather than proselytizing or competing (Sumedho, 1996: 35, 10).

Bell (1991: 168) described how Ajahn Sumedho carefully explained to local people at Chithurst that the Forest Sangha were 'mainstream representatives of an established world religion' rather than an obscure cult, and villagers were reassured at a meeting that the monks were quiet neighbours who would not proselytize ('Buddhists and their teaching come to tiny Chithurst', 1979: 24). The BBC *Everyman* programme 'The Buddha comes to Sussex' (1979) gave wide publicity to the new Chithurst community. Ten years later Denison (1989: 19) reassured *Independent* readers that visitors to Amaravati would encounter 'no recruitment, no request for payment, no cult of anybody's personality...[and] no evangelising'. The Amaravati temple-opening in 1999 included an open day for local people, attended by the Bishop of Hertford, the local MP and many others (Eden, 1999: 68). Ajahn Amaro described this as a wonderfully English occasion, with banners, 'tea and cucumber sandwiches on the lawn', and people from 'shops, surgeries, offices and local agencies', many of whom had long wished to visit the monastery, but with typical reserve 'had not wanted to intrude'. He concluded that 'it seemed that the way of the Buddha and the way of the English were fully at one' (Amaro, 1999: 6).

The Forest Sangha is sometimes criticized for ignoring social problems. Goswell argued that monastics act with compassion for all beings but are engaged with the inner life rather than providing social services. Many lay Buddhists are involved with social or charitable action, and urging monastics to be likewise engaged 'is like arguing that pure science should be abandoned in favour of the applied kind' (Goswell, 1988: 3/292). There may be an implicit value-judgement here about monastic and lay status. The Forest Sangha Theravāda position, according to Bell (1991: 304–5), is that 'putting the world to rights has no part to play in achieving ultimate liberation'. This is expressing it rather starkly, and she acknowledged that the personal morality and simple lifestyle of monks and nuns is a beneficial example in a materialistic and competitive society (Bell, 1991: 307). Ajahn Sumedho has encouraged followers to reflect on the causes of third world problems, where starvation is often the result of 'human greed, selfishness and stupidity'. From a worldly viewpoint the *sangha* may appear inactive, but in a mysterious way monastic life embodies 'the power of goodness' (Sumedho, 1991: 37, 173).

As regards finance, the Forest Sangha relies exclusively on voluntary donations. Ajahn Sumedho emphasized that there was no question of fees at Chithurst, as the monastics were not 'making a business out of teaching the *Dhamma*' ('Chithurst Newsletter', 1983c: 183). At Amaravati, teaching, food and accommodation are all provided free, and Amaravati Publications prints books for free distribution, often sponsored by individuals or groups. Contributions are encouraged, though never solicited by monastics. Suggested donations are displayed in the Amaravati Retreat Centre, which operates separately and charges for weekend or longer retreats. At festivals a lay trustee may remind people of the monastery's regular costs and project appeals, and encourage further donations. This may seem a naïve approach to financing monasteries, but it is a deliberate attempt to keep to the *Vinaya* and to encourage generosity, and it has been successful in covering running costs. There have been substantial contributions from Thailand towards the Amaravati temple and other special projects, but the regular donations for daily support come almost exclusively from Britain (Sumedho, 2002).

Previous attempts to establish an English *sangha* failed partly because the relationship between monastics and lay people was misunderstood, with monks seen as 'lecturers on Buddhism for whom the Trust provided board and lodging' (Sucitto, 1998b: 3). By contrast, the Forest Sangha is a monastic *community* which encourages lay people to participate in a range of activities. Following the *Vinaya* discipline, supported by lay people and acting as exemplar and teacher, the monastic may be seen as a researcher discovering information for others to use 'or as a scout who can find a trail for others to follow' (Sucitto, 1992b: 10). By 1982 there was 'a wider understanding of the value of *bhikkhus* as monastics rather than purely as *Dhamma* teachers' ('Chithurst Newsletter', 1982: 199), but differing perceptions of monastic and lay roles remain.

British lay people may expect monastics to be teachers, priests, social workers, psychotherapists and personal meditation supervisors. In particular, they often expect teaching in return for supporting monastics, though Ajahn Candasiri suggested that this may be given 'through example, through living our life with integrity', instead of always delivering talks, as the monastic's duty is 'to free the heart' rather than entertaining or inspiring people (Candasiri, 2002). While she enjoys meeting lay people and leading retreats, she is wary of those seeking a formal teacher–disciple relationship, as her main priority is the nuns' community. When the monastic *saṅgha* became overstretched in the early 1990s, the lay community began to take more responsibility for organizing their own retreats and teaching, such as *upāsikā* weekends and found that experienced lay people could take on these roles.

Sometimes monastics may have concentrated too much on supporting lay people's practice rather than developing their own, but if they become more inward-looking this can also cause problems. It is difficult to strike a balance here, particularly with fluctuating monastic numbers and increasing expectations from lay people. The oscillation between a highly engaged and a more contemplative monastic *saṅgha* is likely to continue if potential teachers continue to disrobe, though fortunately those who leave often develop as lay teachers instead.

Medhina, one of several lay supporters given a Pali name, described the 'Fourfold Sangha' (monks, nuns, laymen and laywomen) as being 'like the four legs of a table – four interdependent parts that together create the whole' (Sutcliffe and Sutcliffe, 1995: 20). Amaravati exemplifies the interaction between monastic and lay roles. Ajahn Sucitto described it as 'a place of plans and visions and experimentation', which might have become either a monastery or 'some hybrid Buddhist Centre with a resident Sangha around its edges' and where lay retreats, family camps and other activities have created a different atmosphere from 'the settled homogeneity that is a norm for forest monasteries' (Sucitto, 1995: 3). While Chithurst concentrated on monastic training, Ajahn Viradhammo (1996: 16–17) acknowledged the important contribution of lay residents working at Amaravati, pointing out that the unusual mixture of monastic and lay people 'creates a very rich sense of community'. Lay people have also begun to take on more of the management of the centre, and sometimes give talks at local schools as representatives of the Forest Sangha.

However, Amaravati remains primarily a monastic training centre, where lay people can also come and contribute (Candasiri, 2002), and to reverse these roles would threaten the benefits that the monastic *saṅgha* can bring to both communities. There is a creative tension here, with lay people contributing in new ways, and monastics learning to adapt to this new situation, unique to Britain. Perhaps in time monastic and lay perspectives will overlap more and more, each appreciating the other's viewpoint more fully.

Turning to lay organization, the *upāsikā* movement offers clear guidelines for lay Buddhists in contemporary society. There is strong support for the monastic *saṅgha*, with mutual respect between monastics and leading *upāsikās*, but the movement also has an independence, where lay people run events without relying on monks and nuns for teaching and leadership, and so begin to form a community of their own. As well as meditation and workshops, *upāsikā* weekends and study days at Amaravati provide more informal opportunities to discuss Buddhist practice together. Jones (1996: 14) described an *upāsikā* weekend at Amaravati where lay people discussed the concept of *saṅgha*, stressing their 'gratitude to the monastic sangha', but also emphasizing the need for lay supporters to help themselves and each other, especially in local groups. The term 'lay *sangha*' is used frequently at such events, suggesting that lay people are developing their own structures and guidelines, in parallel with monastic conventions. Ajahn Sumedho has also underlined family life as an important opportunity for lay people to give themselves to others, in a society that is increasingly selfish and individualistic. The understanding of attachment and non-attachment can free married couples from wrong views, so that the love between them is no longer 'distorted, clinging and grasping' (Sumedho, 1996: 182).

Local groups vary in their social organization, often having informal leaders who direct chanting, meditation and discussion. For formal teaching, they usually rely on visits from Forest Sangha monks and nuns, taped talks or visits to monasteries. There may be special events as well as these regular activities, including *dāna* meals, weddings, baby blessings, funerals or perhaps the blessing of a new shrine room.

The Forest Sangha may appear out of place in contemporary Britain, though it is perhaps too early to see much social or organizational change. It has established contacts with other Buddhist traditions and Christian communities, based on a common bond between monastics. However, its Theravāda *Vinaya*-based social structure is geared to monks only, and the nuns' order has had to develop separately, with little traditional support. There are good relations with society as a whole, emphasizing a traditional Buddhist monastic identity – world-renouncing rather than world-embracing – which turns away from both social action and commercial activity.

There may sometimes be a tension between lay expectations of teaching and pastoral care and monastic concentration on spiritual practice. Monastics sometimes unconsciously adopt a Thai perspective, expecting relatively undemanding lay support, while lay people unconsciously expect monastics to step into the gap left by the Christian clergy. With relatively little communication between monastics and lay people at an organizational level, such misunderstandings may well persist.

Thai iconography

Each monastic centre and lay group has its own physical setting and its own way of using buildings, artefacts and iconography to support spiritual practice. Ajahn Sumedho has encouraged people to make full use of art and symbols as well as conventions and traditions, not superstitiously 'but with wisdom – for remembrance, for recollection, for mindfulness' (Sumedho, 1996: 36). Renovations at Chithurst, Harnham and Amaravati show existing structures being adapted for Buddhist practice: an abandoned Victorian house, a derelict farm cottage, and run-down school buildings were each transformed into English versions of a Thai forest monastery.

The opening of Amaravati in 1984 marked a high point in the Forest Sangha's presence in Britain. Set in 30 acres in rural Hertfordshire, the wooden-clad former school buildings were adapted to provide a large meeting room, kitchen, accommodation for monks and nuns, a lay retreat centre, library, workshop and office. The fields have a *stūpa* and paths for walking meditation, and a woodland area is being developed for private retreats.

Amaravati's new temple was inspired by those in north-east Thailand, its huge pyramidal roof leading up to a bronze finial flame as a traditional symbol of enlightenment; but red brick and tiles, light stone and timber also harmonize with local buildings. (The new meditation hall at Chithurst was similarly designed to express the 'forest monastery' tradition within a timber-framed aisled barn (see Sucitto, 2005: 34).) The main entrance is flanked by two large *devas* painted in traditional Thai style, blessing and protecting the temple. Inside, the roof is supported by huge wooden columns and beams, with tall windows on three sides. A massive Thai-style golden Buddha sits opposite the entrance, in the preaching *mūdra*. The central floor area has space for about 80 meditators. The outer area can accommodate many more, or a larger audience seated on chairs. The overall impression is of a vast but intimate space, bringing together English vernacular architecture and Thai Buddhist imagery.

There is also a chapel of rest with a large reclining Buddha on etched glass panels, encouraging people to reflect on death and liberation, to arouse a sense of spiritual motivation. Monks and nuns have separate vestries, and sit on opposite sides of the central area, as do lay men and lay women, reinforcing the gender separation.

This is the first Buddhist temple built in Britain combining vernacular and oriental architecture, rather than copying Asian structures: Eden (1997: 269) described this as 'a significant development of the Buddhadhamma in the West'. The title of the celebration booklet *Opening the Doors to the Deathless* (1999) echoes the newly enlightened Buddha's words on deciding to teach, and hints at the role of the material in Forest Sangha practice: opening the temple doors is a metaphor for awakening, for a personal opening towards enlightenment.

The Amaravati Retreat Centre has a large shrine room with a Thai Buddha image, and smaller images and pictures throughout the kitchen, dormitories and corridors. Lay retreats include weekends exploring the role of the creative arts in Buddhist practice.

At Harnham, the Newcastle lay group converted a derelict farm cottage, invited a monk to live there and the small *vihāra* evolved gradually into a monastery. A new Dhamma Hall was constructed, with a large Thai Buddha image and a traditional Thai temple painting of the Buddha's enlightenment. Thai iconography is augmented by donations such as a wooden Kuan Yin (Avalokiteśvara, the bodhisattva of compassion), Chinese temple dragons and a Burmese marble Buddha. A lay retreat centre is also being built at Harnham, again converted from farm buildings.

Forest Sangha lay groups usually meet in a rented public room or a private house, with different implications for the physical expression of their practice. One typical group meets in a small church hall, adapting the space with a Buddha image, candles, flowers and incense, which members bring from home for the evening, helping to create a feeling of the group's own sacred space. In a private house there may be a separate shrine room, used only for group meetings and daily meditation, with a similar but perhaps more elaborate shrine. In one such room, a framed leaf from the *bodhi* tree at Bodh Gaya reminded meditators that they were symbolically sitting with the Buddha, and enlarged photographs of Buddhist sacred places in India recalled the Buddha's life.

While Forest Sangha monasteries are adapted from existing buildings, traditional Thai iconography appears in furnishing and decoration, often reflecting financial donations from British Thais. The exception is the new Amaravati temple, whose deliberate use of British and Thai architecture gives a visual message of the fusion of the two cultures. Artefacts used in lay groups reflect the aesthetic preferences of individuals rather than copying a Thai style. A Tibetan image might well appear on a lay group's shrine, though it would certainly be viewed as the historical Buddha rather than a celestial Buddha or bodhisattva.

The physical setting, however elaborate, is seen as the context rather than the focus of teaching and practice: buildings, shrines and pictures have little intrinsic importance but are used to create suitable conditions for meditation. The overriding sense is usually one of quiet simplicity, rather than colourful interpretation of Buddhist teaching and narrative, reminiscent perhaps of Protestant church decoration rather than more elaborate Catholic iconography.

Conclusion

The Forest Sangha in Britain has expanded from a handful of monks in London into a substantial monastic community supported by lay groups. At first it appears to be a conservative Theravāda monastic tradition, closely modelled on the Thai forest *sangha*. It uses traditional meditation and devotional practices, with an emphasis on mindfulness and calmness. Teaching centres on the Four Noble Truths, especially the Eightfold Path, using the Buddha's life story (from the Pali texts) and Ajahn Chah as exemplars. It follows fixed *Vinaya* rules which support a hierarchical social structure, sometimes separating monks and nuns, monastics and lay people, and men and women into different categories, as well as proscribing both social action and commercial activity. Together with the widespread use of Thai iconography and the choice of rural locations, this may suggest that the Forest Sangha has adapted relatively little to life in modern urban Britain.

However, the tradition now exists in a context radically different from rural Thailand, and a number of significant adaptations have been made, in response to new monastic or lay needs. While the *Vinaya* rules remain fixed, interpretation may vary with a pragmatic approach to change. Obvious adaptations so far include warmer clothing, chanting in English as well as Pali, simpler etiquette for relating to lay people, and – most importantly – the creation of the nuns' order. Unencumbered by the full *bhikkhunī* rules, the nuns' community is skilfully developing its own rule, adapting and expanding the Ten Precepts for monastic life in contemporary Britain.

There are less obvious adaptations as well. Teachers who emphasize mindfulness and the illusory nature of the self, and who downplay or ignore cosmological and mythical elements, are consciously or unconsciously reworking Theravāda teachings for a Western audience obsessed with the ego and unable to relate readily to the supernatural. The emphasis on investigating emotions openly (including negative feelings) may encourage the reserved British to examine their hearts more fully. Individual monastics may use elements or narratives from Mahāyāna Buddhism (such as *mantras* or bodhisattvas) to augment their practice. Ajahn Sumedho is gradually superseding Ajahn Chah as the tradition's living exemplar in Britain. Despite its Thai iconography, the Amaravati temple is a bold attempt at British Buddhist architecture.

Unlike the Thai community, British lay supporters of the Forest Sangha are usually more interested in meditation than generosity, and may feel initial resistance to devotional practice such as bowing and chanting. They may use a range of (less exclusively Theravāda) Buddhist narratives, and may be more catholic in their use of iconography, choosing statues and pictures from different Buddhist countries. Moreover, they may expect monastics to fill a wide variety of spiritual and social roles, from teacher and meditation supervisor to friendly psychotherapist.

These expectations, based partly on the familiar pastoral roles of the Christian clergy, may sometimes create a tension between lay people and monastics. Monks and nuns need time to develop their own spiritual practice, and may become overstretched or discouraged if they are continually responding to lay needs. The *Vinaya* rules also make it difficult for monks to respond to the spiritual aspirations of women in modern Britain. There may sometimes be differing perceptions here. The monastic community may have a Thai model in mind, where lay people's priority is to support the monastic *saṅgha*, while British lay people, with no experience of Christian monasticism, expect to be treated as full members of the *saṅgha* themselves.

Perhaps the overriding characteristic of the Forest Sangha in Britain is the constant practice of mindfulness, in formal meditation and everyday life. Paying full attention to the present moment is more important than the seeming duality between monastics and lay people, men and women or the ego and the world the ego creates. While pragmatic adaptation to a British context is certainly part of the Forest Sangha, it is seen as largely peripheral to the quest for spiritual liberation.

4

THE SAMATHA TRUST

Historical background

The Samatha Trust, like the Forest Sangha, springs from Thai Theravāda Buddhism, but it is a wholly lay organization, with no formal links to any branch of the monastic *sangha*. While some highly traditional elements have been retained, other areas have been consciously adapted for use in Britain. Boonman Poonyathiro (b.1932), known as Nai Boonman, a Thai layman who had spent 15 years as a monk, helped to establish the first Thai temple in London in the early 1960s (Denison, 2001: 46). English Sangha Trust (EST) members heard of his experience and understanding of *samatha* meditation, and at their invitation he began teaching in 1963 at the Hampstead Buddhist Vihāra, and subsequently at Cambridge University Buddhist Society (Boonman, 2004: 50, 52).

In 1971 he led a week's retreat in Cambridge, with sitting and walking meditation punctuated only by meals, brief walks outside, individual guidance and evening talks. Although practising meditators, few participants had been on such an intensive retreat before, and some found it a powerful experience. Boonman explained he had intended to 'test how far westerners could experience meditation in one week' and felt the retreat had been successful in showing them both the difficulties and the rewards of mental training (*One Year After*, 1972: 13).

Several students felt particularly drawn to the *samatha* meditation Boonman taught; and the Samatha Trust was founded in 1973 'to support the teaching of this form of meditation practice in various parts of the country and to establish a national centre' (www.samatha.org). Nai Boonman himself returned to Thailand in 1974, though he remained one of the five trustees (Boonman, 2004: 56). Active groups developed in Cambridge, London and Manchester, where a former Methodist Church was first rented and then purchased from the City Council, acting as the Trust's main centre for some years. Groups were soon meeting in several towns and cities, and in 1987 the Trust bought Greenestreete, a Welsh hill farm with nearly 90 acres of land, and set about converting it into a meditation centre (*Buddhist Meditation*, n.d.). It opened in 1991 with an invitation to join various residential courses, offering guidance from experienced teachers ('The Samatha Trust', 1991: 263).

The Greenestreete barn was converted into a large Shrine Hall, with a smaller shrine room and a library, and the opening was celebrated in 1996 with 'two days of ceremonies, dhamma talks and blessings', attended by Nai Boonman and senior monks from 'England, Thailand, Sri Lanka, Cambodia and Burma, as well as over 300 Samatha members and friends' (Denison, 2001: 47). Boonman has since returned to England each summer to teach meditation and lead retreats (Rose, 2004). By this time there were 19 introductory groups in England and Wales, half of them in the north or North Midlands, as well as a programme of weekend and week-long courses for experienced meditators at Greenestreete. The Manchester Centre continues as the other main centre, with two shrine rooms, meetings rooms and a library, and offers regular beginners classes, study groups and meetings for meditation and chanting (Voiels, 2003).

There were about 50 accredited Samatha Trust Teachers by 2001, with up to 400 members (Denison, 2001: 47–8). Current numbers may be rather higher, with about 500 members and others (including some Asian Buddhists) attending festivals at Greenestreete or Manchester, so that perhaps as many as 1,000 people have some contact with the movement.

Classes and groups met in 26 towns and cities by 2002, usually separated into a beginners meditation class and a second group for more experienced meditators, often led by the same teacher. There are also continuing courses at Greenestreete and Manchester. While Thai connections were initially due to Nai Boonman, Denison (2001: 49) explained that Samatha Trust branches in Cambridge, London and Manchester have continued to develop these links, 'with several members staying in Thailand for varying periods to deepen their meditation practice'.

Lay Samatha meditation and devotion

The Samatha Trust places great importance on structured meditation. Their website explains how *samatha* meditation is based on calming the mind, using the breath as a meditation object: this is said to lead eventually to an understanding of the habits which cause suffering, and so to behaviour which is 'kinder to ourselves and those around us' (www.samatha.org). In developing awareness of the breath, one also allows it 'to become finer and more subtle, with its flow smoother and more even' (*Abhidhamma Adventures*, 1996: 81). These are ancient techniques, as the 'development of calm leading to the practice of insight is a central tradition of Buddhist meditation and was the form of practice followed by the Buddha himself' (Shaw, 1991: 58).

The practice begins with detailed meditation instructions, derived originally from Nai Boonman's monastic practice in Thailand and used by all Samatha Trust teachers. Beginners will typically take between 6 months and a year of regular meetings and practice to work their way through these (Voiels, 2003); and will then move on to further practices 'to integrate meditation with one's life as a whole... Flexibility to move between an inner and an outer focus for practice will in time allow for both to be held in mind simultaneously' ('Method and Inspiration', 1996: 11).

Samatha Trust meditation is taught as a series of graduated stages, based on the length of the breath and the way the breath is observed. This begins with breathing 'the longest comfortable breath without straining' to a count of nine, followed in turn by breathing to a count of six, then three, then one as 'the shortest comfortable breath'. These four stages, known as the 'Longest of Counting', the 'Longer of Counting', the 'Shorter of Counting' and the 'Shortest of Counting' in each case involve 'tracing the sensations down as you are breathing in, from the nose down to the navel, and on the outbreath from the navel back to the nose' (Harvey, 2003). After 'Counting' has been mastered, one moves on to add 'Following', a more careful continuous mindful tracking of the breath (but without counting), and 'Touching', where the attention focuses on the sensation of the breath at the nostrils. Both of these have the four lengths of breathing, making twelve stages in all.

Nai Boonman has explained that although his meditation teaching has always been based on traditional *ānāpānasati* or mindfulness of breathing, 'the technique of how to know the in-breaths and out-breaths I invented myself, no one had taught the same method before' (Boonman, 2004: 50). The 12 stages are thus a personal adaptation from traditional practice, albeit one made by an experienced Thai ex-monk rather than Samatha Trust members themselves.

New meditators are guided through these stages, spending a week or two adding each new one to the series, and always moving from the longest to the shortest breath and then back to the longest again. While the practice always begins and ends with the Longest of Counting, experienced students will be able to move more directly to more subtle stages. However, all the stages must be learnt before taking these 'shorts cuts'; and this can only be done through direct personal instruction from a Samatha Trust teacher (Harvey, 2003).

Counting initiates both mindfulness and concentration, which are then further developed through Following and Touching respectively, and teacher and meditator will then work together to choose the most appropriate shortened path through the twelve stages. With good concentration and mindfulness on the breath, eventually the meditator will reach a fourth stage known as 'Settling', when a mental image or *nimitta* (Pali (P.) 'sign') starts to arise, typically a visual image of a patch of colour or a simple shape, though it often varies. An article in *Samatha* explained this process:

> Change to the settling. Mindful of the breath, turn the attention to the
> visual field, gently applying the mind. There is always an object of some
> kind...Mindfulness of breathing in the settling sustains something; it's
> like a growing medium providing food for seeds to germinate.
>
> ('Practice', 2002: 16)

A typical beginners class – perhaps running through most of an academic year – usually consists of meditation instruction, a guided *samatha* meditation period and a dhamma talk and some discussion (Voiels, 2003). Individuals will then speak privately with the teacher to discuss progress or difficulties. This 'reporting' is seen as an integral part of the process, and all new meditators establish this formal relationship with their teacher (Stanier, 2003). Senior Samatha Trust teachers have confirmed that personal reporting was practised at the Hampstead Vihara before Nai Boonman arrived there and indeed dates back to ancient times, with senior monks offering guidance to junior monks (Harvey, 2004), though here it has been adapted into a fully lay context. The Samatha Trust appears to be the only tradition where lay teachers offer personal meditation guidance to all students as the norm, though some beginners are reluctant to report regularly, perhaps unwilling to admit they have not been meditating at home.

The beginners meditation period is gradually increased from 5 minutes to perhaps 30 or 40 minutes during the year, depending on the group and the teacher, and it occasionally consists of a guided *mettā* (loving-kindness) meditation rather than the mindfulness of breathing practice. There may also be some walking meditation and later on perhaps some insight (*vipassanā*) practice. Simple chanting may be introduced at some stage, but there is otherwise no formal ritual and the atmosphere is perhaps more of an evening class than a spiritual group.

Meetings of a typical group of experienced meditators have a similar pattern, though the meditation, dhamma talk, discussion and individual reporting are more often preceded by chanting, usually in Pali. This includes paying homage to the Buddha, taking refuge in the Buddha, the Dhamma and the Sangha, and reciting the Five Precepts (in the same form as Forest Sangha chanting) and other chants from the *Chanting Book* (Samatha Association, n.d.). Guided meditation lasts for 30 or 40 minutes, with the whole group taking the same shortened route through the stages of practice, which may be different from their usual one.

Further meditation instruction is given to individuals in the experienced meditators group through reporting (regular members are usually more ready to engage with this process) or perhaps to the group as a whole. Sometimes the talk itself may involve chanting, to enable students to internalize the subject or to present it in a devotional rather than an analytical context. The content and atmosphere of such meetings depends on the style of the teacher: some still appear as a group under instruction, while others may feel like a group of spiritual friends, perhaps with different levels of experience. Some have relatively little sustained ritual or formal ceremony, while others have a more devotional feel to them.

Interviewees emphasized the importance of daily mindfulness of breathing, the development of *mettā* practice and walking meditation (Stanier, 2003). The personal reporting relationship remains important even for teachers, who continue to report either to their own initial teachers, to other more experienced meditators or even to 'someone with the same level of experience as you' where this can bring a helpful reflection to support mindfulness (Harvey, 2003).

Importance is also given to chanting (particularly in a group), which is seen as 'a form of practice in its own right in that it requires a balancing of mindfulness and concentration' ('Method and inspiration', 1996: 11, 12), and traditional chants from several Theravāda countries are used. The *Chanting Book* contains a series of Pali chants, including the refuges and precepts, salutations and offerings to the Three Jewels, frequently chanted *suttas*, and verses on the parts of the body, dependent origination, the ten perfections, the *jhānas* and verses of blessing. Unlike the Forest Sangha *Chanting Book* (1994), few of these are translated into English, perhaps so that the chanting can have a calming effect emotionally before the particular meaning is also learnt. Learning the chants in Pali encourages one to 'learn the feeling of the sound...rather than the precise translation' (Voiels, 2003).

The Manchester Centre is probably the only place where such group chanting in Pali is done regularly, and the monthly *pūjās* on Sunday mornings and on full moon days are closely modelled on Thai monastic practice (Voiels, 2003). This is an unusual example of English lay Theravāda practice remaining more traditional than its monastic counterpart, as Forest Sangha chanting at Amaravati is often in English, especially when lay people are present.

Experienced meditators will regularly chant the refuges and precepts in Pali before meditating, both individually and in their group meetings. Stanier (2003) also described a class chanting *pūjās* or *suttas* (such as the *Mettā Sutta* or the *Maṅgala Sutta*) as 'a good way of settling the mind, arousing a good feeling in the heart'.

Further activities at Greenestreete and the Manchester Centre include beginners' weekends and courses for experienced members. Depending on the individual teacher, a beginners weekend may be a fairly relaxed event, where perhaps only the first few stages of meditation are taught, or a more intensive course, covering 'a range of stages which would normally take several months to learn in a class' (Harvey, 2003). Other weekend courses at Greenestreete have focussed on walking meditation, chanting, the *deva* realms, the foundations of mindfulness, the ten perfections, the five *skandhas*, the four *brahma-vihāras*, *dukkha*, karma and dependent origination. There are also week-long courses of more intensive practice for experienced meditators, working weekends and occasional courses on topics outside Buddhism such as t'ai chi. At the Manchester Centre there are groups studying various Buddhist topics, such as *suttas* or *abhidhamma*, and Pali classes, though other topics have also included Western astrology and female mystics in various religious traditions (Stanier, 2003).

Despite the complex structure of Samatha Trust meditation, the separation of beginners from experienced meditators, the importance attached to Pali chanting and the wide range of other activities and interests, the basic practice still remains relatively simple, according to Stanier (2003), with the most important activities being 'daily breathing mindfulness practice, and reporting to a teacher'.

Lay Theravāda teaching and study

The Samatha Trust shares a common body of teachings with the Forest Sangha, which may fairly be described as orthodox Theravāda, but these are introduced and studied in rather different ways in this lay tradition. Rose (2004) pointed out that some of the traditional teachings in the Pali canon were 'pretty much *only* guidance for monks' rather than for lay people so that a careful choice has to be made in deciding what is relevant.

A beginners group will be very much a *meditation* class, with initial instruction often restricted to meditation and mindfulness, and perhaps the five hindrances as obstructions to meditation. There is typically little emphasis on Buddhist teachings, though the Five Precepts may be discussed as guidelines for moral behaviour. Particular teachings may be introduced gradually later on, but always 'to help and inform and direct the practice' rather than for their own sake: as Voiels (2003) explains, 'it's the practice through which you understand the dhamma'.

The Trust's journal *Samatha* gives a broad indication of the character of Theravāda teaching and practice which is emphasized. Topics include meditation and chanting, observing and guarding the senses, *mettā* practice and the ten perfections. Other articles cover the Four Noble Truths, the Eightfold Path, the four *jhānas*, Buddhist mythology and *devas*, Pali *suttas* and Jātaka tales, and the thirty-two marks of a great man. There are poems and stories, cartoons and a running detective story about tracking down 'a dame called Citta' in the 'winding streets of Sankharaville' (i.e. looking for the mind among the confusion of volitional activities).

Handouts distributed to beginners at one group range from general Buddhist teachings (such as the five hindrances, the Five Precepts, right speech and developing loving-kindness) to more specifically Samatha-based material such as mindfulness and concentration, the stages of breathing practice and simple chanting. Stanier (2003) confirmed the emphasis on both mindfulness of breathing and on 'the importance of right action – *dāna*, *sīla*, the cultivation of wisdom'. Members of the advanced group visited had been looking at the seven factors of enlightenment, the *Satipaṭṭhāna Sutta* and the thirty-two marks, and these were seen as typical subjects for dhamma talks and discussion.

While courses at Greenestreete are linked firmly to practice rather than academic study, the inclusion of such topics as *dukkha*, karma, the foundations of mindfulness, dependent origination, the five *skandhas*, the four *brahma-vihāras*, the ten perfections and the *deva* realms clearly points to a traditional Theravāda emphasis in teaching.

Both individual members and groups may read Forest Sangha publications and so assimilate the teachings of Ajahn Chah and Ajahn Sumedho (Stanier, 2003), but the libraries at Greenestreete and Manchester include material outside Theravāda Buddhism from Mahāyāna and Zen to Christianity and other religions, including some of the more esoteric traditions. The Samatha Trust remains firmly in the Theravāda tradition, but study groups have looked at other Buddhist schools, the Christian mystics and further spiritual traditions at various times (Rose, 2004), showing a liberal approach which encourages investigation.

Study groups of experienced members regularly look at Theravāda texts in translation – often using the recent Wisdom translations of the *Dīgha Nikāya* and *Majjhima Nikāya* – though there are also Pali language classes at the Manchester

Centre for those who wish to study texts in the original. There are one or two *abhidhamma* experts as well (Stanier, 2003; Voiels, 2003). There are no 'core texts' to which members are directed: they are free to study whatever interests them, though it is always explored 'in the light of *samatha* practice' rather than for academic interest (Harvey, 2003). Having said that, Samatha Trust members may appear both more studious and more traditional than Forest Sangha monastics, few of whom focus on textual study in either English or Pali.

Some study groups generate publications such as *Abhidhamma Papers*, a series of essays and discussions on applying the *abhidhamma* texts to meditation and daily life. *Abhidhamma* is seen to offer 'an analytical method through which all our experience may be examined and understood', according to Rowlands (1982: 11), as it deals with 'four kinds of realities': various kinds of impermanent consciousnesses or states of mind, the mental factors which allow us to experience these states, the matter or forms which consciousness experiences and Nirvana, which is beyond description except as 'the supreme happiness' (Rowlands, 1982: 12). The essays and discussions deal in some detail with unskilful and skilful mental factors, attachment to the 'three roots' of greed, hate and delusion, the various thought processes involved and questions of cause and effect. It is unusual to find lay Theravāda Buddhists writing so confidently on technical matters such as these.

Similar themes were later taken up in *Abhidhamma Adventures* (1996), again originating from an *abhidhamma* study group. It is intended as a teachers' guide, adopting an exploratory and experimental approach, with an imaginative combination of reflections, questions and meditation exercises, as well as games and group activities. *Abhidhamma* itself is playfully defined as not only 'an instruction manual' but also 'a magician's spell book … a pre-packed balanced meal … a box of wonderful tricks' (*Abhidhamma Adventures*, 1996: 2–3). Each chapter deals with one main area of the *abhidhamma*, explaining mental factors which may be universal or particular, unskilful (such as greed, hate and delusion) or skilful (such as mindfulness, compassion and wisdom). The final chapter deals directly with the nature of *citta*, the ever-changing 'mind, or heart, or mind-and-heart' (*Abhidhamma Adventures*, 1996: 149), listing and describing the various types of unskilful and skilful *citta*.

While the Forest Sangha tends to ignore or downplay the importance of Theravāda cosmology, several Samatha Trust members have shown an interest in it, with one group studying the *deva* realms and producing *A Handbook of Devas* (n.d.). Perhaps this reflects a difference between these two interpretations of the Theravāda tradition. The Forest Sangha, based on *vipassanā* meditation, tends to emphasize impermanence and not-self, downplaying the differences between levels of beings, while the Samatha Trust, based on *samatha* meditation, is more interested in the altered states of consciousness, different levels of which are reflected in the *deva* realms (Harvey, 2003).

These publications on *abhidhamma* and *devas* show Samatha Trust groups examining areas of Theravāda teaching which are less familiar in the West, rather than downplaying them in favour of the familiar Four Noble Truths and the Eightfold Path. This inquisitive approach reflects the interests of individual teachers, but also owes something to Nai Boonman's intellectual and spiritual curiosity, which led him to study mysticism, psychic powers and astrology (as well as Buddhist philosophy and Pali) during his years as a monk (Boonman, 2004: 20, 24). Such an approach also points to a commitment to study and teaching which characterizes the Samatha Trust as a whole.

Sutta groups meet regularly at the Manchester Centre, usually led by a teacher, and occasionally at other groups as well. Again this is seen as 'investigation into Dhamma' rather than study, according to Voiels (2003) since its purpose is 'to get to the heart of the Dhamma through the *suttas*', rather than to acquire knowledge about texts, so that study becomes part of one's spiritual practice. This is reinforced by asking new members to practise for a year before they start using material in the library.

Such groups may explore *suttas* or *abhidhamma* texts, or may instead spend time learning chants such as the *Mettā Sutta* or the *Mangala Sutta*. According to Stanier (2003) group study is seen as 'an important way of supporting meditation practice', and an opportunity in itself to practice mindful listening and right speech.

The Samatha Trust has an unusually academic background, which has influenced its activities and membership. The original class with Nai Boonman was at Cambridge, and early groups often sprang up in universities. Several current teachers (such as Lance Cousins, Peter Harvey and Rupert Gethin) are academics and Pali scholars teaching Buddhism in British universities, and there is a high proportion of teachers and professional people amongst its teachers and membership, reflecting the predominantly middle-class interest in British Theravāda Buddhism.

Within the Samatha Trust there is a kind of informal 'lineage' of teachers. Nai Boonman taught the original enthusiasts (including Cousins and Denison), and they taught many of the other existing teachers, who in turn might recommend that an experienced meditator in their group be considered as a teacher. However, this process is decentralized and informal: members will often attend retreats given by a particular teacher, whether or not they report to them. Moreover, this is an oral tradition, in that neither teachers nor meditators have any written descriptions of the practice to refer to. There is no instruction handbook for teachers, though providing one has recently been discussed (Rose, 2004). Some teachers may offer handouts for their students, but these cannot take the place of personal instruction and individual reporting (Harvey, 2003). This is unusual, as most other traditions have detailed written instructions of how to practise.

The Samatha Trust places a high value on traditional Theravāda teachings, but sees no need to downplay aspects which might be seen as problematic in the West. Teachers and members often have the confidence to choose teachings which seem particularly helpful to lay people, rather than accept a pattern which may apply primarily to monastics.

The figure of the Buddha

Perhaps more than other traditions, the narrative element of Samatha Trust practice focuses almost exclusively on the historical Buddha. Even in a beginners meditation group, which has little emphasis on Buddhist narrative, the life story of the Buddha will be briefly described, perhaps in the middle of the course. Advanced groups will give considerable emphasis to the person of the Buddha, with stories from the Pali texts being used to illustrate the teachings.

Interviewees confirmed that most long-term members would get to know the Buddha's life story well, and that this was the most important narrative (Stanier, 2003; Voiels, 2003). While such information would initially come from talks at group meetings, committed members will also read the texts for themselves, drawing on *suttas* and commentaries for stories about the Buddha which 'help to inform attitudes and practice' (Harvey, 2003).

One example of how such narratives are used is the *The Suttanta on the Marks*, where a translation from the *Dīgha Nikāya* is presented as an opportunity to reflect on the Buddha's qualities as 'an important part of Buddhist meditative practice', and one which can guard against 'dogmatism or rigid views' (McNab *et al.*, 1996: 5). Similarly, in *Thirty-Two Marks* (1995: v), readers are invited to use the 'thirty-two marks of a Great Man' to observe and investigate the characteristics of their own body and mind. In a story told as if for a child, a sleepy prince leaves home on a spiritual quest for wakefulness and is gently introduced to teachings on morality, meditation and wisdom. The thirty-two marks are then linked more directly to this threefold path, to the four *jhānas* and finally to the Eightfold Path. Each of the Buddha's marks is seen imaginatively as relating to spiritual progress, from the 'well-planted feet' which resemble 'the first steps one takes towards the Dhamma' to the 'turban crown' which symbolizes 'insight into the real nature of things: anicca, dukkha, anattā' (*Thirty-Two Marks*, 1995: 106–7).

While this example shows how the narratives are used, it is not a central teaching, but 'just one that groups became interested in' (Voiels, 2003). Apart from the extensive use of narratives surrounding the Buddha himself, members may well refer to narratives about the Buddha's disciples, though these will be chosen to inform the practice rather than out of reverence for Sāriputta or Moggalāna. Individual members might also find some of the *deva* stories or Jātaka tales useful (Harvey, 2003; Voiels, 2003).

Unlike the Forest Sangha, there is little emphasis on the life and teaching of contemporary figures. Nai Boonman is highly respected among teachers and experienced members as the person who first taught this form of meditation in Britain: the *Samatha Newsletter* carries details of his current activities in Thailand and his summer visits to Greenestreete, and his recent autobiographical essay *From One to Nine* (Boonman, 2004) has been read with interest. However, he is not seen as either the founder or the leader of the Samatha Trust, and members may not initially even be aware of his role. The two remaining founder members, Lance Cousins and Paul Denison, are respected as senior teachers, and might be quoted from time to time, but they are not revered as spiritual leaders (Voiels, 2003).

There is certainly a deep reverence for the Buddha amongst Samatha Trust members, but even the narratives about Gautama are studied for their implications for practice, rather than a feeling of hagiography. It is perhaps significant that the large Buddha in the Greenestreete Shrine Hall is sculpted in the *Dhammacakra mudrā*, the teaching pose 'which symbolises the Buddha's First Sermon' (Denison, 2001: 49), rather than in the calm meditation posture one might expect from a *samatha* tradition.

Calming the mind

The practice dimension already described gives helpful suggestions on how it feels to practice in this tradition. We have seen *samatha* meditation being used to calm the mind, *mettā* meditation to generate loving-kindness, and chanting to encourage feelings of calm, energy, joy and devotion.

An introductory leaflet explains that *samatha* means 'calm, peace or tranquillity' and that Samatha practice draws on our 'inner resources for developing deep states of calm', leading to improved concentration, less emotional turmoil, a sense of joy, increasing self-confidence and openness to others, and greater 'mental clarity and awareness, which enable one to understand the workings of one's mind and emotions, and respond to life in more skilful, and subtle, ways' (Harvey, 'Introduction to Samatha Meditation', n.d.: n.p.). A passage from *Abhidhamma Adventures* (1996: 107–10) underlines the importance for practice of 'skilful mental factors' which include confidence, mindfulness and self-respect, stilling the body and mind, and compassion, sympathetic joy, and wisdom.

This may represent something of an 'official' version of feelings which should ideally be generated, but interviewees tended to support it from personal experience. Newcomers may be interested in meditation rather than Buddhism, and although their practice may bring the wish for deeper involvement, this is often due to the trust and confidence of experience, rather than any leap of faith (Harvey, 2003; Stanier, 2003).

It is hardly surprising to find that Samatha practice is more associated with calmness than with devotional fervour. Voiels (2003) spoke of 'a deep peacefulness' in meditation and suggested that 'the still cool forest pool is an image which conveys something of the qualities of the Samatha Trust'. Stanier (2003) underlined the importance of serenity and of becoming 'calmer and more focussed' through her practice, and Harvey (2003) also emphasized calmness and mindfulness as important qualities in Samatha practice.

However, interviewees also reported feelings of great happiness and joy experienced during meditation. Voiels (2003) spoke of intense feelings which might arise and could be described as 'an overflowing of emotion', Stanier (2003) referred to 'occasional bliss states', which might be 'pleasant and encouraging' as long as one does not chase after them and Harvey (2003) suggested that qualities like joy and happiness often build up as one approaches the 'Settling' stage in the meditation and as the *nimitta* arises.

Such joyful states may also arise during chanting practice. Harvey (2003) reported that a 'joyful devotion can come in through the chanting', and Voiels (2003) pointed out that while there is no 'fervent devotional chanting' in this tradition, it can nevertheless be 'very powerful, it does have quite a strong effect'.

In response to a question on how to deal with negative emotions, interviewees referred repeatedly to the teaching on the five hindrances (sensual desire, ill will, sloth and torpor, restlessness and worry, and doubt or 'fear of commitment' (Harvey, 1990: 249)), which Harvey (2003) described as 'pretty central to Samatha theory'. These hindrances are seen as 'unskilful states' to be gradually abandoned, 'heart-mind states' even more persistent than fleeting emotions (Voiels, 2003).

Members may examine in turn the nature of the hindrances, the unfortunate results they have and counteractive measures, such as developing the 'five factors of *jhāna*' (applied thought, examination, joy, happiness and 'one-pointedness of mind' (Harvey, 1990: 250)). Stepping back to be mindful of the hindrances, being aware that feelings will pass and 'not taking yourself too seriously' are further reflective practices recommended to understand and deal with negative emotions (Harvey, 2003).

A beginners' class will often have the feeling of a group under instruction, perhaps more like a yoga class than anything more spiritual. There may well be a quiet and peaceful atmosphere, though newcomers may sometimes become bored waiting in silence for others to finish their prescribed period of meditation. Advanced groups may be set in a more devotional framework, and while there may still be something of the atmosphere of a class rather than a spiritual group, there is also a shared sense of commitment to Buddhism and a personal experience of a spiritual path.

The Five Precepts

A strong link is made in the Samatha Trust between personal feelings and ethical behaviour. It is the avoiding of negative states and actions, as well as meditation and chanting, which are seen to bring peace and happiness. In a beginners class the Five Precepts will be introduced at some stage during the course, perhaps with an explanatory handout. This is done as an invitation, and members are neither required nor expected to take the precepts formally or to adopt them as moral guidelines. In an experienced group, as we have seen, the precepts are chanted in Pali at each meeting, and members are generally expected to be committed to them. In this way basic Buddhist ethics are understood and accepted. On full moon days at the Manchester Centre, some members will take the Eight Precepts for the day, and others may do so when on strict retreat at Greenestreete (Voiels, 2003).

However, the Five Precepts are seen as broad moral guidelines, and there are no specific prohibitions in this tradition. Although not strictly required by the first precept, vegetarianism is very much the norm at British Buddhist centres: Greenestreete was the only centre visited where meat was served at a communal meal, perhaps recognizing that only a minority of newcomers would be vegetarians. Interviewees confirmed that the Five Precepts are seen not as a series of prohibitions, but more as 'a way of reminding oneself about basic rules for daily conduct' (Stanier, 2003). Right speech, however, was often seen as particularly important (Harvey, 2003).

Even on retreat at Greenestreete, where there is 'a very clear sense of observing *sīla*' (P. 'morality'), Voiels (2003) still felt that 'it's not good to be fanatical about particulars'. Harvey (2003) also underlined the danger of a judgemental approach to the precepts, where for example the abstainer becomes so 'attached to not drinking' that he criticizes everyone who does drink.

Voiels (2003) suggested that ethical guidelines spring from 'a strong sense of *saṅgha*, a sense of real regard and trust', rather than the more literal approach of 'having a code that you keep'. Although Samatha Trust members chant the Five Precepts together and ethical behaviour is essential to support meditation practice, the important aspect is to develop 'an integrity which you can recognize', based on how members trust and relate to each other. It is tempting to see this as a distinctive lay approach, contrasting with monastic adherence to the *Vinaya*, but the notion of mutual trust as more important than keeping rules is probably more about going beyond the form and into the real spirit of the practice.

Asked about the encouragement of specific virtues in this tradition, interviewees referred in particular to loving-kindness, right speech and generosity as being emphasized and encouraged (Stanier, 2003). As well as financial support, generosity could include 'doing things for the tradition', such as giving time to clean or maintain one of the centres (Harvey, 2003). This might be seen as an adapted version of the *dāna* usually associated with supporting Theravāda monks, though monks do visit both Samatha Centres and are supported by lay people during their stay there.

A decentralized lay organization

The overall organization of the Samatha Trust is not dependent on any central administration or individual leader. Trustees oversee finance and strategy, a management group runs the Greenestreete Centre, members and teachers each have their own annual meetings and there are also 'Seekers of Ways' or 'Sowers', who develop and push forward modes of teaching and practice (Harvey, 2003). Rose (2004) added that although there are no 'authoritative leaders in the middle telling you what to do', the senior teachers are still respected as 'people to turn to for advice and guidance'. There is no resident lay community at Greenestreete, partly for lack of accommodation, but also to keep the centre independent of any particular individual or small group.

As we have seen, most Samatha Trust branches are divided into two groups, meeting separately but usually led by the same teacher. Voiels (2003) made the distinction between 'an instruction class for beginners' and a 'study group' of more experienced members. Beginners classes often meet weekly, and students may tend to interact with the leader rather than with each other, giving the group a feeling of a class under instruction rather than a meeting of spiritual friends.

At a large branch such as the Manchester Centre there are beginners classes almost every evening, with a different teacher for each class, though individuals usually remain with the same teacher throughout, to maintain continuity and regular reporting to see how their meditation is going (Voiels, 2003). Some group members enjoy reporting to their teacher, while others find it awkward, especially if they have not been meditating. Teachers will always try to act with kindness to their students but will concentrate on the meditation practice rather than become involved in more general advice or counselling. As well as the teacher, there is usually an assistant or 'disciplinarian' to help organize the reporting sessions, while maintaining a quiet atmosphere in the group, encouraging mindfulness and right speech (Voiels, 2003).

The advanced group or study group consists of experienced members – often middle-aged – who may know each other better and have a stronger feeling of spiritual friendship. Meeting perhaps monthly or fortnightly for meditation, chanting and study, the style of the group may be less formal, though this will often depend on the particular teacher. Individuals will normally remain with the same teacher throughout, as 'every meditator has one person whom they would regard as "their" teacher' (Stanier, 2003).

According to Voiels (2003), there may be no clearcut distinction between the two groups, but instead 'a point at which they stop being a beginners class and become more like a group'. Members of the advanced group will usually gain more confidence in their own practice and so become less dependent on the teacher, though again this will vary considerably.

The teacher's role remains important throughout. Interviewees described how a teacher is seen as a spiritual friend or as 'someone who treads the path a bit ahead of you', rather than an authority figure or guru (Voiels, 2003), or perhaps as a 'guide' or a 'lead explorer' rather than a teacher in the formal sense (Harvey, 2003). Denison (2001: 46) has explained that Nai Boonman was skilled in 'training and encouraging his meditation students themselves to begin to teach meditation as they gained enough experience'. Lance Cousins and Paul Denision are seen as the two remaining 'first generation' teachers. Further teachers become 'accredited' after being informally examined by two existing teachers, perhaps at a Greenestreete retreat, who will look for an understanding of the teaching, experience of meditation and for 'spiritual maturity' (Harvey, 2003). Voiels (2003) explained how this process may happen informally over a period of time, with an experienced meditator perhaps first taking sessions at a retreat and maintaining personal contact with their own teacher who can see if their practice and commitment is sufficiently developed. A formal invitation is then given, after which the person is authorized to teach as a Samatha Trust teacher. This is in effect an informal type of lineage transmission, more often seen in monastic practice.

The Samatha Trust is financed by subscriptions from British members and donations from members and visitors (Stanier, 2003). Although there are strong connections with Thailand, this has not produced the kind of Asian benefactors who support the Forest Sangha. The large golden Buddha in the Shrine Hall at Greenestreete was a gift from Thai Buddhists, but the purchase of the farm and land (and the Manchester Centre) was funded completely by British members. The Trust is a relatively low-budget organization where no charge is made for teaching, but members and visitors are asked to make donations to cover the hiring of rooms (Voiels, 2003). Even residential courses at Greenestreete – which until recently were charged for at fixed rates – are now funded by asking for donations towards running the centre.

The attitude of Samatha Trust members to society as a whole may be glimpsed from another publication originating from a study group. *The Universal Monarch* is a series of essays, stories and poems, which reflect on Pali texts dealing with the king who 'represents the highest ideal of the household life, of the man or woman who, married with children, with material possessions, wide responsibilities and much work to do, is nonetheless ruled by dhamma' (*The Universal Monarch*, 1987: 1). The ideal ruler and the ideal kingdom from the Buddha's time are clearly seen as relevant for personal and social life today, underlining the theme of making spiritual progress in family life rather than as monastics. Stanier (2003) confirmed that she saw the strength of Samatha Trust groups as their willingness to address, as lay people, 'the challenges of being a Buddhist – whatever that means – in a secular world'.

There are contacts with various Theravāda monastic communities in Britain, including both the Forest Sangha and Asian monks. At the opening of the new shrine hall at Greenestreete, for example, Sri Lankan monks performed an all-night *paritta* chanting, while Ajahn Viradhammo came from Amaravati to give a talk (Harvey, 2003). Monks and nuns will sometimes be invited to the Manchester Centre or elsewhere, and groups in the Birmingham area have developed firm links with local Burmese and Thai *vihāras*: the Thai monk Maha Laaw has taught them a number of Pali chants (Voiels, 2003). However, senior Samatha Trust teachers have been careful not to align the movement with any particular Theravāda school (Rose, 2004).

In this way the Samatha Trust draws on 'the broader Theravādan tradition' (Harvey, 2003), though such links tend to fluctuate and are sometimes rather tenuous. Outside the Theravāda tradition there are fewer contacts. Members of the Cambridge and Manchester groups have sometimes visited local Tibetan Dechen groups, though Tibetan and Zen groups would not normally be invited to celebrations at Greenestreete. Interviewees suggested that most local Samatha groups tend to have little contact with those from other Buddhist traditions, and there was a certain wariness of both the FWBO and the NKT.

The social and organizational dimension of the Samatha Trust may be seen as an interesting blend of traditional Asian Theravāda Buddhism and more modern Western ideas. There are contacts with Thailand and Theravāda monastics in

Britain, teachers have an important role and a lineage of accreditation, Pali texts are referred to for exemplars for daily living, and there is some suspicion of non-traditional forms of Buddhism. However, all this is seen in a completely lay context, where individual initiative is more important than central authority, where members are fully integrated into modern society and where informal structures may seem closer to British educational practice than to communal Buddhist monasticism.

Images of calmness

Apart from Greenestreete and the Manchester Centre, Samatha Trust groups usually meet in hired rooms or on university premises, with no permanent Buddhist artefacts or decoration. In a beginners group there may be no visual clues to identify this as a Buddhist meeting, while an advanced group will often set up a small Buddha image, with candles and incense. Both groups sit on the floor to meditate, and members may bring their own cushions or meditation stools, though ordinary chairs are used outside the formal meditation. A few groups meet in members' homes, where there may be a shrine room specifically for meditation practice, and committed members may also have shrines in their own homes.

Greenestreete is a former farmhouse with 8 bedrooms and further accommodation in 4 small huts in the extensive grounds. The adjacent barn has been converted into a large shrine hall, a smaller shrine room and a library. The large shrine hall has a massive gilded Buddha, over 8 feet tall, specially commissioned from Thailand, seated in the teaching posture and surrounded by smaller Buddhas, tables and vases, all in the Thai style. The small shrine room also has a Thai gilded Buddha and a standing Buddha which appears more Burmese, and there is further Thai iconography throughout the centre.

The Manchester Centre's main shrine room has a large gilded Thai Buddha, flanked by smaller Buddhas given by the Thai community. This room is used for *pūjas*, dhamma talks and large meetings. Stanier (2003) felt that the Buddha *rūpas* 'engender a sense of awe as well as warmth', helping to create an atmosphere 'very conducive to mindful practice'. On one wall a painting by a Western artist shows the path of purification, symbolically depicting the 3 fires and the 5 senses. A general meeting room (with no shrine) is used for beginners meetings, and a further room has a huge wall hanging of a *bodhi* tree on one wall, sewn by local members, as a highly recognizable symbol of the Buddha's enlightenment. This room also has an unusual example of Buddhist stained glass – appropriately enough in a converted church – showing the wheel of Dhamma and other images from the *Satipaṭṭhāna Sutta*.

Although much of the imagery at both Greenestreete and Manchester is in the Thai style, the Buddha images – the central iconographic feature of this tradition – are chosen primarily for their '*samatha*' feeling of calm and peacefulness and so may be from other Theravāda countries as well.

Conclusion

The Samatha Trust may appear as a parallel to the Forest Sangha, fitting neatly at the conservative end of a 'spectrum of adaptation' in British Buddhism. Each dimension shows evidence of traditional Asian Theravāda Buddhism. This includes structured *samatha* meditation and Pali chanting, orthodox Theravāda teaching (including an interest in cosmology) and close study of Pali texts, a firm emphasis on the life of the historical Buddha, traditional use of the Five Precepts (and the five hindrances teaching) to avoid unwholesome states and to promote moral behaviour, an informal lineage of respected teachers who guide students in their practice, and Buddha *rūpas* as a focus for devotion. Indeed, Pali chanting, textual study and Theravāda cosmology may suggest that the Samatha Trust is even more traditional than its monastic counterpart.

However, this interpretation ignores important adaptations in each dimension which give this tradition a distinctly British flavour. These include personal guidance from lay meditation teachers, with separate beginners classes and advanced groups, an emphasis on unusual elements of the teaching, as well as the Eightfold Path, interpreting texts and narratives imaginatively to inform contemporary practice in the secular world, a sense of confidence in the practice rather than faith in Buddhism, a communal ethics based on mutual trust rather than on individuals keeping rules, and an integration with the secular world, with no central residential community.

One final element again combines Asian and Western strands. An unusually high proportion of Samatha Trust teachers and members work in schools and universities, some of them teaching religious studies. The pattern of study groups and publications has a slightly academic flavour to it, though this is always used to support practice rather than research. Among committed members there is an emphasis on imaginatively – sometimes even playfully – exploring the implications of traditional teachings for the life of lay Buddhists in contemporary Britain.

The Samatha Trust combines a strong emphasis on calmness and mindfulness with elements of joyful devotion. It combines a highly structured meditation with a loose organizational structure, and it is a wholly lay movement which nevertheless retains some characteristics of Thai monasticism. The complex mixture of elements here shows the difficulty of placing this tradition on a simple 'spectrum of adaptation' and suggests that a more sophisticated model may be needed for comparing the different traditions of Buddhism in Britain.

5

SERENE REFLECTION MEDITATION (SRM)

Historical background

Both the Serene Reflection Meditation tradition (SRM) and its monastic core, the Order of Buddhist Contemplatives (OBC), are firmly based in Japanese Sōtō Zen Buddhism, though there have been conscious adaptations in bringing the tradition to the West. SRM traces its origins back to two Japanese Zen Masters: Dōgen (1200–53) first brought the Sōtō Zen tradition from China to Japan, and Keizan (1268–1325) later adapted the practice to Japanese customs, also founding Sōjiji monastery, where the SRM founder would train over six centuries later.

Peggy Kennett (1924–96) came from a Christian background, studied music and became a church organist. Disillusioned by the Church of England's attitude to women, she began to study Theravāda Buddhism, and after joining the Buddhist Society in 1954 became 'an enthusiastic member of Humphreys' popular Zen Class' (Kay, 2004: 121). When Keidō Chisan Kohō Zenji (1879–1967), the abbot of Sōjiji, came to London in 1960, she helped make arrangements for his visit, and when he invited her to become his disciple in Japan, she readily agreed (MacPhillamy, 2000: xi). In late 1961 she left England for 'an intensive course of the study and practice of Soto Zen' in Japan, with the Buddhist Society's blessing ('Buddhist News', 1961: 130).

Her 7 years of training in the East are described in *The Wild, White Goose*, an edited version of her contemporary diaries (Kennett, 2002: x–xi). En route to Japan in 1962 she paused to give lectures in Malaysia and was ordained in the Chinese Rinzai *saṅgha*. After 3 months she continued to Japan and was welcomed into the Sōtō tradition by Kohō Zenji, who received her as his personal disciple, despite opposition to a foreign woman from some of the other monks (Kennett, 2002: 10, 37–8).

At Sōjiji she endured hostility, physical pain and ill health, but after only 6 months she experienced her first *kenshō* or 'enlightenment experience'. In 1963 she was given 'Dharma Transmission' by Kohō Zenji and thus formally recognized as a Sōtō Zen lineage holder (Kennett, 2002: 39f., 128–9). He later certified her as a *rōshi* (Zen Master) and, as the first Western woman with this title, she developed 'a small, but committed group of Western disciples' at her own temple (Kay, 2004: 123).

In 1964 Christmas Humphreys wrote asking for a Zen teacher for England, but when Kohō Zenji nominated Rōshi Kennett as the 'Buddhist Bishop of London', Humphreys rejected her and 'specifically requested a Japanese male Zen *Rōshi* instead' (Kay, 2004: 124). Buddhist Society representatives came to examine her suitability, but pronounced the Sōtō school's teaching methods and lack of interest in the scriptures as 'unacceptable in Britain' (Kennett, 2002: 256f., 270). It seemed clear that she would not be welcome in London.

She was awarded the Sei-kyoshi certificate (a monastic equivalent of a Doctor of Divinity) in 1966, but in the following year Kohō Zenji died, while she herself was ill in hospital. With little support in Japan, she left to teach in America in 1969, certificated by the Japanese Sōtō Zen administration as 'their official representative when going to America and England' (Kennett, 2002: 470, 498–9, n. 170).

She founded the Zen Mission Society (ZMS) in San Francisco, gathering lay supporters and ordaining disciples, and introducing a period of postulancy to ensure full commitment (Kay, 2004: 124). Kohō Zenji had declared that Westerners who practise Zen 'must colour it for themselves just as the Japanese did', (Kennett, 1973a: v) so the adaptation process had official sanction. In 1970 Shasta Abbey was established in California, and Rōshi Kennett visited Britain on a teaching tour, which Rev. Master Daishin described as the 'first significant impact made by Sōtō Zen Buddhism in Britain' (Morgan, 1994a: 137). Her lectures and meditation retreats stimulated considerable interest: a dozen people received lay ordination and five more returned to America with her to be ordained (Kay, 2004: 125).

One of these, Daiji Strathern, returned to look for a base in England and purchased a Northumberland farmhouse with his own money (Kay, 2004: 125). He became the first prior when Rōshi Kennett visited in 1972 to lead retreats and to inaugurate Throssel Hole Priory as 'the first Sōtō Zen Buddhist monastery in Britain' (Morgan, 1994a: 137), independent from Shasta Abbey. The accommodation was spartan but 'a lot more comfortable than the average Japanese temple' (Kennett, 1973b: 5), and there were soon six monks in residence. (OBC monastics – male and female – are called 'monks' or 'priests': I have used 'monks' throughout, sometimes adding 'and nuns' to underline that women are included.)

British followers hoped that Rōshi Kennett would remain at Throssel Hole: but with limited strength, and unsure of the welcome from 'some elements of the Buddhist establishment in Britain', she chose to return to America (Morgan, 1994a: 140). In 1973 she published *Selling Water by the River* (Kennett, 1973a), a detailed description of Zen training which aroused great interest, and visited Britain again, though in poor health. Her scheduled 1974 visit was cancelled, though the London Zen Priory was opened: Kay (2004: 125) linked this with disagreements between Rōshi Kennett and Daiji Strathern, but Rev. Master Daishin (2004) reported that these only began later.

Soon Throssel Hole offered a programme of weekend and week-long retreats, and there were six lay groups meeting in private houses ('Soto Zen Meditation

Groups', 1974: 5). With relatively inexperienced monks, an expanding lay congregation, a need for more accommodation and little prospect of further visits from Rōshi Kennett, the small monastic community may well have felt overstretched.

Rōshi Kennett's health deteriorated further, and early in 1976 she entered an intensive private retreat to prepare for death. Here she experienced a further *kenshō*, which her chaplain later described as 'a massive spiritual opening accompanied by visions and recollections of past lives' (MacPhillamy, 2000: xiv). These unusual experiences were described in her autobiographical *How to Grow a Lotus Blossom* (Kennett, 1977) and had a profound effect on her subsequent teaching and the development of the ZMS.

Kay (2004: 164) described the 'Lotus Blossom' years between 1976 and 1983 as a 'turbulent and unstable' period where responses to Rōshi Kennett's visions varied widely. Some monks and nuns accepted her visions and even had similar experiences themselves, while others rejected them and left the movement. Remote from these events, the small British community was plunged into 'uncertainty and crisis' as several influential disciples chose to leave, including Daiji Strathern and the senior monk at the London Zen Priory, which had to close (Kay, 2004: 167f.). Naturally this undermined support for the movement in Britain.

Meanwhile, the ZMS became the 'Reformed Sōtō Zen Church' in 1976, and within it the OBC was formed in 1978 to unify and regulate the various monastic communities (Morgan, 1994a: 142). Throssel Hole Priory was purchased from Daiji Strathern and became a charitable trust. In 1977 the five remaining British monks moved to Shasta Abbey for an extended period of training, while a succession of American monks acted as prior at Throssel Hole and supported British lay trainees (Morgan, 1994a: 141). Rōshi Kennett was initially reluctant to assume responsibility for the British congregation (Kay, 2004: 173), but she soon promised to write regularly for the *Journal of Throssel Hole Priory* and to take 'a far more active part in what happens in Britain' (Kennett, 1978a: 11).

The controversy of the Lotus Blossom period gradually subsided, and the movement entered what Kay (2004: 182) called 'a new period of growth, relative stability and routinisation' in the early 1980s. Rev. Daishin Morgan (b. 1951) was certified as a *rōshi* at Shasta Abbey, and became the prior of Throssel Hole when he and the other British monks returned in 1982. Monks and nuns could again be ordained in Britain, and the monastic community gradually expanded (Morgan, 1994a: 141). This prompted the growth and commitment of the lay congregation, and according to Kay (2004: 182), 'marked the beginnings of Throssel Hole Priory's autonomous, and largely self-regulating, development'.

In 1983 it was decided to translate 'Rōshi' as 'Reverend Master' to emphasize English terms ('Announcement', 1983: 4), and Rōshi Kennett became known as Rev. Master Jiyu. A lay ministry programme (begun in America) was introduced in Britain, with the first lay ministers certified in 1984 (Kay, 2004: 203). A new monastic meditation hall was completed by 1988, a new priory opened in Reading, and in 1992 there were 30 monks and nuns at Throssel Hole, with 40 lay ministers, 30 meditation groups and a total congregation of 'about a thousand' ('Throssel Hole Priory: 1972–1992', 1992: 17; Batchelor, 1994: 136).

Rev. Master Jiyu-Kennett died at Shasta Abbey in 1996 and Rev. Master Daizui MacPhillamy was elected as Head of the Order. Kay (2004: 215) reported that strengthened connections between the various monasteries helped to negotiate this crucial phase successfully. Rev. Master Daizui visited Britain in 1997 and conferred abbey status on Throssel Hole, formally recognizing it as an independent training monastery ('The Conferring of the Charter of Throssel Hole Buddhist Abbey', 1997: 12–14). Further priories were opened in Telford and Edinburgh, and smaller centres in Rochdale, Exeter, Aberystwyth and Pembrokeshire. In 2000 an OBC Conclave met at Throssel Hole to review the *Rules* and consider new proposals including liturgy and ceremonial, monastic discipline, the lay ministry and the master–disciple relationship (Hollenbeck, 2000: 41).

The SRM tradition remains a substantial movement in British Buddhism, with 30 monks and nuns at Throssel Hole, several more at other centres, over 50 lay ministers and 26 affiliated groups. Between 25 and 30 people receive lay ordination each year, and the total congregation is probably over 1,000. These figures suggest that many SRM trainees practise on their own, perhaps with occasional retreats at Throssel Hole, rather than with a local group.

Sōtō Zen meditation and ceremonial

The OBC have called meditation 'the foundation of our religious practice', with *zazen* or 'serene reflection meditation' described as simply sitting still with the mind alert, 'neither suppressing nor indulging the thoughts and feelings that arise' (www.OBCon.org). This echoes Dōgen's *Rules for Meditation*, which are recited daily at the abbey and in meditation group meetings. Dōgen taught that the enlightened mind saw that meditation training was not separate from enlightenment, but when duality is allowed to creep in, this perspective disappears: 'when the opposites arise, the Buddha Mind is lost' (Kennett *et al.*, 1996: 1). Seated in a quiet room in loose clothing, trainees are told to bring the mind under control, assume an upright posture, keep the eyes open and then 'sit steadily, neither trying to think nor trying not to think; just sitting, with no deliberate thought, is the important aspect of serene reflection meditation' (Kennett *et al.*, 1996: 2).

This form of meditation has no further levels or more complex practices for experienced practitioners. Rev. Master Daishin explained how Sōtō Zen introduces the whole form of meditation from the start, without the preliminary practices used in some other traditions: this reflects the 'sudden aspect of enlightenment' where meditation is done 'to realise the Buddha that we already are', rather than achieving Buddhahood gradually (Morgan, 2004). The only addition Rev. Master Jiyu has made to this traditional method is a form of 'circular breathing' with 'inhalation up the back of the body and exhalation down the front' (Kennett, 1977: 187) which is used to begin meditation and to bring the attention back when it wanders.

Dōgen's instructions for sitting in the lotus posture have been removed to avoid leg and back injuries in Westerners and meditators often sit on a chair or meditation bench, keeping the back upright. Rev. Master Daishin reported that using chairs for meditation – and removable sections in the monks' meditation platforms for those who cannot sit cross-legged – would horrify some Japanese temples, while others have quietly begun to introduce chairs themselves (Morgan, 2004).

Seated meditation is often alternated with 5 or 10 minutes of *kinhin* or walking meditation, moving slowly with the body still erect, the hands clasped together above the navel, bringing the mind back to the walking when it wanders off. Trainees are also encouraged to do everything 'with the mind of meditation', bringing the attention back to each activity so that eventually 'meditation truly becomes a twenty-four hours a day activity' (Morgan, 1996a: 29).

Interviewees confirmed that monks and lay people are taught the same meditation practice. The monastic community may have more personal guidance to find the balance between censoring their thoughts and indulging them, but lay people are also encouraged to acknowledge thoughts and feelings which arise, allowing them to pass without engaging with them.

As well as the emphasis on meditation, this is a highly liturgical tradition, with daily services and festival ceremonies throughout the year. Rev. Master Jiyu explained in *The Liturgy of the Order of Buddhist Contemplatives for the Laity* (*Liturgy*) that she transcribed all the ceremonial she learned in Japan, so that lay people can 'join fully in the Buddhist liturgy both when in a temple and at home' (*Liturgy*, 1990: i). Rev. Kōshin Schomberg (1997: 113) explained that all the ceremonial translated and taught by Rev. Master Jiyu is 'a vehicle for expressing the mind and heart of meditation': the traditional Buddhist practice of bowing, for example – either ceremonially before a Buddha statue or simply greeting each other with palms together in *gasshō* – is used to help trainees recognize 'that all beings are Buddhas' (Morgan, 1994a: 145). Kay (2004: 185) confirmed that despite 'modifications and adaptations', much OBC ceremonial is similar to traditional Japanese Sōtō Zen practice.

The daily Morning Service includes chanting the *Avalokiteshvara Scripture* (from the *Lotus Sūtra*), the *Scripture of Great Wisdom* (the *Heart Sūtra*), and the Sōtō Zen ancestral line, running from the Buddha to Rev. Master Jiyu. Dōgen's *Rules for Meditation* are recited during Mid-Day Service, and Evening Office (previously 'Vespers') includes a further invocation of Avalokiteśvara in 'The Litany of the Great Compassionate One' (*Liturgy*, 1990: 47–88, 97–100, 108–11). These scriptures and texts are also used in lay meditation groups.

Festival ceremonies commemorate the birth, enlightenment and death of the Buddha, the life of Zen Masters such as Bodhidharma, Dōgen and Keizan, and bodhisattvas such as Avalokiteśvara, Samantabhadra and Mañjuśhrī, who are seen as 'the personifications of attributes of enlightenment' (Morgan, 1994a: 144). These are colourful events, with monks processing round the ceremony hall sprinkling water, wafting incense and strewing paper lotus petals. The lay congregation will participate by chanting and processing to offer incense in turn at the altar. Other services include naming, wedding, funeral and memorial ceremonies, and even the funeral service encourages mourners to participate, from offering incense to filling the grave, to help them 'let go of their loved one at death' (Cush 1990: 29).

Some Buddhist terms are translated unusually. In the *Scripture of Great Wisdom*, *śūnyatā* (Skt 'emptiness') is given as 'pure', bringing a unfortunate moral overlay to this important concept, and the origin and cessation of suffering are described as 'accumulation' and 'annihilation' (*Liturgy*, 1990: 73–4). There are also many examples of archaic language. For a man in danger (male pronouns are always used), 'no injury will e'en a single hair of him sustain' if he thinks of Avalokiteśvara, who is later invoked as: 'Thou hast the Wheel within Thine hand, hail! Thou Who hast the lotus, hail!' (*Liturgy*, 1990: 49, 109). Rev. Master Jiyu described the marriage service as 'a compromise between Sōtō and Church of England', and several familiar phrases from the 1662 *Book of Common Prayer* are included (*Liturgy*, 1990: i, 92).

The use of seventeenth-century English has become increasingly rare in the Church of England since the introduction of the *Alternative Service Book* in 1980, and it is strange to see it preserved in contemporary Buddhist liturgical language. The chanting is in medieval plainsong, accompanied by an electric organ, with Buddhist hymns for most festival ceremonies. This has been criticized as close to Christian worship, but Rev. Master Daishin defended the liturgy as 'entirely Buddhist' in content, adapting traditional Mahāyāna chanting with 'musical forms that are familiar and easy on the Western ear' (Morgan, 1994a: 144). Although the content of the liturgy is translated from Japanese Sōtō Zen ritual, its style owes much to Rev. Master Jiyu's personal background in Anglican music, and some Western ears find this easier than others.

Interviewees explained that changing the liturgy would be a major task, and there is no real demand for wholesale revision. A new translation would need approval throughout the Order, and each abbot may already omit sections that seem less appropriate. The language will change eventually, but the Order is conscious of Rev. Master Jiyu's central role here and would be cautious when altering her words.

This pattern of meditation and ceremonial is maintained in a full retreat programme at Throssel Hole. Regular introductory weekend retreats include detailed meditation instruction, and talks explaining the Refuges and Precepts, as well as 'the importance of gratitude and compassion... [and] how to establish a practice at home' (Morgan, 1994a: 145). Further weekend or three-day retreats give a brief period of more intense practice and may coincide with festivals such as the Buddha's enlightenment or emphasize specific aspects of training such as the Ten Precepts.

There are also several week-long retreats. For those who wish to receive lay ordination, the Ten Precepts Retreat (Japanese (J.) *Jukai*) emphasizes the 'searching of the heart' in preparation for making 'a formal commitment to becoming a Buddhist', by promising to keep the Ten Precepts and receiving a token *kesa* (a thin black scarf worn round the neck) as a symbol of 'the robe of Shakyamuni Buddha' (Morgan, 1997: 18). Ceremonies here include acknow-ledging past wrong actions, a symbolic journey around the buildings and grounds and the community's recognizing the new lay ordainees as Buddhas (*Liturgy*, 1990: 6–46). Lay ordainees are expected to keep the Ten Precepts for life, but may still study with other teachers if they wish.

Summer *sesshins* or further 'searching the heart' retreats are periods of more intensive meditation and practice with the minimum of distractions, though they are now usually not as 'demanding and uncompromising' as early retreats at Throssel Hole (Morgan, 2004). The Feeding of the Hungry Ghosts Retreat, for example, allows trainees to remember those who have died or who are suffering, offering them loving-kindness and wishing them well, while the New Year Retreat is more relaxed, allowing time for reflection on both past and future.

Kay (2004: 198) explained how the monks lead 'a disciplined and structured communal life of meditation, manual labour, study, lectures and ceremonial observance'. Meals are usually taken in silence after reciting verses which emphasize receiving food gratefully and remembering the precepts even while eating (*Liturgy*, 1990: 95). Food preparation and serving is seen as a spiritual discipline in itself, rather than a distraction from spiritual practice.

Rev. Master Daishin described the fortnightly 'Spiritual Examination Ceremony' or *shōsan*, where each novice asks the abbot a short question 'direct from the heart' to help focus their mind on spiritual training. Each winter and spring there is a closed retreat where monks leave their ordinary work for a period of more intense practice to help 'deepen the experience of meditation' (Morgan, 1994a: 143). However, the current monastic schedule shows 'a gentle rather than an ascetic quality', with 'a marked softening' in recent years as the community's practice has matured and their commitment deepened. Most weeks include a 'renewal day' where monks can 'rest, reflect and relax', perhaps watching television drama or news together in the evening, partly to remain in touch with contemporary society (Morgan, 1994a: 144–5).

Kay (2004: 132) pointed out that OBC monks provide 'religious teaching, spiritual guidance and inspiration' for lay people, rather than the 'ancestral or funerary rituals' performed by Japanese monks. Monks regularly visit lay medi-tation groups, lead retreats and give talks, as well as offering spiritual counselling (*sanzen*) in person or by letter or telephone, even at night in emergencies. British lay trainees have contributed articles to the *Journal of the Order of Buddhist Contemplatives* on 'training in the world' and on family life, but also increasingly on ways in which the monastic routine 'can be skilfully used to support lay training or otherwise adapted to the demands of lay life' (Kay, 2004: 196).

As well as attending retreats, lay trainees may stay at the monastery during most of the year, joining the monastic routine for a few days or longer periods. Curry (2004) explained how, as well as communal meditation, dharma talks and spiritual counselling, supervised working meditation can help to undermine fixed views about one's own ability or how things should be done.

A typical local group will meet weekly for liturgical chanting, periods of sitting and walking meditation and a taped talk or an informal discussion over tea, unless a monk is visiting to give a talk. Kay (2004: 200) found that groups adopted 'a rigorously contemplative emphasis of practice not immediately accessible to newcomers', though this may underestimate the efforts of lay ministers and others to welcome visitors and new members.

Lay trainees usually meditate regularly at home, perhaps once or twice each day, and may recite scriptures and make offerings at a home altar, if appropriate in their family setting. As well as formal meditation, they are encouraged to make daily life a spiritual activity by reducing self-indulgence and keeping the precepts, and activities such as religious reading, mealtime verses, bringing the mind back to stillness, meditating with others and visiting the priory (Stevens, 1980: 2–6). There are parallels here with the *upāsikā* training in the Forest Sangha.

As no other OBC monks have trained in Japan, it is difficult to tell exactly how far Rev. Master Jiyu has adapted Japanese Sōtō Zen practice. Meditation instructions are taken directly from Dōgen and ritual has been copied meticulously from Japanese forms, but unusual translations and Anglican music give the tradition a different flavour from its Japanese parent. This approach reflects Rev. Master Jiyu's view that Zen 'must be its own master in its own country' (Kennett, 1973b: 3), with a Western Zen keeping true to the essence while leaving behind what Kay (2004: 138) calls the 'culturally incidental'. However, it might be queried by British Buddhists who wish to leave behind both Christian belief and the 'culturally incidental' in Christian ritual.

Sōtō Zen teachings

Sōtō Zen teachings were first formulated by Dōgen, whose concentration on monastic practice and observing the precepts might appear puritanical, and Keizan, who used ceremonial to encourage lay practice. However, there is also what Rev. Master Daishin called a 'common heritage with all other schools of Buddhism', including the Four Noble Truths, *anicca*, *anattā*, karma and rebirth (Morgan, 1994a: 136). SRM teachings often appear similar to Theravāda Buddhism. Rev. Master Daizui highlighted the Three Refuges, faith and trust, following the precepts, and developing compassion, love and wisdom as 'fundamental and essential', with meditation as 'the engine that drives all the rest' (MacPhillamy, 1997b: 6–7). His leaflets on 'The Eightfold Path' (MacPhillamy, 2001) include Sōtō Zen precepts and meditation instructions but could otherwise appear almost unaltered in Forest Sangha or Samatha Trust literature.

Four specific teachings are repeatedly emphasized in SRM literature: the practice of meditation, living by the Ten Precepts, developing and expressing the heart of compassion and the 'Buddha Nature' of all beings. This 'Buddha Nature' is an idea not found in Theravāda Buddhism, and is described by Rev. Master Jiyu as 'one's own true nature' or 'True Self', though not in the sense of 'a separate soul' (Kennett, 1999: 304).

Articles in the *Journal of the Order of Buddhist Contemplatives* give a broader idea of teachings seen as important. These range from general subjects such as karma, meditation, the Ten Precepts, the *Saṅgha*, and the Eightfold Path to more specific topics such as Buddha Nature, emptiness, Avalokiteśvara and other bodhisattvas, Sōtō Zen scriptures and ceremonies and the master–disciple relationship.

The most detailed account of Sōtō Zen teachings is given in Rev. Master Jiyu's *Zen is Eternal Life* (first published as *Selling Water by the River*). She begins with the Buddha's life story and brief descriptions of *anattā*, karma, rebirth, the Four Noble Truths and *anicca* (Kennett, 1999: 3–13), firmly anchoring Zen doctrine in early Buddhist teachings. She insists that 'the Bodhisattva ideal was exemplified in the life of Shakyamuni Buddha Himself' rather than a later development and that Nirvana is a mental state which results from spiritual effort 'rather than a reward in the hereafter' (Kennett, 1999: 16, 19).

Meditation is strongly emphasized, but trainees also need to develop the compassion which transforms selfish motivation, the love which allows them to have complete faith and trust in 'the Buddha Nature of the teacher', and the wisdom of an intuitive understanding which sees beyond duality (Kennett, 1999: 40, 47, 54). The Rinzai use of *kōans* as puzzles which every student must solve is rejected: by contrast 'Sōtō studies the individual and artistically suits the teaching to his or her needs' (Kennett, 1999: 70).

A substantial section introduces and translates Dōgen's teaching, which encourages disciples to lead simple and 'immaculately pure lives', following the precepts without being bound by them, and practising silent meditation like the Buddha himself (Kennett, 1999: 92–3). The *Shushōgi*, a concise compilation of Dōgen's essential teachings emphasizes impermanence, the need to acknowledge past mistakes, taking refuge in the Three Treasures, receiving and following the Ten Precepts, awakening the bodhisattva's heart of compassion, using the Four Wisdoms of charity, tenderness, benevolence and sympathy to help others and showing gratitude for the teachings (Kennett, 1999: 94–103).

Selling Water by the River was subtitled 'A Manual of Zen Training', and it became 'the main textual resource for the teachings and practices of the ZMS during the early period' (Kay, 2004: 127). However, while the *Shushōgi* was compiled to help lay people follow the Sōtō Zen precepts as an *alternative* to formal meditation, Rev. Master Jiyu insisted that *both* elements are essential daily practices for monastic and lay trainees. This contrasts with contemporary Sōtō teaching in Japan. As with the Forest Sangha, the emphasis on lay meditation is an integral part of adapting Buddhist monastic traditions to a Western context.

Interviewees confirmed the importance of the Four Noble Truths and the Eightfold Path, as well as specific elements such as the Refuges and Ten Precepts, Buddha Nature, the bodhisattva ideal and the development of gratitude and compassion. The Three Treasures or Three Refuges were seen as particularly important. Rev. Master Daishin explained that taking refuge in the Buddha, Dharma and Sangha means trusting the Buddha Nature, listening to 'the teaching of the Buddha Nature in all things' and recognizing 'the Buddha Nature within others' (Morgan, 1994b: 12).

There is considerable emphasis on faith in the SRM tradition. Rev. Master Jiyu insisted that spiritual growth in Buddhism 'requires faith in the Eternal, faith in the Teaching, faith in its priesthood and faith in one's master' (Kennett, 1986: 4). Although she drew attention in *The Wild, White Goose* to her need for 'blind faith' while training in Japan (Kennett, 2002: 44), she later contrasted the 'absolute faith', which leads to 'bigotry, fear, and frequently the giving up of the will', with the more flexible 'perfect faith' where both master and disciple are willing to ask for each other's help 'with a positive attitude of mind' (Kennett, 1983: 26). Rev. Master Daizui explained that one may begin Buddhist training without faith, taking the Dharma as a 'working hypothesis', but eventually one must recognize 'that there is Something in the universe that is greater than oneself and that this Something can be trusted' (MacPhillamy, 1997b: 10).

The understanding of enlightenment and the Buddha Nature is crucial to SRM teaching. Rev. Master Daishin underlined Dōgen's teaching that 'there is no distinction between training and enlightenment'. Since all beings have the Buddha Nature, enlightenment is not seen as a remote goal: whenever people look beyond their selfish wishes towards the Eternal, 'this is the activity of enlightenment here and now' (Morgan, 1983b: 3).

'Buddha Nature' was originally used to describe the ultimate reality which embraces all things. However, after Rev. Master Jiyu's 1976 visions, articles began to appear in the *Journal* using new terms such as 'the Cosmic Buddha', 'the Lord of the House' (or simply 'the Lord') and, occasionally, 'God'. Kay (2004: 140, 166, 161) called this a 'quasi-theistic language' which implies 'a monotheistic, and explicitly Christian, cosmology', where the Cosmic Buddha represents 'the personalisation of the impersonal absolute'.

The new language rang alarm bells for some trainees, and the teaching has been repeatedly clarified. A 1983 *Journal* note states firmly that although the ultimate reality is referred to as the Cosmic Buddha – and by Keizan as 'the Lord of the House' – this personifying of the Dharma does *not* imply 'a personal deity or creator-god' but is simply 'a natural human response to experiencing the infinite and compassionate heart of Buddha' ('To Our Readers', 1983: 3). Rev. Master Daishin explained that the Buddha Nature is neither an internal soul nor an external god, but 'enlightenment itself' which 'embraces all of existence'. Those who can let go of the idea of being separated from ultimate reality will find that they have always been 'in the hand of the Eternal Buddha' (Morgan, 1996b: 31, 36). This was not a Christian version of Zen, as Rev. Master Jiyu insisted that there was no saviour figure and frequently clarified this kind of language by emphasizing the core teachings on emptiness (Morgan, 2004).

As well as this new terminology, Rev. Master Jiyu's third *kenshō* prompted an emphasis on past lives, following her description of the need for 'cutting the roots of karma' and purifying the residual 'karma of former lives', so that remaining seeds cannot germinate (Kennett, 1993: 29, 43). While both these elements were controversial at the time, they may not have amounted to 'significant doctrinal and practical transformations and innovations', as Kay (2004: 157) has claimed, and their importance has gradually faded, particularly in recent years. While respecting Rev. Master Jiyu's personal experience of past lives, Rev. Master Daishin has found that interest in them can sometimes become obsessive and felt that in downplaying both past lives and theistic language 'we are returning more to the mainstream of the Zen tradition' (Morgan, 2004).

In common with many Mahāyāna traditions, the SRM tradition emphasizes the importance of the master–disciple relationship for spiritual training. The *Shushōgi* reminds those who recognize a true Zen Master to ignore his appearance and behaviour, and simply bow to him 'out of respect for his great wisdom' (Kennett, 1999: 101). Rev. Master Daishin explained that while basic teaching and practice may be learned independently, training with a master can help the disciple 'gain an intuitive sense of the depth of the teaching' (Morgan, 1994a: 137). Where there is mutual trust and recognition of each other's Buddha Nature, the disciple can both ask questions openly and accept correction where needed (Morgan, 1994b: 11). Monks also have 'a collegiate sangha refuge' in the relationship with senior monks as 'their uncles and aunts in the Dharma' (Morgan, 2004).

Some of the most important scriptures used in the SRM tradition are translated by OBC members in *Buddhist Writings* (1998). The selections include three chapters from the *Lotus Sūtra*, the *Scripture of Brahma's Net* (containing the Mahāyāna Precepts) and also teachings by Bodhidharma and Keizan on meditation. Rev. Master Daizui encouraged readers to treat scriptures with great respect, but not with the fundamentalist approach of 'a fear-based attachment to words' (*Buddhist Writings*, 1998: xv). Rev. Master Raymond described the *Scripture of Great Wisdom* as 'the essence of the Mahāyāna view of Ultimate Reality', adding that all the scriptures recited daily give practical help in illuminating the path. Monks tend to read these scriptures with a contemplative rather than an academic approach, 'trying to let the meaning sink in' (McGowan, 2004).

Rev. Master Jiyu preferred to teach informally on Dōgen rather than giving a systematic analysis, and Rev. Master Daishin confirmed that there is little academic study in the SRM tradition, though he felt there might now be a need to develop 'a stronger philosophical underpinning' of the movement's understanding of Buddhism. Formal classes are rare, though he has recently led discussions on Dōgen's *Rules for Meditation* (Morgan, 2004). Novices have a recommended reading list, while senior monks may read more widely if they wish, and lay people on retreat may be encouraged to read short scripture passages as well as listen to oral teaching (Curry, 2004; Watson, 2004).

With an emphasis on meditation, the Ten Precepts, Buddha Nature and compassion – and on teachings common to most Buddhist schools, and the master–disciple relationship – SRM teaching seems close to that of its Japanese parent tradition. While the insistence on lay meditation may be a Western development, the downplaying of Rev. Master Jiyu's theistic language and past-life experiences may represent a return to more traditional Sōtō Zen teachings.

The Buddha, Bodhisattvas and Zen Masters

Narratives of the Buddha and other figures, the Sōtō Zen lineage, the life of Rev. Master Jiyu and the 'Cosmic Buddha' are all important in this tradition. We have already seen the significance of the Buddha, Dōgen and Keizan from their prominent role in *Zen is Eternal Life* and in SRM ceremonies and teachings, and this was confirmed by interviewees, who spoke of the Buddha's life in particular as an inspirational narrative. However, such figures are seen as illustrating teachings in the present, rather than as examples from an idealized past.

Bodhisattvas such as Avalokiteśvara, Samantabhadra and Mañjuśhrī are emphasized in *Zen is Eternal Life* as the embodiment respectively of compassion, love and wisdom (Kennett, 1999: 36–65), and these were also mentioned by interviewees as figures inspiring devotion. Avalokiteśvara was seen as particularly important, though perhaps more as a mental attitude than an actual figure. Rev. Master Daishin explained that calling upon Avalokiteśvara as 'the manifestation of compassion and mercy' is not an appeal for magical help but simply one expression of 'taking refuge within the Eternal' (Morgan, 1986: 12), though this may hint at a monistic view untypical of Japanese Zen.

The role of lineage is seen as vital in the SRM tradition, bringing legitimacy and continuity from the Buddha to Japan, and eventually to the West. *Zen is Eternal Life* included sections of Keizan's *Denkōroku* or *Transmission of the Light*, which described Zen Masters from the Buddha to Dōgen (Kennett, 1999: 217–96); and the ancestral line of Zen Masters is chanted daily. Rev. Master Daishin described the Zen tradition as transmitting the truth of enlightenment 'from Master to disciple in an unbroken lineage from Shakyamuni Buddha to the present day' (Morgan, 1994a: 133).

Kohō Zenji is still revered in the SRM tradition, both as Rev. Master Jiyu's master and as the key figure linking the Japanese lineage with the West. Rev. Master Jiyu claimed that he gave her direct authority 'to create a Western form of Zen', her role as his 'Dharma-successor' enabling her to 'separate the essential principles of *Sōtō* Zen from their Japanese cultural forms', according to Kay (2004: 137, 138). Even during the Lotus Blossom period, she claimed that she and her teachings remained firmly 'within the *Sōtō* Zen lineage' through her master–disciple relationship with Kohō Zenji (Kay, 2004: 175).

Interviewees confirmed that Rev. Master Jiyu's personal narrative remains an important factor in the SRM tradition, while warning against accepting all her teachings uncritically or attempting to copy her experience. The accounts of her Zen training in Japan (*The Wild, White Goose*) and her later visions (*How to Grow a Lotus Blossom*) became particularly influential as narratives of the founder's life.

The role of visions and similar experiences appears ambivalent in the Zen tradition. They are often seen as *makyo* or illusory, and treated as 'transitory and unreliable', according to Rawlinson (1997: 368), though Kay (2004: 149–50) pointed out that Dōgen recorded meeting bodhisattvas in his dreams, and Keizan had visions of past lives. In *How to Grow a Lotus Blossom*, Rev. Master Jiyu explained that visions seen in meditation may indeed be 'valid experiences' rather than illusions, but Zen Masters would not speak of them to avoid confusing new trainees, and they should never be actively sought in meditation (Kennett, 1977: 4, 7). Her own visions included climbing a glass mountain between the roads to cheap pleasure or worldly success; the abyss of despair, walking by a calm lake, a series of past lives, towers appearing as a mandala, following Śākyamuni Buddha in a lotus pool, a celestial ordination, columns of light symbolizing eternal meditation, the cleansing water of the spirit and a union with the Cosmic Buddha (Kennett, 1977: *passim*).

She presents these visions as her spiritual autobiography rather than something to be believed or a path for others to follow (Kennett, 1977: 173). Rev. Master Daizui emphasized that she was preparing for death rather than looking for visions, underlining that experiencing *kenshō* 'or *any* religious experience, is neither the purpose nor the end of religious training' (Kennett, 1977: 185). However, the second edition included later visions, offering guidance to those in 'the more experienced Buddhist population' who have had such visions and memories (Kennett, 1993: 179), perhaps implying that they are more common than is usually supposed.

Kay (2004: 149, 155–6) argued that Rev. Master Jiyu's experiences 'display undeniable Christian parallels', pointing out that she was familiar with the Christian mystics and suggesting links between her visions and the Christian mystical tradition. However, the mountains, towers, water and spiritual union are general symbols which may be found in Buddhist texts as well as Christian mysticism.

Rev. Master Jiyu described *kenshō* in traditional Zen terms as 'a Transmission outside of the scriptures and doctrines', where there are no theories and where 'beliefs and doctrines are superfluous'. However, she went on to claim that

> The kenshō of Zen and the spiritual marriage of Christianity are identical.
> It is interesting that the Buddhist goes up one side of Mount Sumeru and
> discovers that the men or women he meets on the top came up one side
> of Mount Carmel or Mount Sion.
>
> (Kennett, 1978b: 20)

Kay (2004: 161) concluded that the Christian terminology became so explicit in the Lotus Blossom years that Rev. Master Jiyu seemed to be 'asserting the deep and essential *identity* of the two traditions'. This may confuse the goal with the path: the mystical *experience* of the Buddhist and the Christian may be similar, but their spiritual *practice* remains radically different. However, some disciples clearly had grave doubts about the visions and the way they were described.

Rev. Master Jiyu's influence on the movement may have begun to change since her death. Rev. Master Raymond suggested that a more diverse approach might be emerging, with greater confidence in 'the unfolding of each individual's training' and perhaps new ways of expressing the teaching (McGowan, 2004).

There remains the narrative of the Cosmic Buddha, which has an important role in the SRM tradition as an attempt to explain mystical experience through a personification of ultimate reality. Rev. Master Jiyu realized that speaking directly about the existence of the Cosmic Buddha might raise difficulties with those students who had 'unfortunate experiences' with the notion of God (Kennett, 1978a: 10). We might also see it as undermining the Mahāyāna concept of 'skilful means', where teaching is adapted to what the student *needs*, rather than expressing what the master has *experienced*.

Her direct style sometimes presents her personal experience as the only way of describing the spiritual path, rather than one of many. Soon after her third *kenshō*, she wrote: 'Anyone who has ever had kenshō *knows* that the Cosmic Buddha exists... I was overjoyed when I first knew for certain that He existed... from here on it is "full speed ahead and damn the torpedoes"' (Kennett, 1978a: 11). Such uncompromising language might tend to polarize rather than unite her students. However, she also described the Cosmic Buddha in terms of mystical experience rather than theistic belief: the Lord of the House is said to be 'eternally in meditation', always helping and teaching, without gender or form, neither a being nor not a being, neither a god nor not a god and without beginning or end (Kennett, 1977: 178).

Most of the narrative elements here appear consistent with the Japanese Sōtō Zen tradition, and even Rev. Master Jiyu's third *kenshō* experiences may be seen as the wholly legitimate visions of an authentic Zen Master. However, there remain those who are uncomfortable with any remotely theistic language, and the 'Buddha Nature' is often used as a less controversial description of ultimate reality.

Kenshō, faith and compassion

The Zen tradition sometimes uses experiential language to describe occurrences in meditation. Linked to the *kenshō* experiences already described, SRM emphasizes the role of 'Transmission' in describing the realization of one's own true nature, the 'True Self' which is identified with the 'Buddha Nature' rather than as a separate soul. In a formal sense, the master recognizes that a disciple is mature enough to take responsibility for his or her own training, but as Rev. Master Daizui explained, this is not only a ceremony, but also the 'revolutionary spiritual understanding or *kenshō* which makes possible the Transmission in its deeper meaning' (MacPhillamy, 1978: 11). In Rev. Master Daishin's words, the Transmission truly takes place when 'the Master experiences the disciple's certainty' (Morgan, 1994a: 136), and it is this spiritual realization which enables a monk to become a true 'Dharma heir' in the Sōtō Zen lineage.

It is easier to give a flavour of such experiences than to describe or explain them. Rev. Master Jiyu spoke after her first *kenshō* of 'living in a totally different dimension' where her books no longer made sense and everything had to be learned again. Looking into Kohō Zenji's eyes during her Transmission ceremony, 'it was not Zenji Sama I saw but Shakyamuni Buddha', as she felt 'the life of Buddha itself' flowing between them (Kennett, 2002: 91, 131).

On a more sombre note, Rev. Master Jiyu gave one reason for sharing her Lotus Blossom experiences as helping to dispel the fear of death and to express the joy which can be experienced when close to death (Kennett, 1977: 8). Kay (2004: 150) pointed out that while Rev. Master Jiyu described her retreat as 'a time of spiritual preparation for her imminent death', others have seen it as 'a period of emotional and psychological breakdown and fragmentation'. Perhaps these explanations need not be mutually exclusive.

Articles in the *Journal* deal with a variety of emotional responses, including suffering and despair, desire, anger and doubt, or faith and acceptance, patience, trust, compassion and letting go. We have already seen the importance of faith in the SRM tradition, and Rev Master Jiyu's response to the experience of knowing the Cosmic Buddha was one of overwhelming joy and love (Kennett, 1978a: 11). Rev. Master Daishin confirmed that the Sōtō Zen ceremonial also encourages devotion – though some devotional hymns may feel 'too rich' in comparison to the *Scripture of Great Wisdom* and there is a need for balance (Morgan, 2004).

We have also seen that developing and exhibiting compassion is strongly encouraged. Rev. Master Jiyu emphasized the 'Four Wisdoms' of 'charity, tenderness, benevolence and sympathy' as representing the bodhisattva's aspirations to help others (Kennett, 1999: 99). These are similar to the Pali Canon's four 'foundations of social unity', described by Harvey (2000: 109–10) as 'giving... kindly speech... helpful action... [and] impartial treatment' or more broadly to the *brahma-vihāras* of loving-kindness, compassion, sympathetic joy and equanimity, expressed as the 'four immeasurables' in Tibetan Buddhism. Interviewees suggested that these Four Wisdoms are not goals to aim for, but qualities we already possess, which will naturally express themselves if we act with an open heart.

When dealing with strong emotions, Rev. Master Daishin recommended calling upon Avalokiteśvara, perhaps asking for the compassion to see desire in its true perspective, or 'reaffirming our faith' in the Eternal to help overcome fear (Morgan, 1986: 17). However, he also explained how the trainee gradually learns through meditation simply 'to recognise a feeling as a feeling', so that one can acknowledge anger without needing 'to act in ways that are angry'. Feelings which arise are neither good nor bad: by simply accepting them, rather than feeding, judging or analysing them, one can let them subside (Morgan, 2004).

Interviewees reported that even powerful negative emotions could be dealt with by the simple meditation practice of 'just sitting' until they give way to more positive feelings. Spiritual counselling is available for trainees with emotional difficulties, though this often means listening and letting people express their feelings, rather than giving advice. Curry (2004) summed up the connection between emotions and SRM teaching, speaking of her personal experience of 'overwhelming feelings of both sadness and joy', and being encouraged to allow feelings to pass without rejecting or clinging to them: ' the ability to accept everything that comes to me is the most important response'.

The Ten Great Precepts

There has always been a strong emphasis on moral behaviour in the SRM tradition. In the early 1970s, Rev. Master Jiyu warned that Zen is firmly opposed to 'permissiveness, promiscuity, drug taking, and other abuses' (Kennett, 1973b: 4). Although this tone has softened over the years, Rev. Master Daishin explained that the precepts are still 'the very essence of Buddhism'. Based on the Three Refuges, they are not only moral rules but also 'the very life of Buddha', as they are 'the natural expression of compassion' (Morgan, 1997: 13–14).

SRM publications refer to 3, 10, 16 and 48 precepts, with varying levels of importance. The Three Pure Precepts are simple and broadly based: 'Cease from evil...Do only good...Do good for others' (Morgan, 1997: 16). These may be seen as a Mahāyāna version of the Pali *Dhammapada*, 'Avoid doing evil, learn to do good, make your own heart pure' (verse 183), where a pure heart is one filled with compassion.

The Ten Great Precepts appear frequently in SRM literature, often with explanatory comments on their nature and significance. Trainees are warned to avoid killing or harming living beings, stealing or taking what is not given, sexual misconduct (translated as 'Do not covet'), false speech, drink or drugs ('Do not sell the wine of delusion'), speaking against others, pride and devaluing others, meanness in 'giving either Dharma or wealth', indulging anger and defaming the Three Treasures by denying 'the Buddha Nature in yourself or in others' (Morgan, 1997: 14–15).

The first five are almost identical to the Theravāda Five Precepts, and Harvey (1990: 207) suggested that all ten are based on the 'ten skilful actions' described in the Pali *Sevitabbāsevitabba Sutta*, that is 'the seven factors of right action and right speech, plus avoiding covetousness, malevolence and wrong views'. Despite different wording, the order is similar, and it seems likely that Zen's Ten Great Precepts have their origins in early Buddhism.

These Ten 'Bodhisattva Precepts' are formally undertaken in both lay and monastic ordination and, unlike those in the Pali *Vinaya*, are the same for both monks and lay trainees (though the precept on sexuality is interpreted differently). The 16 precepts comprise the Three Treasures, the Three Pure Precepts and the Ten Great Precepts. According to Rev. Master Daishin, the essence of the Ten Precepts is said to be expressed in the Three Pure Precepts, while the Three Refuges embody the Buddha Nature as 'the final authority in Buddhism' (Morgan, 1997: 16).

The *Scripture of Brahma's Net* describes in detail the Ten Great Precepts and 'Forty-eight Less Grave Precepts' which have a subsidiary role. Disciples are to avoid intoxicants, meat eating, and cheating, slandering or abusing others. They should respect teachers and friends, encourage others to keep the precepts, care for the sick, adopt right livelihood, avoid worldly attachments, attend Dharma talks, and ask for spiritual guidance if needed. Monastic teachers should give true Buddhist teachings, offer the precepts and teachings without discrimination, keep the monastic rules and ensure harmony in the Sangha (*Buddhist Writings*, 1998: 136–82).

Some of these lesser precepts are built into the OBC *Rules* and inform monastic practice, but only the Ten Great Precepts are recited in the fortnightly monastic Renewal of Vows ceremony, somewhat like a simplified version of the Theravāda *pātimokkha* recitation, though with a silence for *sanghē* (J. 'contrition') rather than the need for confession.

Celibacy and abstaining from alcohol are the only formal preceptual obser- vances which distinguish OBC monks from lay trainees. Most Sōtō Zen 'monks' in Japan are married, and Rev. Master Jiyu initially ordained several married couples, but she came to feel that this diluted the monastic tradition, and chose to revert to celibacy as 'the more traditional method' (Morgan, 2004). This transi- tion took some time and was not without controversy, though it is now fully accepted. All ordained Order members and postulants make an explicit commit- ment to complete celibacy and, like Theravāda monastics, should not be alone in private with a member of the opposite sex (*Rules of the Order of Buddhist Contemplatives*, 2000: 30).

The OBC monastic discipline is based on traditional Sōtō Zen scriptures and other 'widely accepted Buddhist sources, both Mahayana and Theravada', where they are compatible and useful (Kennett, 1991: 4). The OBC *Rules* (2000: 3) confirm that they sometimes rely on the Pali *Vinaya* as well as the 'Mahāyāna Vinaya' in the *Scripture of Brahma's Net*. Monastic behaviour is also guided by Dōgen's monastic rules, which have been adapted as appropriate, while recognizing 'the necessity of staying true to the source of the tradition' (Morgan, 1994b: 10).

There are disciplinary regulations on serious breaches of the precepts, such as falsely claiming a *kenshō*, killing, theft, sexual intercourse, striking another monk, giving false teaching or advice, or 'wilfully causing disharmony in the Sangha' (*Rules*, 2000: 11), for which monks may be suspended or excluded from the Order. These are similar to the serious offences in the Pali *Vinaya*. Further rules forbid the abuse of 'any position of power, authority, or trust' and any form of sexual harass- ment. Members are expected to avoid 'giving even the appearance of such wrong- doing', and there are procedures for investigating allegations (*Rules of the Order of Buddhist Contemplatives*, 2000: 14–17). Serious rule-breaking is extremely rare, and lesser infringements are often dealt with informally, encouraging monks to understand their mistakes.

Rev. Master Daishin confirmed that the OBC *Rules* are seen mainly as 'house rules rather than ... the rules of Buddhism' and can be changed by agreement, while Dogen's monastic rules for eating and sleeping in the meditation hall might be described as 'etiquette' (Morgan, 2004). The distinction made between these and the Ten Precepts allows a more flexible system than in Theravāda monasticism.

Lay people who follow the Ten Precepts in their daily life will – like Western lay people in other monastic traditions – often interpret them as positive guide- lines for personal and family living, 'motivated by the wish to do good rather than fear of breaking rules' (Curry, 2004). As members of the Order, lay ministers are expected to follow the Ten Precepts more strictly, abstaining from drugs and alcohol, avoiding 'non-Buddhist practices' such as magic or astrology, and never imposing their will on others (*Rules of the Order of Buddhist Contemplatives*, 2000: 39–41), but even here the emphasis is on developing moral behaviour rather than following rules.

Monastic and lay tradition and adaptation

The SRM tradition has a complex organizational structure. From the start, Rev. Master Jiyu declared that her disciples were 'British Buddhists... studying British Zen', with no need to create an artificial 'oriental environment, sitting on the floor and using chopsticks' (Kennett, 1973b: 5). More recently, Rev. Master Daishin described Throssel Hole as both 'a monastic training monastery and a retreat centre for a lay congregation', with many similarities to Japanese Zen monasteries, but also with adaptations to suit the different 'cultural and social climate', and where there is 'a growing opportunity to make a contribution to the religious life of Britain' (Morgan, 1994a: 142, 149).

The OBC is described as 'the lineage family association for the disciples and descendents of Rev. Master Jiyu-Kennett' (MacPhillamy, 2003: 142), though it remains part of the wider 'Sōtō Zen Church' through continued links with Japanese monks. Rev. Master Daizui described the Order's three main purposes as providing rules and procedures for Order members, ensuring that practice and teaching remain true to the tradition passed on by Rev. Master Jiyu and maintaining 'unity and harmony' in the Order and the lay congregation (MacPhillamy, 1997a: 18). The Order has designated administrative roles and an advisory council, with individual abbots responsible for their own monastic and lay communities. Monks and nuns, lay ministers and postulants are all members of the Order, while they remain active trainees. Ordination is for life: Rev. Master Daishin will not ordain someone who plans to be a monk 'for a few years', though he respects the 'different setting' of those who do offer temporary ordination, such as the Karma Kagyu tradition at Samye Ling (Morgan, 2004).

As we have seen, the monastic routine is often guided by Dōgen's *Monastic Rules*. His instructions may appear pedantic, with minute detail on correct behaviour in the meditation hall and meal-time procedure, but they are designed to help monks to learn an attitude of respect for each other and their surroundings. Even the 'Instructions to the Chief Cook' include the reminder that he and 'all temple officers' must continually cultivate a mind of 'gratitude, love and generosity' (Kennett, 1999: 159).

While much of the ceremonial has been taken directly from Japan, many social and organizational aspects have been developed on a pragmatic basis to promote harmony and minimize problems. For example, monks may 'wear ordinary clothes in a situation where the robes might cause difficulties' (Cush, 1990: 26), and there are regulations for those who have 'returned to lay life' (i.e. disrobed), with possible reordination on request (*Rules of the Order of Buddhist Contemplatives*, 2000: 19–22).

Kay (2004: 128) found that the stages of OBC monastic life reflected 'the traditional, hierarchical system of Sōtō monasticism'. After an initial year as a postulant, candidates are ordained as novices and enter a disciplined phase where they have to 'learn what it is to be a monk', letting go of their previous behaviour and attitudes (Morgan, 2004). (Unlike the Theravāda *saṅgha*, only a single master is needed to ordain monks in Japanese Sōtō Zen (Kennett, 2002: 480, n. 40).) After a further year they become Head Novice for a brief period, organizing work routines and beginning to take 'responsibility for the spiritual welfare of others' (MacPhillamy, 1978: 12). Some years later monks will receive 'Dharma transmission', when their full commitment is formally recognized by their master. Transmitted monks train to become 'parish priests' who can 'run temples, conduct... ceremonies and give pastoral counselling' (*Rules of the Order of Buddhist Contemplatives*, 2000: 4). After 2 further years of monastic training – making at least 7 in all – a monk may be given a formal role as a Teacher of Buddhism. The title of Master (previously *Rōshi*) is only given when the monk's own master sees that the disciple has both experienced *kenshō* and 'digested the experience and demonstrated a commitment to deepen their training' (Morgan, 1994b: 11). The Zen Master may then ordain and train monks and even accept lay disciples by mutual agreement. Each stage is usually initiated by the abbot rather than the individual monk and involves wearing a different coloured *kesa*, with juniors in black robes and seniors in brown.

Throssel Hole Abbey is run by a small group of trustees, with the abbot in charge, though decisions have always been agreed by consensus (Morgan, 1994a: 147). The abbot's secretary handles daily administration, with a council of senior monks meeting periodically to consider policy matters. Department heads such as the Chief Cook, the Sacristan and the Bursar each have their own staff, but these roles are spiritual as well as administrative, since even chopping vegetables is seen as part of training. This is probably less hierarchical and more community-based than a traditional Japanese monastery.

The unique relationship between disciple and master helps to 'keep the monks on track' in the absence of a formal *Vinaya*: it may be 'quite friendly and informal' or sometimes more stern, depending on the need for guidance (Morgan, 2004). There is a vertical relationship, where the abbot stands in 'the line of masters and ancestors' as an authoritative figure, and a horizontal relationship 'where we are all equal in Buddha Nature': both aspects work together in an effective master– disciple relationship, since the master represents both 'the Buddha and a human being at the same time' (Watson, 2004).

Rev. Master Daishin explained how the 'monastic core of Sōtō Zen... exists in order to serve the lay community': these two 'broad vocations in Buddhism' are mutually interdependent, with lay trainees seeing the monastery as 'a source of teaching, a place of retreat and a spiritual anchor' (Morgan, 1994a: 137, 145). Lay members underlined the need for a cooperative rather than hierarchical relationship between monastic and lay communities, to encourage the latter to 'develop and mature' ('Groups Weekend: Nov 23–25 1990', 1991: 25), and Rev. Master

Jiyu's recently published oral teachings include a substantial section on lay life, with comments on marriage and children, spiritual practice at home and at work, and community involvement (Kennett, 2000: 194–257). Lay people are encouraged to visit Throssel Hole for retreats and festivals or for longer periods, and committed lay trainees as well as monks may benefit from the master–disciple relationship (Morgan, 1994b: 12). The overall pattern here is one of mutual cooperation, encouraging lay people to participate as much as possible while still allowing the essential focus on monastic training.

Experienced lay trainees may be invited to train as lay ministers, allowing them to serve others by supporting a local group and offering meditation instruction (though not formal teaching) (Morgan, 1991: 24). Both the lay minister's training (which includes retreats and learning various ceremonial functions) and the role itself are still developing and changing (Morgan, 1994b: 10), and Curry (2004) described being made a lay minister as not so much taking on formal responsibilities as 'a way of furthering my practice'.

The OBC *Rules* (2000: 39–40) explain that the most important role of lay ministers is to 'exhibit the Four Wisdoms in everyday life and... encourage others to do the same'. They must practise only OBC teachings, though they may still visit other groups within or outside Buddhism. Their license to practise will not be renewed if they break the Ten Precepts or abandon their ministry. Lay ministers wear a black robe with a turquoise *kesa*; and groups are expected to have a lay minister or another member authorized to give meditation instruction before becoming formally affiliated.

Gender issues have always been important in the SRM tradition. Dōgen emphasized that Buddhist teaching insists on 'the complete equality of the sexes' (Kennett, 1999: 99); and Rev. Master Jiyu was keen to underline the teaching that 'women's spirituality is identical with that of men', roundly criticizing Christian churches who refused to ordain women (Kennett, 1981: 6).The OBC *Bylaws* (2002: 10) forbid discrimination, stating that men and women 'may advance equally in the priesthood becoming full priests and teachers', and Rev. Master Daishin (1984: 7) has criticized the reluctance in some Buddhist schools to give women full recognition as monastics, pointing out the benefit of woman teachers in helping male disciples consider their own prejudices. Using male pronouns in the liturgy and referring to female monastics as 'monks' may appear unfortunate to contemporary ears, though this reflects Rev. Master Jiyu's background rather than any conscious discrimination. Her oral teachings have been posthumously edited to include 'gender neutral pronouns' (MacPhillamy, 2000: xix).

Although *Journal* articles include social issues such as engaged Buddhism and the treatment of animals, there may be an ambivalence here. Rev. Master Jiyu sometimes spoke out on social issues such as 'abortion, euthanasia and... animal rights and welfare', as Kay (2004: 206) reported, but she also warned trainees against emotionalism, idealism and civil disobedience. While not criticizing Buddhist schools who embrace social activism, she argued that demonstrating or picketing are 'not the way of our tradition' (Kennett, 2000: 228), though it is worth remembering that her own tradition included British as well as Japanese conservatism. Monasteries must not support political or social action, however worthwhile, though individual monks may engage in educational or other approved secular activities. At Throssel Hole monks and lay trainees have been involved with Angulimala, the Buddhist Prison Chaplaincy Organization, seminars on Buddhism have been run for religious education teachers (Morgan, 1994a: 148) and tree planting has grown into a major ecological project with Forestry Commission backing.

Throssel Hole is a registered charity financed almost entirely by voluntary donations. The original fee system for retreats became too complex, so there is now no charge for teaching, meals or accommodation, and returning to 'the traditional basis of relying on donations' actually increased the monastery's income (Morgan, 1994a: 146). There are fundraising events to support new building work, and there is income from the sale of books, tapes, meditation equipment and altar furnishings. Monks may keep their own property, enabling a few to contribute to their upkeep (Morgan, 1994a: 146–7). The OBC *Rules* (2000: 27) explain that monks should live simply, not seek paid work or state benefits, use resources wisely and make suitable arrangements for their own assets 'according to their individual conscience'.

Kay (2004: 200) has fairly described the SRM tradition as having a 'characteristically low level of promotional activity'. Rev. Master Daishin (1994a: 146) confirmed that trainees are encouraged 'not to thrust their belief and practice onto others', but to use their training to help them 'live peacefully with others' rather than attempting to convert them. Lay trainees often said they were attracted to the tradition by the welcome they received on introductory retreats, rather than by reading SRM literature.

Apart from some initial difficulties in Britain, the SRM tradition has maintained good relationships with other organizations. Rev. Master Jiyu originally discouraged contacts with the Buddhist Society – once referring to Christmas Humphreys as 'the Pope of Eccleston Square' – and criticized British Buddhists for their half-hearted approach and their fascination with oriental culture (Kay, 2004: 126, 133–4). However, this attitude soon softened, and by 1979 she and Throssel Hole dissociated themselves from British Buddhist publications which criticized other religions ('Disclaimer', 1979: 15). Rev. Master Daishin suggested that understanding other traditions helps to establish the ethical norms which make it 'much harder for abuses to flourish' (Morgan, 1994b: 9). Rev. Master Daizui has written recently of his respect for 'all forms of Buddhism' and indeed all the great religions, 'each being good for different people' (MacPhillamy, 2003: xiv) and this inclusivism is typical of current SRM attitudes.

Although Order members are restricted to following SRM teaching and practice, individuals are not discouraged from studying other teachings or visiting other religious traditions. Throssel Hole 'maintains friendly relations with other Buddhist traditions' in Britain, sometimes joining their festival days (Morgan, 1994a: 148), and visitors from these traditions are also welcomed in meditation groups.

Visits to Throssel Hole by senior Forest Sangha monks prompted comments on 'the similarity between Zen and Theravada practice' and how much the two communities had in common ('Priory News', 1979: 18). There have also been visits from teachers in other Zen traditions and from Samye Ling monks. Rev. Master Daishin has maintained personal contacts with Ajahn Sumedho and other Forest Sangha monks, as well as leading Friends of the Western Buddhist Order figures: despite criticizing the FWBO in the past, he still respects the 'genuine spirit' of their very different approach (Morgan, 2004). Throssel Hole joined with other groups in 1994 to form the Network of Buddhist Organisations (NBO) as 'an initiative to promote fellowship and dialogue', recognizing that there is much to be gained by cooperation and pooled experience ('The Network of Buddhist Organisations' 1994: 34).

This positive attitude extends beyond Buddhism to include Christian–Buddhist retreats and visits from a Catholic priest to lecture on the Christian mystics. Rev. Master Daishin has argued that commitment to a Buddhist tradition should not involve rejecting the past, and encouraged trainees with a Christian upbringing to offer their 'respect and gratitude to Christianity and its teachers', rather than treating it with hostility (Morgan, 1983a: 7).

Like the Forest Sangha, Throssel Hole has adopted a friendly approach to the wider community, inviting local residents to look round the monastery and speak to monks informally, allowing a festival ceremony to be filmed and broadcast, and publicizing a recent open day and art exhibition on local television. Rev. Master Daishin has given talks in Hexham about Zen Buddhism and an interview for the local paper describing daily life at the Abbey.

Kay (2004: 171–2) refers to Rev. Master Jiyu's 'strategies' in developing and preserving what he calls 'Kennett's movement', almost as if she were directing a preconceived plan. This personal focus may underestimate the genuinely experimental nature of the organization, where patterns emerge and develop piecemeal, responding to the needs of trainees rather than to the will of the founder.

A mixture of styles

Throssel Hole Buddhist Abbey is a substantial monastic complex set in 40 acres of hillside and woodland in a secluded Northumberland valley. A mixture of original farm buildings and new construction gives separate accommodation for monastics and lay visitors, kitchen and dining areas, and a bookshop.

The monastic meditation hall is arranged on traditional Japanese lines, each junior having a raised platform or *tan* for meditation, eating and sleeping. A central statue of Mañjuśrī seated on a lion represents 'enlightened wisdom' and the 'untamed self', which seem to be separate but are actually one (Cush, 1990: 26). The windows are decorated with images of 'Bodhisattvas and protectors of Buddhism' seated within 'a vast heavenly sea of lotuses', reminding monks of their own sitting place in this symbolic ocean of compassion ('The New Meditation Hall', 1988: 32).

The ceremony hall can seat up to 50 lay people for meditation and many more for lectures. Its rich symbolism reflects much of the tradition's teaching and practice. A prominent Japanese-style main altar represents Mount Sumeru, the symbolic central axis of the world, its shape reminding trainees that while the first few steps may be easy, they will eventually reach 'the sheer face and the overhanging steps' where they will have to 'let go of the self' in a leap of faith (McGowan, 2004).

Seated on a lotus on the altar is a large gilded Buddha with a Western face, his right arm raised in the 'fear not' *mudrā*, surrounded by candles, artificial flowers (to avoid cutting live plants) and offerings of water and fruit. Above is a painted sky with clouds symbolising the Dharma (a reminder of Rev. Master Jiyu's additional name *Hōun*, 'Dharma Cloud') and flying *garuda* birds representing the spiritual ascent towards the central symbol of enlightenment, a flaming jewel set on a lotus: clouds, birds and flames all suggest dynamic movement rather than a static picture.

Behind the main altar are side shrines depicting Avalokiteśvara – a calm androgynous figure surrounded by the flowing water of compassion – and the fierce-looking Achalanatha ('the immovable one'), surrounded by flames of greed, hate and delusion, representing the determination to pursue the spiritual path. Large lotus-covered canopies are suspended above the Buddha on the altar and the abbot or other celebrant in the centre of the hall, as symbolic parasols linking and showing the importance of these two figures (McGowan, 2004).

Lay residents sleep in the hall, their bedding and belongings kept in cupboards whose doors are painted with golden *bodhi* trees, recalling the Buddha's enlightenment and again emphasizing the sitting place of the trainees. While some elements of iconography appear traditionally Japanese, others show a mixture of styles, often appearing as a Western adaptation of Japanese, Chinese or Indian symbolism.

Other priories copy this iconography on a smaller scale. Meditation groups will set up a temporary altar for their meetings, usually with a Buddha statue, artificial flowers, a candle and incense (representing the light and pervasiveness of the Buddha's teaching), and a small bowl of water (symbolizing the cleansing action of meditation). Lay trainees often have a similar altar in their own home

Conclusion

The SRM tradition is an unusual mixture of traditional Sōtō Zen and adapted elements, reflecting Rev. Master Jiyu's determination that 'we here in England need our own Buddhist identity' (Kennett, 1973b: 3). The British movement developed slowly at first, but since the return of the British monks from America in 1982 it has expanded into a substantial organization with several monasteries and lay groups throughout the country.

There is a strong emphasis on traditional Zen meditation and on moral behaviour based on the Ten Precepts, which are seen as embodying the Three Refuges. The important ceremonial is closely based on Japanese practice, though its English translation draws on outdated Christian ritual. Teachings such as realizing the Buddha Nature, developing faith and compassion, and the crucial role of the master–disciple relationship, all reflect traditional Sōtō Zen teaching. However, the links made with Theravāda teachings and the insistence on lay meditation both appear as Western adaptations, and the use of theistic language and past-life experiences (though now less prominent) relate closely to Rev. Master Jiyu herself.

The reverence paid to the Buddha, bodhisattvas and Sōtō Zen lineage masters again appears traditional, though Rev. Master Jiyu's personal narrative has been influential and sometimes controversial. The explicit description of her later *kenshō* experiences – using the figure of the Cosmic Buddha instead of the more traditional Buddha Nature – may have suggested a theistic understanding of ultimate reality as the norm.

The organizational dimension of the movement has an experimental approach rather than a planned development. Monastic routine, the ranks from novice to Zen Master and the master–disciple relationship all follow Sōtō Zen tradition, and the reintroduction of celibacy may be seen as a return to traditional monastic practice. However, the roles of postulant and lay minister are genuine adaptations, the latter reflecting the explicit view that monastic and lay communities are equally important. The insistence on gender equality is seen as originating from Dōgen (rather than current Japanese practice) but also reflects Western values.

Much of the symbolism of the tradition is expressed in iconographical form as a focus for devotional activity, but although the figures and motifs are often drawn from Japanese Zen, their style may be Indian, Chinese or Western. With no ethnic Japanese involved in the SRM, there is no equivalent of the Forest Sangha's Thai iconography.

Kay (2004: 137) underlined Rev. Master Jiyu's insistence on developing a Western form of Zen which does not idealize Japanese religion and culture, and where 'adaptations are legitimated by direct reference to the essence of *Sōtō* Zen'. As a recognised Zen *rōshi*, with her master's approval for bringing the tradition to the West, she appeared to have both the experience and the authority to make such adaptations. While the SRM tradition is certainly a westernized form of Buddhism, it retains many traditional Japanese elements, and while Rev. Master Jiyu has transplanted many of the authentic teachings and practices of the Sōtō Zen lineage, their presentation in the SRM tradition reflects much of her own somewhat idiosyncratic personal approach.

If adaptations such as plainsong chanting, archaic language and Christian terminology remain, so does a much greater emphasis on lay as well as monastic training. The defining characteristics of the SRM tradition remain the four elements of practising serene reflection meditation, following the Ten Precepts, realizing the Buddha Nature and developing compassion, together with the distinctive ceremonial which expresses and encourages this training. While these are all now practised within a British context, they are still firmly consistent with traditional Japanese Sōtō Zen teaching and practice.

6

SŌKA GAKKAI INTERNATIONAL UK (SGI-UK)

Historical background

Sōka Gakkai International (SGI) is a worldwide movement for 'developing the positive human potentialities for individual happiness and for global peace and prosperity' (SGI, 1996: 2). It is inspired by the Buddhism of Nichiren (1222–82), a Japanese monk who taught that chanting the name of the *Lotus Sūtra* was the only true practice of Buddhism. As well as religious activities, SGI sponsors exhibitions, conferences and publications on world peace, human rights and environmental issues, and many cultural events (SGI, 1996: 10–17). The British branch, formerly known as Nichiren Shōshū of the United Kingdom, was renamed Sōka Gakkai International of the United Kingdom (SGI-UK) in 1993 and this name will be used throughout.

This is a controversial tradition which has been criticized as authoritarian and intolerant, often without supporting evidence. Sōka Gakkai has been described in the British press as a dangerous cult and by a senior Western Theravāda monk as an aberration which should be opposed by other Buddhists (Wilson, 2000: 370; Scott, 1995: 12). SGI-UK is indeed sometimes regarded with suspicion by other British Buddhists, and so it is particularly important to examine the movement fairly and without prejudice.

Sōka Gakkai ('value-creating society') grew from an educational movement started in Japan in 1930 by Tsunesaburō Makiguchi (1871–1944), and revived after the Second World War by his disciple Josei Toda (1900–58), who strongly encouraged 'vigorous proselytising' or *shakubuku* (to 'break and subdue' false teachings) (Wilson and Dobbelaere, 1994: 10–11, 256). This approach was somewhat modified by Daisaku Ikeda (b. 1928), who became president in 1960, founded Sōka Gakkai International in 1975 and expanded SGI into a worldwide movement as a lay branch of Nichiren Shōshū Buddhism. Batchelor (1994: 150) described Sōka Gakkai as 'the largest lay religious organization in the world', and Bocking (1994: 127) referred to the strong funding, the 'wide range of international activities' and the centralized organization of a movement which saw itself as 'on the verge of becoming a world religion'.

Sōka Gakkai came to Britain in 1961 with the Japanese wives of London-based English businessmen, and there were few British converts at first (Wilson, 2000: 355). SGI-UK had only 200 members when Richard Causton (1920–95) became leader in 1975, though it then grew rapidly, claiming 3,000 members and 130 branches in 1986 (Macaulay, 1986: 11; Causton, 1995: 1). The *Middle Way* is almost silent about Sōka Gakkai. A 1987 report refers disparagingly to the 'now-famous "chanters" ', whose practice is seen as self-seeking, egoistic and 'a most unBuddhist way of proceeding' ('Nichiren Shoshu', 1987: 70). A brief history is given, but neither Japanese nor English SGI headquarters replied to requests for further information.

By 1988 SGI-UK had about 4,000 members and the movement had spread from the London area to cities and towns across England (Wilson and Dobbelaere, 1994: 13–14). Taplow Court in Berkshire was purchased as a national headquarters, and an extensive refurbishment programme began. This neo-Elizabethan mansion with an 85-acre estate is used to host conferences, exhibitions and arts and music festivals and since 1989 has housed the Institute of Oriental Philosophy European Centre, with a substantial library for scholars and a lecture and seminar programme. SGI-UK claimed about 5,000 members in 1990, almost two-thirds of them in the south-east, with half of the 'headquarters' in members' homes in London (Wilson and Dobbelaere, 1994: 39–40).

Allwright reported that there had been tension since 1980 between SGI and a Japanese Nichiren Shōshū priesthood 'increasingly unable to open itself to the needs of a diverse and international membership', and in 1991 High Priest Nikken 'excommunicated the entire SGI membership in an attempt to destroy the movement altogether', making it a purely lay organization (Allwright, 1998: 109). (Wilson and Dobbelaere (1994: 232–45) gave a detailed account of this 1991 split and its effect in Britain.) According to Bocking, while Japanese members still expect priests to perform funeral rites, those from Britain and other 'protestant' cultures may see the split not as a 'tragic division' but as a 'positive opportunity to cleanse the movement of elements deriving from traditional Japanese Buddhist culture' (Bocking, 1994: 120, 122). In 1994 the first joining ceremonies took place since the split, with 220 new members receiving their *gohonzon* – a copy of a sacred scroll – from Ricky Baines (then Vice General Director) rather than from a priest (Waterhouse, 1997: 103).

In 1995 Scott described SGI-UK's 'relatively high profile' in Britain, with 6,000 members claimed, and pointed out that SGI-UK had joined the Network of Buddhist Organizations NBO, which might either 'soften, or confirm, the initial image of Nichiren dogmatic sectarianism' (Scott, 1995: 12). In the same year Richard Causton died and Ricky Baines took over as General Director, though one of the two Deputy Directors is still Japanese, reflecting the continued influence of the parent movement on its national organizations.

SGI continues to expand worldwide. According to Waterhouse (1997: 92) the international movement claims 'up to sixteen million members' in Japan, with 30,000 in Europe, and perhaps 6,500 in Britain, while Allwright (1998: 108) claimed 'over ten million members in Japan as well as around a million in 128 other countries'. In 2000 Wilson gave the total UK membership as '6,500 to 7,000 members', with perhaps 4,000 active and another 3,000 coming to discussion meetings (Wilson, 2000: 373), and SGI-UK may well be the largest Buddhist organization in Britain.

Chanting *Nam-myōhō-renge-kyō*

Sōka Gakkai is probably the only Buddhist tradition with no practice of silent meditation, its place being taken by individual or communal chanting. SGI-UK described their practice of Nichiren's Buddhism as 'faith, practice and study'. Faith involves morning and evening chanting of the phrase *Nam-myōhō-renge-kyō* ('Homage to the Lotus Sutra of the Mystic Law'). This *Lotus Sūtra* invocation, known as the *daimoku* or as 'chanting', is usually preceded by the *gongyō* or 'assiduous practice' (often referred to as 'the prayers'), where two sections from the text of the *Lotus Sūtra* are chanted. Chanting is said to be 'the powerhouse of faith. The act of chanting is faith itself' (SGI-UK, 1993: 8). Study focuses on Nichiren's teachings, as contained in his letters to his disciples and practice involves both applying these teachings to one's own life and introducing others to Nichiren Buddhism (SGI-UK, 1993: 8–9).

Causton explained the basic practice as the repeated chanting of *Nam-myōhō-renge-kyō* while sitting or kneeling upright, with the hands together, the eyes open, chanting aloud 'with a clear and relaxed voice'. Regular morning and evening chanting is important, for 10 minutes or so at first, with members advised to set up 'a precise and clear rhythm and to listen to the sound of your *daimoku*' (Causton, 1995: 246–7). The chanting is usually conducted with considerable energy for 20 minutes, with a deep resonance building up during the session. Wilson and Dobbelaere (1994: 175) found that over half the members chanted twice a day, with 9 out of 10 chanting at least once a day on average.

During chanting members are encouraged to 'concentrate solely on precise pronunciation and a steady rhythm', though it is recognized that personal concerns will often come to mind. Chanting is described as praying for answers to problems, and members are assured that continued practice will bring insight and hope: eventually 'a solution will definitely present itself' (SGI-UK, 1993: 11). Causton (1995: 247) described how 'your current preoccupations or desires will probably come into your mind as prayers, to be bathed, as it were, in your intuitive Buddha wisdom'.

The two sections of the *Lotus Sūtra* chanted as *gongyō* emphasize that 'all people have innate Buddhahood' and reveal 'the eternity of life', according to Allwright (1998: 91–2), who claimed that the practice of *gongyō* 'refreshes the universal self... We experience the eternal, unchanging nature of the universe. We return our lives to the ultimate truth'. Waterhouse (1997: 113) reported that *gongyō* includes appreciative prayers to Buddhist guardian deities, to the *Dai-Gohonzon* (the original scroll inscribed by Nichiren), to Nichiren and his priestly successors, and prayers for the spread of Buddhism and for the dead.

Causton explained that these scriptures are recited fast, in 'classical Chinese pronounced according to Japanese phonetics', using a chanting book with a romanized script for Westerners. While it may seem strange to use 'a language no one understands', he argued that this is a spiritual rather than intellectual practice, enabling all SGI members to chant together, and 'deep within our lives, our Buddha nature understands and responds to it' (Causton, 1995: 249–51). The recitation of *gongyō* may be established by using audiotapes or by chanting slowly at first with help from experienced members. New members usually start with *Nam-myōhō-renge-kyō*, learning the full *gongyō* later to complete the practice and help them focus on the chanting. Chanting is always in this romanized Sino-Japanese rather than in English: one interviewee explained that 'nothing would happen, it wouldn't work! You have to chant *Nam-myōhō-renge-kyō* for you to be a Nichiren Buddhist'.

Chanting is usually done by individuals or families in their home, in front of the *gohonzon*, inscribed with the mantra *Nam-myōhō-renge-kyō*, summarized teachings and the names of Buddhas and bodhisattvas, in Chinese and Japanese characters. The *gohonzon* is mounted in a wall cupboard or *butsudan* and treated as a shrine when the doors are opened.

According to Causton (1995: 28, 191), chanting *Nam-myōhō-renge-kyō* means 'putting yourself in harmony, or rhythm, with the universal Law', progressively weakening the bonds of karma and so changing 'even the worst karma into good fortune'. New members are encouraged to chant for specific personal wishes – including a better job or house, or improved finances or health or relationships – as 'an important initial step in proving to ourselves that the practice works', though after such confirmation they may focus more on 'the happiness of other people or overcoming our own weaknesses or failings' (Causton, 1995: 248). As well as a method of focussing the mind, chanting is seen as 'the way to direct our whole life along a more creative, fulfilling path': one is not encouraged to attempt consciously to solve problems while chanting but simply to 'relax and enjoy the chanting' (SGI-UK, 1993: 11).

As Waterhouse pointed out, *Nam-myōhō-renge-kyō* may be seen in a wider Buddhist context as 'a tantric transformatory mantra', with the emphasis on sacred sound rather than intellectual meaning. However, she found SGI-UK members preferred to emphasize the effort made in chanting: they were uneasy with the concept of a 'magical' mantra, but seemed to be unclear as to whether the power of chanting 'resides in the mantra itself or in the life of the individual' (Waterhouse, 1997: 114). There are no overtly devotional practices such as bowing or prostrations, though incense, fruit and water are offered to the *gohonzon*. As well as chanting, there are important monthly study and discussion meetings, seen as virtually compulsory for committed members, where the local leader may invite members to share their experience about practising (Wilson and Dobbelaere, 1994: 16).

New members originally received their *gohonzon* in a joining ceremony, *gojukai*, where they recited *gongyō* and promised to 'practise properly and not to follow any other religion' (Cush, 1990: 104). These ceremonies could only be performed by a Nichiren Shōshū priest, and were suspended after the 1991 split, with no new *gohonzons* issued (Wilson and Dobbelaere, 1994: 26). In 1994 copies became available from another source, and both Taplow Court and many individual SGI-UK members exchanged their existing *gohonzons* for new ones not associated with High Priest Nikken (Waterhouse, 1997: 104–5). In place of the priest-led *gojukai* ceremony, new members now receive their *gohonzon* from lay leaders in a modified ceremony, though accepting the *gohonzon* still signifies agreeing to practice faithfully. Lay leaders also perform marriages and funerals, again with the reciting of *gongyō*; though Buddhist festivals have largely been replaced by more secular cultural events such as concerts (Wilson and Dobbelaere, 1994: 19). Members also spend time supporting the movement, either locally or by coming to Taplow Court to help run the centre for a week. Many SGI-UK members have been to the SGI European Centre in southern France for training courses, and before the 1991 split some also visited Japan to worship in front of the *Dai-Gohonzon* at Taiseki-ji (Wilson and Dobbelaere, 1994: 177).

Much of this shows considerable commitment, though Waterhouse (1997: 127) found SGI-UK members felt that 'essential requirements for the practice of SGI Buddhism are reducing in scope' and may be limited to chanting *Nam-myōhō-renge-kyō* to the *gohonzon* rather than the full *gongyō* practice. Like other Buddhist traditions, there seem to be varying levels of engagement with the practice, though in SGI this may be more explicit.

Nichiren's teachings on the *Lotus Sūtra*

Sōka Gakkai places more emphasis on correct belief than most other sub-traditions, arguing that according to Nichiren the causes of human suffering are the 'misleading philosophies on which people base their lives' (SGI-UK, 1993: 5). Bocking (1994: 122) described 'a well-developed doctrinal dimension', unusual for a Japanese religion, with an emphasis on study and 'rational explanations' which reflected the fact that its founders were teachers.

The description of Nichiren Buddhism as faith, practice and study informs SGI belief as well as practice. Causton (1995: 243) described how this involves belief in the power of the *gohonzon*, the twice daily chanting of *gongyō* and *Nam-myōhō-renge-kyō*, attempting to spread this form of Buddhism and the study of Nichiren's teachings. There is an unusual emphasis on proof: '*documentary* proof' or 'the written evidence that all Buddhist teachings lead to the Lotus Sutra' is said to show that Nichiren's Buddhism is both orthodox and suitable for all, '*theoretical* proof' is said to show that '*Nam-myōhō-renge-kyō* perfectly eluci-dates the mysteries of life and death', and '*actual* proof' shows how chanting improves people's lives. Causton described this 'actual proof' as a new teaching of Nichiren, rather than connecting it with the empirical approach recommended by the Buddha (Causton, 1995: 258, 31).

Both Causton (1995) and Allwright (1998) have given detailed accounts of Sōka Gakkai philosophy, and interviewees confirmed that these accurately reflect the relative importance of specific teachings. Causton (1995: 39–50) first described the 'Ten Worlds' or ten states of life said to be experienced by us all. The 'Three Evil Paths' are *Hell* (physical and mental suffering, which allows us to empathize with others), *Hunger* (physical or mental desires, which should be creatively redirected rather than repressed) and *Animality* (the instinctive behaviour of eating, sleeping, sex and aggression). The remaining three of the 'six lower worlds' are *Anger* (including arrogance and conflict, but which may stimulate beneficial change), *Tranquillity* (a neutral peacefulness, which may also mean laziness or passivity), and *Rapture* (our reaction to fulfilled temporary desires). *Learning* and *Realization* represent the intellectual and spiritual understanding taught by the Buddha, and *Bodhisattva* is the state of universal compassion which wishes 'to replace suffering in others with happiness'. Finally, *Buddhahood* is the 'absolute happiness' which all people can attain, enabling them to exhibit the positive aspects of the other nine worlds (Causton, 1995: 50–61, 68). These may be seen as psychological readings of the traditional six realms of rebirth and of the spiritual achievements of enlightened beings: Waterhouse (1997: 108) has pointed out that these and other SGI teachings are borrowed from the Tendai (Ch. T'ien t'ai) school, brought from China in 805 by the Japanese monk Saichō.

Myōhō-renge-kyō is the Japanese version of the Sanskrit *Saddharma-puṇḍarīka-sūtra* ('the Lotus of the True Dharma'). Causton (1995: 97–8) gave one meaning of the chanted *daimoku* or invocation of the *Lotus Sutra* as 'I devote my life to the Mystic Law of the Lotus Sutra', but he also suggested that the title of any Buddhist *sūtra* 'encapsulates the entirety of the teaching that follows', so that the elements of *Nam-myōhō-renge-kyō* may be used to explain the teachings further.

Myōhō not only means 'Mystic Law', but signifies the unity between *myō* (ultimate reality, enlightenment, the unseen or latent) and *hō* (everyday life, delusion, the seen or manifest) (Causton, 1995: 102; Allwright, 1998: 80). This encompasses several further teachings. The Three Truths (again borrowed from Tendai) are seen as physical existence, the spiritual life and the Middle Way which joins them. The Oneness of Mind and Body emphasizes the unity between 'the physical and spiritual aspects of life', while the Oneness of Life and its Environment underlines that individuals and their surroundings are 'all part of the great cosmic life-force' (Causton, 1995: 104, 106, 118). Thus individuals 'can change the world' as well as change themselves through chanting: unexpected money or a new job are 'merely your environment reacting *directly* to your chanting' (Causton, 1995: 121, 125).

The Eternity of Life teaches that living things are not created or destroyed, as life and death are only 'alternating aspects in which our real self manifests itself' (Causton, 1995: 138). The traditional five *skandhas* or 'Five Components' combine to form 'the life entity or nucleus', and although this is said not to be a soul, Nichiren taught that it has always existed, and that it 'continues unchanged throughout the individual's life; disappears but remains unaltered at death; and then reappears in a different form in the future' (Causton, 1995: 139, 145). Each rebirth of this constant 'true self' is merely a change of identity, with death as part of 'the eternal process by which an individual life entity constantly refreshes and renews itself before reappearing in a different guise' (Causton, 1995: 150). This may not be a soul theory which contradicts traditional *anattā* teaching, but it seems to undermine classical Buddhism's rejection of eternalism, especially any eternal 'self'.

Renge or 'lotus flower' symbolizes both our Buddha nature emerging from everyday life and the important teaching of 'the simultaneity of cause and effect'. Although *karma* still applies to past, present and future, chanting *Nam-myōhō-renge-kyō* causes the immediate experience of 'the Buddhahood that is innate within us' (Causton, 1995: 165, 192). Allwright (1998: 36) confirmed that Nichiren's Buddhism has 'no stages to go through. We can experience Buddhahood immediately'.

Kyō or 'sutra' is seen as 'the voice or teaching of a Buddha', and as 'sound, rhythm or vibration' it may also be interpreted as chanting (Causton, 1995: 195). According to Allwright (1998: 82), it also implies both the 'voices of all living beings' and 'the eternity of life'. In this context, the teaching of *ichinen sanzen* or '3000 realms in a moment of life' explains how changing oneself can also change the environment, through the complex interaction between the Ten Worlds, the Ten Factors of Life (appearance, nature, entity, power, influence, inherent cause, external cause, latent effect, manifest effect, consistency) and the Three Realms of Existence (individual, society and environment) (Causton, 1995: 197, 202). Finally, *Nam* or 'homage to' is a devotional invocation to the *Lotus Sūtra*, the Buddha, all beings and 'life as a whole', hinting at the attitudes and actions needed to 'attain Buddhahood in this lifetime' (Causton, 1995: 221, 212).

The *gohonzon* or 'object of fundamental respect, worthy of honour' is seen as a mandala which embodies *Nam-myōhō-renge-kyō* (SGI-UK, 1993: 18). Causton (1995: 226) described it as 'the prime point of faith, practice and study' and as 'the *object of worship*', though it is not worshipped as an idol, but as a symbolic representation of enlightenment: 'Through chanting Nam-myōhō-renge-kyō, we fuse our lives with the Gohonzon and draw out and experience our own enlightened life-condition' (Allwright, 1998: 86). Members chant at home facing the *gohonzon*, which has no divine or magical powers, according to Causton, but which represents 'the physical embodiment of the state of Buddhahood'. It also embodies the life of Nichiren, who is said to have been 'enlightened at birth', and is seen as 'the external cause to awaken the Buddhahood dormant in all people throughout the world' (Causton, 1995: 231, 233, 242). However, the *gohonzon* may be referred to in SGI literature either as 'a symbolic representation of what is already latent within an individual' or as 'an object which has its own intrinsic power' (Waterhouse, 1997: 106). Members are sometimes ambivalent about its exact status, and it seems unclear as to whether the *gohonzon* itself or the person kneeling in front of it is the agent of change.

SGI-UK has a national programme for studying Nichiren's teachings, which are collected in the *Gosho* ('writings worthy of the greatest respect') (Causton, 1995: 264). Members all study the same *Gosho* each month, following a text and commentary published in *UK Express* and presented at study meetings by accredited leaders (Waterhouse, 1997: 110). Individuals may read whatever they wish, but leaders will remind them that all teachings other than those of Nichiren are provisional, and interviewees saw this as compassionate guidance rather than an exclusive approach. Study is seen as spiritual rather than academic: Causton (1995: 265) described it as 'reading a line or phrase of the *Gosho* each day in order gradually to assimilate its profound meaning'.

Waterhouse found that Nichiren's more uncompromising statements (such as the dire consequences of the slightest departure from his advice) may be 'given a liberal interpretation' by leaders to avoid challenging members' perceived obligations. While speculative discussion is discouraged, some members would prefer 'a more rigorous approach', perhaps reintroducing the 'more advanced programme' which was dropped as leaders felt it was undermining group study, and which 'might include information on other schools of Buddhism' (Waterhouse, 1997: 111, 112). There seems to be a tension here between a centralized didactic approach and the wish of some individuals for a wider pattern of study.

The *Lotus Sūtra* has a unique status within SGI, following Nichiren's claim that it contains the ultimate Buddhist teaching within its title, so that all who chant *Nam-myōhō-renge-kyō*, 'even without understanding its meaning, realise not only the heart of the Lotus Sutra, but also the essence of all the Buddha's teachings' (quoted in Allwright, 1998: 83). Interviewees confirmed this crucial interpretation of the *sūtra* and its title. Both Nichiren and SGI argue that the *Lotus Sūtra* itself does not need to be studied, as only chanting *Nam-myōhō-renge-kyō* can lead to enlightenment, and the emphasis in meetings is often on Nichiren's interpretation or President Ikeda's lectures, rather than the text itself. Allwright (1998: 13) stated clearly that the Buddha himself taught the *Lotus Sōtra* towards the end of his life, and interviewees were often unaware of the accepted academic view that the *sūtra* was compiled several centuries later.

According to Waterhouse (1997: 113), most members chanted the *gongyō* in romanized Sino-Japanese with 'no interest in the content of the Lotus Sūtra', and some were even unaware of the accessible translations, though others have copies of the recommended English version by Burton Watson (*The Lotus Sūtra*, 1993). Nichiren's writings are all studied in SGI's own translations, and while some members are prepared to address questions of provenance and interpretation, they seem to be in a minority.

Apart from the *Lotus Sūtra*, no other scriptures are studied in the groups, though Nichiren occasionally quotes from other Mahāyāna texts. Individuals might follow up these references in English translations, though it would be seen as inappropriate to study them in depth, and leaders would encourage members to focus on the *Lotus Sūtra*. At least one interviewee recognized that this was 'a faith approach' which could be challenged from an intellectual viewpoint.

While SGI firmly supports freedom of religion, Causton (1995: 284) argued that the most foolish act is to 'slander the True Law', and only the *Lotus Sūtra* explains that 'slandering the True Law' means 'to fail to recognise the Lotus Sūtra as Shakyamuni's highest teaching'. This exclusive interpretation of a text rich in symbolic value may explain why Nichiren was so critical of other Buddhist schools and why SGI-UK remains relatively isolated from other Buddhist traditions in Britain.

SGI teaching includes at least something of Nichiren's uncompromising attitude towards other religions. Causton explained Nichiren's view that 'wrong religions' (involving either 'provisional' or 'heretical' teachings) lead only to suffering. Indeed Nichiren claimed that Śākyamuni (and all other Buddhas) proclaimed that 'neither the Lotus Sutra nor the other sutras lead to enlightenment. Only *Nam-myōhō-renge-kyō* can do so... To mix other practices with *Nam-myōhō-renge-kyō* is a grave error' (quoted in Causton, 1995: 292). This again shows a committed practitioner's view: the Buddha's recommendation to chant the title of the *Lotus Sūtra* comes from Mahāyāna apologetics rather than from history.

Interviewees also showed this committed attitude. Śākyamuni Buddha is said to have left behind teachings which Nichiren later rediscovered and revealed for use in the modern world. Their teachings may thus be viewed as practically identical; though a more critical view would see them as radically different. The importance of Nichiren may have been further strengthened by the split with the priesthood, according to Waterhouse (1997: 131): with the authority of tradition removed, SGI may rely even more heavily on Nichiren's writings.

While the doctrinal dimension is clearly important in SGI teaching and practice, the question of adaptation to a modern Western context is ambivalent, as it has mainly taken place in a Japanese-based SGI rather than in SGI-UK itself. There is a firm emphasis on faith in the *gohonzon*, the efficacy of chanting *Nam-myōhō-renge-kyō*, the teachings of Nichiren, and the capacity to change one's life. There are also highly philosophical areas, such as the mental states of the Ten Worlds or the complexity of the *ichinen sanzen* doctrine, the suggestion of eternalism or the simultaneous appearance of cause and effect. There are problematic questions of interpretation, such as whether the *gohonzon* has symbolic or intrinsic power, whether the efficacy of chanting can be proved and whether it has a quasi-magical effect which operates without the practitioner's understanding, with the title of the *Lotus Sūtra* used as a mantra. The organization continues to emphasize a simple faith-based approach, though some members would welcome a more critical attitude towards the teachings.

Nichiren and the role of chanting

Important narratives within SGI-UK include those of the Buddha, Nichiren, President Ikeda, the split with Nichiren Shōshū and the results of chanting. Most members would accept that the Buddha – always referred to as 'Shakyamuni' within SGI – spent the final years of his life teaching the *Lotus Sūtra*, which supersedes all other teachings. This is presented as a factual account by Causton (1995: 26), Allwright (1998: 13) and elsewhere in SGI-UK literature, without reference to the complex Mahāyāna apologetics by which the *sūtra's* authors establish its credentials and embed them into the text. Causton (1995: 64) followed Nichiren in claiming that 'the inherent limitations of Learning and Realization' led the Buddha to proclaim that nobody could attain enlightenment prior to the teaching of the *Lotus Sūtra*, though of course this ignores the frequent accounts of enlightenment in the Pali canon. *The Art of Living* gives a brief account of the life of the Buddha, though the account of the life of Nichiren which follows is more substantial (SGI-UK, 1993: 25, 28–31), reflecting the conscious downgrading of the historical Buddha in this tradition.

According to Causton (1995: 26), Nichiren is 'the Buddha for our present age', for whom the historical Buddha 'prepared the way'. Nichiren was able 'to transform profound theory into practical action', realizing and revealing the 'ultimate truth' of Buddhist practice. While other Mahāyāna traditions view the historical Buddha in the context of various mythical Buddhas, it is unusual to see him presented as the forerunner of a later historical Buddha, particularly in a doctrinal rather than a devotional context.

Nichiren is seen as 'the only person who revealed a way for ordinary people to obtain enlightenment in this lifetime', according to Vicky Abel (quoted in Cush, 1990: 103). His denunciation of all other forms of Buddhism is treated as the legitimate condemnation of those who 'went against the teachings of Shakyamuni', as only the *Lotus Sūtra* could save them (SGI-UK, 1993: 28). He is said to have opposed other teachings out of compassion, suffering continual persecution (Allwright, 1998: 104); but his persistent intolerance makes him an unusual role model for contemporary Western Buddhists.

Cresswell (1994: 7) described how SGI-UK members 'acknowledge Nichiren as their master', since he revealed the practice of chanting *Nam-myōhō-renge-kyō*, thus 'identifying himself as the leader of the Bodhisattvas of the Earth', that is, those disciples called on by the Buddha in the *Lotus Sūtra* to continue the teaching after his death.

Asked about the relative importance of the Buddha and Nichiren, interviewees said that both were respected, though Nichiren was seen as the master who reinterpreted the Buddha's teachings and revealed this form of Buddhism. They confirmed Nichiren's status within the movement as 'the true Buddha', while pointing out that we are all potential Buddhas. Members learn relatively little about Sākyamuni himself, except to explain the origins of Buddhism, and are usually only aware of him through Nichiren's writings rather than earlier texts.

While SGI-UK describes itself as part of an international movement based on the *Lotus Sūtra* and the teachings of Nichiren, their introductory brochure directs readers to the writings of President Ikeda (SGI-UK, n.d.: 5–6, 18), who is seen within the movement as 'a master for today' (Creswell, 1994: 7). Interviewees saw him as their personal teacher, guiding them by his writings rather than by personal contact, though also speaking of the powerful experience of being in his presence at a public meeting. Critics may see the publicity surrounding Ikeda as a personality cult, and British members may be reluctant to accept him as a living master on par with Nichiren or the Buddha (Waterhouse, 1997: 132), but his role as spiritual leader in both SGI and SGI-UK remains a central and highly influential one.

Following the 1991 split with the Nichiren Shōshū priesthood, there has been some confusion about Nichiren's spiritual lineage, and a new narrative of lay succession has emerged. One interviewee described Ikeda as 'our teacher of today', with an important lineage passed to him through Makiguchi and Toda, and another suggested that the lay presidents of Sōka Gakkai (rather than the Nichiren Shōshū priests) are now the 'true disciples' of Nichiren. This is the first of three examples of new Buddhist movements beginning to reinterpret their recent past, to explain and legitimize a crucial separation from their Asian parent traditions.

Newcomers to SGI-UK are 'encouraged to chant for what they want', in recognition of 'desire as a powerful motivation in our lives' (SGI-UK, 1993: 10). Although Causton (1995: 91) made clear that 'chanting *Nam-myōhō-renge-kyō* is not an instantaneous miracle cure', he included many personal testimonies of practitioners who have conquered anger, illness, alcoholism, low self-esteem and other problems through persistent practice. He claimed that society itself can be changed by more people chanting, with less crime, fewer drug and alcohol problems, and 'a lower divorce rate, a stronger economy and higher standards of living, generally better health, [and] a greater life expectancy'. Nichiren Buddhism is seen as the only religion which can envisage humanity developing enough to 'learn to overcome the many problems which it has created' (Causton, 1995: 260–1).

These are bold claims, made repeatedly in SGI-UK literature. Wilson and Dobbelaere (1994: 181) found that greater happiness, improved relationships, more possessions, and better working lives were described as 'proofs of steps towards salvation, towards buddhahood'. Almost all those who chanted for specific goals believed that they were achieved in some way, though some reported that chanting had helped them change their attitude to the problem they were chanting about (Wilson and Dobbelaere, 1994: 195, 200). Although there may be echoes here of the protective *paritta* chanting of Theravāda Buddhism, or the Mahāyāna *dhāraṇīs*, chanted to preserve Buddhist teachings, the motivation for chanting within SGI-UK seems generally more pragmatic, at least for many members.

The benefits of faith and chanting

Newcomers to SGI-UK were attracted by a variety of factors, according to Wilson and Dobbelaere (1994: 53f.), including friendly and sincere members, changes seen in family or friends who had begun to practise, or the practical benefits expected from chanting. Others were attracted by SGI-UK's simple ritual, emphasis on personal responsibility, approachable leaders or the absence of moral rules. While members might joke about chanting for cars, Waterhouse (1997: 95, 117) underlined the movement's 'reputation for promoting the view that members can chant for material benefits', and there are accounts of people chanting directly for money (Wigmore, 1985: 10; Wilson, 2000: 365). SGI-UK (1993: 11) conceded that people often begin chanting for personal concerns, but they later see that developing compassion for others affords access to 'our Buddha nature, which is one with the infinite power of the universe'.

Interviewees confirmed that while chanting for material things was legitimate, a more spiritual motivation usually developed over time, as the chanting itself transforms personal desires into more compassionate aspirations, including spiritual development, the happiness of others and world peace. Chanting may thus be seen within the Mahāyāna tradition of using 'skilful means' to transform unwholesome desires, though such changes in motivation may mean that individual members are often practising for different reasons. Waterhouse (1997: 117) suggested that those who do not receive the results they seek tend to rationalize this 'by questioning the depth of their faith or the sincerity of their practice'.

Wilson and Dobbelaere found that almost all SGI-UK members chanted for specific goals, including better careers, relationships or finances as 'the most literal interpretation of the idea of value creation'. Although many also chanted for personal health and happiness, only about one-fifth chanted 'for the welfare of others' or for the overall social and political goals of the movement (Wilson and Dobbelaere, 1994: 186–7). While the motivation for chanting may often change and become more spiritual over time, there seems to be evidence of a continued materialistic attitude, perhaps emphasizing the difference between committed practitioners and the wider membership.

The claimed or perceived results of chanting are also important here. Causton (1995: 13) began by promising that those who chant, study and teach others will eventually find their desires 'completely fulfilled' and will develop 'unshakeable happiness and confidence'. Allwright (1998: 47) confirmed that chanting will bring 'optimism, determination and joy'. There may be a link here with traditional ideas on the benefits of *puñña* (P.: Skt *puṇya*, 'karmic fruitfulness' or 'merit'), though these usually accrue through generosity and moral actions rather than through chanting.

According to Nichiren, these benefits are produced in four ways. The 'conspicuous prayer' of chanting for specific things may bring the 'conspicuous benefit' of money or a job, or the 'inconspicuous benefit' of deferred achievements. The 'inconspicuous prayer' of committed practice may bring the 'conspicuous benefit' of a protective ' "deposit account" of good fortune', or the 'inconspicuous benefit' of 'human revolution', where one's life becomes 'filled with the qualities of your true self, which is Buddhahood – wisdom, courage, compassion, purity and the joy of inexhaustible life-force' (Causton, 1995: 194).

Interviewees agreed that faith and devotion were the most predominant emotional responses encouraged in this tradition and emphasized that Sōka Gakkai is very much a world-embracing rather than a world-renouncing movement. Faith in one's own Buddhahood was seen as vital for changing one's life and environment and so becoming more peaceful. One interviewee referred to the importance of the emotional states in the Ten Worlds teaching, each of which may be used to generate positive change in oneself and one's surroundings. Interviewees also emphasized that while negative emotions may need to be understood and expressed, the most important response was to transform them through chanting and so channel them into more positive and valuable behaviour.

Like other Mahāyāna traditions, SGI-UK goes beyond the original teaching that unskilful desires cause suffering. Like Nichiren, the movement argues that 'earthly desires are enlightenment', in the sense that their transformation into wisdom leads to Buddhahood. Even anger 'can be transformed into a passionate desire for peace' (SGI-UK, 1993: 20). Such claims might be misinterpreted as encouraging continued indulgence in 'earthly desires', though the Ten Worlds teaching helps to explain how this emotional transformation takes place. Even negative emotions such as the Hell state enable one to 'sympathise with the suffering of others', while Anger may bring either 'the energy needed to fight injustice' or 'the passionate driving force for personal and social reform' (Causton, 1995: 43, 53).

Although the chanting in a local group may have a powerful sense of reverence or devotion, the discussion which follows often has a more secular mood. Members may tend to emphasize their positive experiences, rather than to reflect on difficulties with their practice, even when prompted by the group leader.

While SGI-UK members do not follow Nichiren in condemning other Buddhist traditions, interviewees defended what might be seen as an intolerant approach. One argued that Nichiren had proved the validity of chanting rather than other practices and simply wished to spread this knowledge. Nichiren was compared to Luther as 'profoundly compassionate' in counselling people firmly against other Buddhist practices which went against the Buddha's teaching and would only lead them astray. Another interviewee felt that anger and intolerance towards what is wrong or corrupt can be justified and that like Nichiren 'we should stand up and be counted'.

A personalized morality

Unlike other forms of Buddhism in Britain, SGI-UK has no explicit moral code for members to follow. Causton (1995: 4) argued that chanting *Nam-myōhō-renge-kyō* shows people 'the existence of Buddhahood within themselves', obviating the need to suppress desire or 'to live by some demanding (and possibly outdated) moral code'. Allwright (1998: 43) claimed that even selfish desires are powerful motivators which can be used as 'fuel to transform our lives and manifest enlightenment'. As lay people in the secular world, SGI-UK members see monasticism as an outdated and unnecessary asceticism, perhaps reflecting attitudes in contemporary Japan, where celibacy has often been replaced by a married priesthood. Similarly, individual members may choose to be vegetarians but there is no restriction on eating meat or drinking alcohol.

While the SGI Charter pledges support for human rights, religious freedom, cultural diversity and environmental protection (Allwright, 1998: 113), it is seen within SGI-UK as 'an organizational statement to the outside world' rather than a personal guide for members, according to one interviewee. Moral issues such as abortion or nuclear weapons are seen as matters for individual decision (Cush, 1990: 105), and even where members endorsed the 'politicized moral values' which support peace or disarmament, Wilson and Dobbelaere (1994: 154) found them 'less disposed towards the regulation of the individual's personal behaviour'. Members rejected the traditional religious norms of 'objective moral rules' in what amounted to a 'privatization of morality', and SGI-UK's 'permissive ethic', together with its promotion of individual happiness and fulfilment, made it ideally suited to 'the secular ethos of post-Christian Britain' (Wilson and Dobbelaere, 1994: 130, 133, 220). British converts are often attracted by this flexible moral approach, rather than by SGI teachings and practices, according to Wilson (2000: 354–5). Interviewees emphasized the feeling of being trusted to make decisions, with personal morality dependent on its contemporary context.

However, although Nichiren's Buddhism has 'no rules to regulate human conduct', Causton (1995: 76) argued that the practice itself soon shows which actions 'create true value for yourself and others and which cause suffering'. Members reported that 'chanting leads to moral behaviour', according to Waterhouse (1997: 120), through increased understanding of others' needs and of the relationship between causes and effects. The movement emphasizes that moral judgements are informed by respect for living beings and an understanding of *karma* or the 'universal law of cause and effect' (SGI-UK, 1993: 7), and interviewees underlined this view. *Karma* was seen as an ethical teaching which encourages both individual responsibility and respect for life, or a 'first precept' which proscribes killing and violence because of their inescapable consequences.

Wilson (2000: 353) argued that SGI-UK has rejected 'inflexible moral rules' in favour of 'very general abstract principles of compassion, integrity, and fortitude'. Within this context, worldly pleasures may be enjoyed rather than rejected, as the individual engages positively with secular culture. As a lay organization with no monastic links, no fixed moral rules, and no restrictions on food, alcohol or sexual behaviour, SGI-UK certainly appears to be at the 'world-embracing' end of the moral spectrum, though again any adaptation here may already have been made by Sōka Gakkai in Japan.

Hierarchy, participation and evangelism

Waterhouse described SGI-UK as 'a highly structured hierarchical organization with several administrative layers', where senior staff in Britain are still 'answerable to the central administration in Japan', though the structure made communication more efficient and leaders were 'respected for their experience rather than for their positions' (Waterhouse, 1997: 92, 130). Cresswell (2004) confirmed that SGI-UK is a complex organization where changes sometimes take place rapidly: although some matters are still referred to Japan, most decisions are made locally.

Robert Samuels, a Vice General Director of SGI-UK, explained that the leadership structure actually 'starts from the bottom', when a group of 10 people practise together and become a District: 2 or 3 Districts may then create a Chapter, and 3 Chapters may create a Headquarters. These are then coordinated by four Vice General Directors, with Ricky Baines as General Director (Samuels, 2002). There is thus what Wilson and Dobbelaere called 'a chain of experience in faith throughout the organization'. District leaders are authorized to train group leaders and to give 'short talks on the principles of Nichiren's Buddhism or on a passage of the *Gosho*', while Chapter leaders 'can give deeper advice and guidance on matters of faith' (Wilson and Dobbelaere, 1994: 36, 167). All leaders are appointed rather than elected, though the leadership role is advisory rather than authoritarian, according to interviewees. The structure is seen as supportive rather than controlling, and members may approach leaders at any level for guidance, rather than being restricted by a formal teacher–disciple relationship.

As well as the hierarchical structure, there are separate sections for men and women, for young men and young women, and for children, though this Japanese-based social pattern is less important than the District meetings which all members attend. At a national level, there have also been more informal groups of members in different professions and ethnic groups, though these now meet only rarely. Wilson and Dobbelaere (1994: 163) found that some members saw a contradiction between the movement's seemingly authoritative structure and its claim to be 'strongly democratic and egalitarian', while younger members were sometimes unhappy with gender divisions which may appear sexist. Stereotyped roles at major events, with young men from the 'Value Creation Group' directing traffic while young women from the 'Lilac Group' provide refreshments (Wilson, 2000: 267), suggest that traditional Japanese patriarchal views may still have an influence.

In 1995 SGI-UK began 'a conscious exercise of reappraisal', acknowledging its poor public image and hierarchical organization (Wilson, 2000: 373). Members who supported adaptation to 'British cultural norms' proposed a simplified structure with fewer leaders and no 'culturally based' gender divisions (Waterhouse, 1997: 129). There are now more women leaders, and Japanese patriarchal culture is gradually giving way to a pattern of gender equality more in keeping with contemporary British society.

Asked if SGI-UK was a British or Japanese organization, several interviewees responded that it was international. SGI as a whole shows 'a remarkable degree of unity in its actions', though there is also 'considerable autonomy' in each national organization (Causton, 1995: 270). Batchelor (1994: 155) claimed that while President Ikeda often spoke about democracy, in SGI 'all decisions descend from above'. This could hardly be applied now to SGI-UK, though senior appointments still have to be approved in Japan. The British branch also remains somewhat Japanese in flavour: many members expressed an interest in Japanese culture or lifestyle, though some felt the movement was 'too Japanese' and had not yet been 'translated to an English way of life' (Wilson and Dobbelaere, 1994: 95). Changing patterns of autonomy, cultural elements and gender roles make the overall picture difficult to see here, with a mixture of Japanese adaptation from traditional Nichiren Buddhism and British variation from SGI.

Wilson and Dobbelaere (1994: 40ff.) gave a detailed account of social patterns within SGI-UK. They found that almost two-thirds of members lived in the southeast, nearly all were 'first generation converts' (like most 'white Buddhists' in Britain), though only a quarter had any previous religious affiliation. (This contrasts with anecdotal evidence from other traditions, where converts often come from a Christian background.) With high rates of university attendance, self-employment, training or practice in the caring professions or performing arts, they were often 'socially outgoing [and] culturally oriented' (Wilson and Dobbelaere, 1994: 119–29, 152), in contrast to the introverted and intellectual caricature of the British Buddhist. Despite the frequent meetings and shared chanting, however, SGI-UK was 'not a congregational organization', and members might often practise without close contact with each other. Unlike some New Religious Movements, the organization appeared open and tolerant, with no pressure to abandon existing relationships, although many members had experienced opposition to their chanting practice, often from their family (Wilson and Dobbelaere 1994: 100, 108–10).

Interviewees confirmed that SGI-UK may be socially broader than other Buddhist traditions in Britain because of its emphasis on working within society, and more cosmopolitan due to its international character, but its image as the fashionable 'designer Buddhism' of the 1970s and 1980s, with famous names and a high media profile, has faded as fashions move on and individuals grow older.

As part of SGI, SGI-UK has received substantial financial support from Japan, including £2.6 million to purchase Taplow Court, a further £2 million for restoration and continued funding for almost all the running costs (Wilson and Dobbelaere, 1994: 21; Waterhouse, 1997: 96). The organization is mainly self-financing on a daily basis, relying on *UK Express* subscriptions, donations and regular giving from members, and sales of *butsudans* to house the *gohonzon*, which range from £50 to more than £1000 (Wilson and Dobbelaere, 1994: 20). Meetings are in members' homes, so the cost of maintaining local or regional centres is saved. However, Taplow Court shows that SGI-UK 'has access to a far greater level of funding' than other British Buddhist organizations (Waterhouse, 1997: 102), and continued financial links with Japan may hinder the movement from adapting freely to its British context.

Early press coverage of SGI-UK, emphasizing the materialism of chanting for money and portraying the movement as a cult, has subsided, but left the organization wary of media contacts, and its public relations are still somewhat strained. SGI-UK now tends to promote its work for peace or its music concerts rather than an overtly religious message. Groups do not advertise their meetings locally, and initial contact tends to be by personal recommendation or more formally through

Taplow Court, though advertised public meetings are sometimes held in London and occasionally elsewhere.

As well as their personal practice, SGI-UK members are also 'working to establish *kosen-rufu*', that is, to 'widely declare and spread' Nichiren Buddhism, including both world peace and 'the widespread acceptance of Buddhist philosophy as the foundation of society'. However, individuals are always encouraged to act 'with compassion and wisdom, with the utmost respect for life', influencing others by enlightened behaviour, rather than as overt evangelism (Allwright, 1998: 97–8).

Causton argued that *kosen-rufu* is the ultimate aim of 'practice for others', usually through 'entirely natural, peaceful methods' – such as explaining the benefits of chanting – rather than aggressive proselytizing. While acknowledging Western suspicions, he claimed that the wish 'to help others overcome their sufferings and gain lasting happiness through practising this Buddhism' is 'the most pure and noble of all causes', enabling practitioners to purify their own karma (Causton, 1995: 256–7). This appears to create a link between successful evangelism and one's own spiritual progress; and he also argued that Nichiren Buddhism would soon become a global religion, and is the only way towards world peace (Causton, 1995: 259).

The early commitment of Sōka Gakkai in Japan to the 'vigorous proselytising' of *shakubuku* has been modified in recent decades, and SGI-UK members clearly recognize that such an approach would be inappropriate in Britain. Bocking (1994: 128) described SGI-UK proselytizing in Britain as 'diligent evangelism', rather than the earlier and more forceful methods used in Japan. However, while some see proselytizing as a compassionate act towards those who are suffering, others still see it as a requirement of membership (Wilson and Dobbelaere, 1994: 106), and Macaulay (1986: 11) reported that there were 'targets set every year for new recruits'. Interviewees confirmed that there is no aggressive door-to-door evangelism in Britain: members would not seek to convert practising Christians or Buddhists, but would 'introduce people who are suffering' to the practice of chanting if they are interested. Local groups may be keen to explain the benefits of chanting to potential new members, but any proselytizing is usually done informally by individuals, rather than through publicity and courses or retreats.

SGI-UK has supported UNICEF, environmental groups and the peace movement, either communally through fundraising, festivals and exhibitions, or through the work of individual members. Wilson and Dobbelaere (1994: 152) found that a third of members were active in organizations such as the Samaritans, Friends of the Earth or Amnesty International. However, Bell (2000: 415) saw a possible discrepancy between the organization's high-profile social engagement and individuals who were more concerned with personal issues. There seems to be a gap between President Ikeda's overall vision and the work of particular Districts, with some involved and others not really interested, according to one interviewee. SGI publicity sometimes presents the movement as a peace organization, whereas it is essentially a religious organization. Members may see the movement's influence rather like concentric circles, those at the core chanting and creating a church, and those further out working for social goals, perhaps practising in other religious traditions or none at all.

There appears to be a certain separation between SGI-UK and the rest of contemporary Buddhism in Britain. In 1988 for example, Causton (1995: 23) described the popular image of Buddhism as 'an abstruse, complex and mystical teaching... studied in monkish isolation' which can only be properly understood 'by highly dedicated intellectuals'. This seems curiously out of touch when there were almost two hundred Buddhist groups in Britain, considerable media interest and unprecedented public awareness about the benefits of meditation.

Causton (1995: 258) argued that Nichiren's followers are not intolerant of other religions, though they see it as legitimate to 'correct misconceptions that even other Buddhists may, in all good faith, hold about Buddhism'. Waterhouse (1997: 99) found that while Nichiren Buddhism has been strongly opposed to other traditions, 'SGI-UK has manifestly softened its attitude towards other Buddhist groups', joining the NBO in 1995 and taking part in interfaith dialogue. Her interviewees expressed 'a respect for other religious paths', though still firmly supporting the SGI view that other forms of Buddhism were 'provisional teachings superseded by the Lotus Sutra'. They often knew little about other Buddhist traditions, though there was also 'a growing contingent of well informed members'. While SGI-UK is now more open towards both other Buddhist traditions and other world faiths, she found that meetings in Bath are not advertised, and neither the public nor other local Buddhists are aware of their presence (Waterhouse, 1997: 100–1, 94).

Interviewees confirmed that there was often little contact between SGI-UK and other Buddhist groups, at least at the local level, partly as members saw the movement as 'the true Buddhism' but also because few of them have any other experience of Buddhism. Some members may be confident enough to study other Buddhist traditions, but they are more likely to be looking at New Age movements or reading self-help books and 'comparing these approaches with their Buddhist practice'. One interviewee who had been chanting for 12 years had not heard the term 'Theravāda Buddhism', perhaps because SGI-UK literature has used the disparaging and outdated term 'Hinayāna' (Skt 'lesser vehicle') until recently. Again there is an unusual insularity here.

Wilson (2000: 373) concluded that SGI-UK has 'little if any relation' to other Buddhist groups in Britain, and its members have little interest in Buddhism as a whole. According to Bocking (1994: 129), the absence of its 'Nichiren Shoshu traditionalists' may allow SGI-UK to begin to relate to other Buddhist groups, 'relaxing its claim to exclusive possession of the truth'. Although the overall organization of SGI has changed somewhat since the 1991 split, perhaps we may conclude with Wilson and Dobbelaere (1994: 230) that the movement's unusual achievement has been 'to maximise lay participation while retaining a firm system of central control'.

Secular culture and the Japanese *gohonzon*

SGI-UK is unusual in having a stately home as its headquarters and in maintaining it as a largely secular building. Taplow Court is seen as a cultural and administrative centre rather than a temple. The main house has been renovated in period style, with no Buddhist iconography or decoration, apart from *gohonzons* in the rooms used for chanting. However, the New Century Hall – a large new building in the grounds – combines secular and religious functions. It has a sanctuary or *butsuma* with a *butsudan* and *gohonzon* and can seat up to 500 people for chanting and ceremonies or (with the sanctuary screened off) for conferences and films.

SGI-UK is a lay movement with no temples, though there is a centre in a renovated house in London, and plans for further centres. Meetings usually take place in members' homes, where the altar is seen as equally precious as the one in Taplow Court. In one room there will be a shrine, which will include offerings of greenery and 'candles for light, incense to purify the air, and fruit. Fresh water is offered every day' (Cush, 1990: 100). The candles and water are said to represent wisdom and purity, respectively. Although there may be Buddha images elsewhere in the home, perhaps for aesthetic rather than spiritual reasons, there will be no Buddha image on the shrine itself. This is to emphasize that the *gohonzon* is seen as 'the *object of worship*' (Causton, 1995: 226), enshrined in a cabinet or *butsudan* ('place of the Buddha'). Allwright (1998: 86) explained that the *gohonzon* functions as a mandala, a 'focus for concentration for meditation'. It is a scroll with Chinese and Sanskrit characters, containing the central inscription '*Nam-myōhō-renge-kyō* Nichiren', the names of Buddhas and bodhisattvas, the ten states of life and 'various protective forces of the universe'. Chanting is directed towards the *gohonzon*, which is described as the 'external stimulus for Buddhahood' (Allwright, 1998: 86–8).

The *gohonzon* may also be seen symbolically as 'something which exists within the heart of the worshipper' (Bocking, 1994: 122), so it is possible to chant without its physical presence when away from home. Ideally the *gohonzon* is enshrined in a separate room, but is often seen in an ordinary living room. Family life may continue as normal even during chanting, perhaps with someone else watching television or talking on the telephone.

Wilson and Dobbelaere (1994: 96, 120) found considerable adaptation to British culture within SGI-UK. Many members work in the visual and performing arts, and music and dance festivals have become an important part of the movement. The 1986 London production of *Alice!*, a musical based on *Alice in Wonderland*, was written, produced, staged and acted by SGI-UK members, and a May Festival in 1990 included 'programmes of jazz, classical music, song, visual arts, a children's day, and dance' (Wilson and Dobbelaere, 1994: 153, 165). The annual Taplow Court Festival has raised funds to support children caught in war zones. World music, massed choirs, modern jazz and rock are all included, and SGI-UK is surely the only British Buddhist movement to book Mark Knopfler from Dire Straits.

Conclusion

SGI-UK's strong Japanese influence, rapid expansion in Britain and reputation for aggressive proselytizing have made it a controversial tradition which has received unfavourable (and often unfair) treatment in the media. It is sometimes portrayed even from within Buddhism as a tradition based on materialism and magic rather than spiritual values and practice.

While it is unusual for chanting to replace silent meditation completely in a Buddhist tradition, there are many Asian Buddhists – and certainly some British converts – who see personal morality or developing compassion (rather than meditation) as their basic practice. Moreover, the use of the *gohonzon* as an object of worship in SGI-UK may not be far removed from the reverence paid to Buddha figures in other traditions, at least in popular Asian Buddhism.

The strong emphasis on doctrine may appear to lead in rather different directions. Consideration of the Ten Worlds encourages reflection and the transformation of negative emotions, while the Eternity of Life seems at odds with Buddhism's traditional rejection of eternalism. The quasi-magical operation of chanting, together with a largely uncritical acceptance of the *Lotus Sutra* and Nichiren's teaching, emphasizes the importance of faith, but sits awkwardly with the wish of some members for a more hermeneutic approach to Buddhist texts and history.

Nichiren clearly overshadows the historical Buddha in SGI. Although great teachers are sometimes visualized as Buddhas during tantric practice and regarded as successors to Śākyamuni as Buddhas in their own right, it is unusual to see the historical Buddha portrayed as a forerunner of Nichiren.

The absence of a formal moral code and the legitimizing of chanting for personal gain are also unusual in Buddhism and certainly attractive to newcomers to SGI-UK. While some on the fringes of the movement may seek material benefits without making real behavioural changes, committed members find that chanting leads naturally towards compassionate and altruistic behaviour, based on personal responsibility rather than fixed rules. This world-embracing attitude may be seen as an example of 'skilful means' rather than a departure from adherence to conventional moral precepts.

A hierarchical international organization based in Japan seems an unlikely candidate for the largest Buddhist movement in Britain, and there remain latent tensions between individual and organizational goals, as well as ambivalent relationships with other Buddhists. However, Wilson (2000: 372) concluded fairly that SGI-UK does not show the 'secrecy, authoritarianism, inflexibility, and entrenched resistance to change' which popular opinion identifies with a cult.

The question of adaptation in SGI-UK is a complex one. While chanting, teachings and proselytizing clearly come from Nichiren, the emphasis on peace, education and culture – and the movement's organizational style and social values – have grown up in twentieth-century Japan, and the role of President Ikeda has developed within SGI. This means that in some respects SGI-UK might be described as a 'pre-adapted' tradition, conforming to changes already made. However, it is also adapting from the pattern of the international movement by promoting British egalitarian social values, a more liberal interpretation of Nichiren's uncompromising teachings and a concern for personal rather than political issues.

The underlying attitude of SGI-UK remains bold, positive and exclusive. Allwright (1998: 70) claimed that those who chant *Nam-myōhō-renge-kyō* have no need for 'difficult meditation or ways of life which are removed from society', and Causton (1995: 294) argued that only the practice of Nichiren Buddhism can reverse the current downward spiral of 'natural and man-made disasters' which leads to global war. If this sounds different from the tolerant and inclusive attitudes we expect to find in Buddhism, perhaps we should question those expectations themselves, before judging Sōka Gakkai for not conforming to them.

7

THE KARMA KAGYU TRADITION

Historical background

The unique combination within Tibetan Buddhism of great complexity, prominent mystical and non-rational elements, and the flexibility to adapt to different temperaments, may explain much of its appeal to Westerners. It certainly makes teachings and practices more difficult to describe, particularly in a European context. There is also the question of whether Tibetan Buddhism is developing outside Tibet primarily to appeal to Westerners, or to preserve a religion-in-exile, and there may be tension between these two purposes. As Western students learn Tibetan teachings, Tibetan Buddhism itself may be changing to accommodate Western sensibilities or 'redefining its boundaries' to include Westerners within its hierarchy, even occasionally recognizing one of them as a *tulku* or reincarnated lama (Tib.: Skt gun) (Rawlinson, 1997: 8, 11).

Of the four main Tibetan schools, the Kagyu (Tib. *bKa' brgyud*, 'Oral Transmission Lineage') traces its origins from Marpa (1012–97) and his disciple Milarepa (1040–1123), who passed on the teachings to Gampopa (1079–1153), author of the famous *Jewel Ornament of Liberation*, who 'organized the teachings and practices into the Kagyu school' (Keown, 2003: 133). The Karma Kagyu, now the largest Kagyu school, was apparently the first Tibetan tradition to develop the concept of 'succession through reincarnation', and has been led by successive Karmapas since the twelfth century (Williams, 1989: 191).

The Karma Kagyu tradition in Britain began with two young Tibetan Buddhist teachers, Chögyam Trungpa (1939–87) and Akong Tulku Rinpoche (b. 1939), both of whom had been recognized in Tibet as *tulkus* (Akong, 1994: 189; Trungpa, 1996: 93). Arriving from India in 1963 to study in Oxford, they were soon invited to give talks around the country. A dwindling Theravāda group they visited in Eskdalemuir agreed to sell them Johnstone House, and in 1967 this became the first Tibetan Buddhist centre in Europe, its name taken from 'Samyé, Tibet's first monastery and lay centre' (Holmes, 1982: 90).

Batchelor (1994: 104) described Chögyam Trungpa as a brilliant but controversial teacher, whose idealistic and restless early Western students often saw Buddhist ideas through 'a haze of psychedelic intuitions'. Trungpa's participation in the lifestyle of 1960s counterculture shocked more traditional practitioners, and when in 1969 he 'returned his monastic vows', married and left for America, Samye Ling gained a local reputation for 'wild parties, free sex and the use of drugs' (Batchelor, 1994: 105).

Trungpa (1996: 95) insisted that in the West Buddhism should be 'free from cultural trappings and religious fascination'. Batchelor (1994: 106) aptly described the 'crazy wisdom' of his teaching and lifestyle as 'a model for Buddhist life that was by turn eminently sane and disturbingly outrageous'. When he died in 1987, the *Middle Way* could not decide whether he was 'bodhisattva or fallen angel – or a combination of both' ('Editorial', 1987: 78).

A Karma Kagyu centre with a stricter regime opened in 1973 in Saffron Walden. Lama Chime Rinpoche originally intended Kham Tibetan House as a monastic centre, but chose to marry and adopt a Western lifestyle. The centre welcomed those 'prepared to make a sincere effort to follow the path of liberation unselfishly' (Loveard, 1973: 89), emphasizing the Five Precepts, silence and mindfulness, and no drugs or alcohol. Lama Chime was its spiritual director for many years, and Marpa House, as it later became known, continues as a Karma Kagyu centre (*BD*, 1994: 69; *RelUK*, 2001: 194).

Early visitors to Samye Ling often had 'New Age' attitudes with only a casual interest in Buddhist teaching. However, there gradually emerged 'a more serious application of traditional practice', as Akong Rinpoche 'led the Centre through a period of quiet internal spiritual consolidation' (Holmes, 1982: 90). During the 1970s a resident community of practitioners committed to meditation and study emerged: the sixteenth Karmapa, head of the Kagyu tradition, visited Samye Ling twice and ten Westerners were ordained there (Oliver, 1979: 114).

The 1980s were a decade of expansion. Lama Yeshe Losal (b. 1943) took full ordination in 1980, and began to practise with great energy (Yeshe Losal, 2001: xvi). By 1982 the community had grown to 50 and a dozen were preparing for a traditional long retreat. One thousand visitors a year (including many non-Buddhists) received guidance from private interviews with Akong Rinpoche, and about 4,000 Buddhists were said to be 'directly associated with Kagyu Samye Ling', including those at centres in Dublin, Glasgow, Edinburgh and Newcastle (Holmes, 1982: 91–2).

Work began on a large Tibetan-style temple. Akong Rinpoche revisited Tibet and took responsibility for several monasteries there, and in 1985 Lama Yeshe Losal returned to Samye Ling, at first in solitary retreat but in 1988 taking over as Retreat Master for the Westerners in the traditional 'cloistered four year retreat' (www.samye.org.uk). Meanwhile the community grew to about 90 people, including a few Western monks and nuns, with about 6,000 visitors a year (Carmichael, 1986: 14).

The massive new temple was opened on the auspicious date of 8 August 1988 with 2,000 visitors, including government and religious representatives, and 300 Karma Kagyu practitioners from Britain and abroad joined the residents in celebrations (Holmes, 1989: 220). The 1984–88 retreat was completed by 16 people, a second 4-year retreat began in 1988 with over 40 candidates, and plans were begun for a full-scale Tibetan Buddhist college at Samye Ling (Holmes, 1989: 223).

The 1990s began with controversy. The sixteenth Karmapa, who had helped bring Tibetan Buddhism to the West, died in 1981, but the seventeenth Karmapa (b. 1985) was not discovered until 1992, and his identity was disputed (Waterhouse, 1997: 201ff.). Akong Tulku Rinpoche was described as playing 'an active mediatory role in the recognition and subsequent enthronement of the new Karmapa' (*25 Years of Samyé Ling*, 1993: 6).

By 1992 there were about 30,000 visitors a year, including Women's Institutes and Rotarians (Quirke, 1992: 14). The Dalai Lama visited in 1993, 34 men and women completed the second long retreat, having lived in 'cloistered contemplation' for 4 years, and the centre's focus had expanded to include alternative therapies, charitable work and interfaith activities (*25 Years of Samyé Ling*, 1993: 5, 8). It was estimated in 1994 that Samye Ling was 'a home base for between 4,000 and 5,000 British Buddhists', though these figures probably included 'casual attenders at the monastery' (Waterhouse, 1997: 184). Counting 30,000 visitors is easier than finding which of them are Buddhists.

Lama Yeshe was appointed Abbot of Samye Ling in 1995, and the centre's religious, therapeutic and charitable activities continued to expand. New kitchen and accommodation facilities were being built, and the lay community was expanding into neighbouring villages. A huge new *stūpa* was consecrated, and by 2001 there were over 50 Western monks and nuns in this tradition, 20 or more of them at Samye Ling, with others in associated centres in Britain and Europe (Yeshe Losal, 2001: xix; Dechi, 2002).

Several further centres have been established. In 1992 Samye Ling bought Holy Island, off Arran in the Firth of Clyde, to develop accommodation for long-term retreats and an interfaith centre. After a decade of renovation and building work, the Centre for World Peace and Health was opened in 2003. Kagyu Samye Dzong London opened in Lambeth in 1998 as an important urban centre for Tibetan Buddhism, with regular meditation classes, courses on both Buddhism and Tibetan culture, and short retreats for beginners and experienced practitioners. According to its teacher, Lama Zangmo, an experienced Western nun, there was 'a huge demand in London for spiritual training', with over 2,000 Londoners on the Samye Ling mailing list (Sharkey, 1998: 30). There are also main centres in Dundee, Glasgow and Dublin, and smaller groups elsewhere.

The overall picture is of a high-profile Buddhist centre at Samye Ling, with ambitious building projects, imaginative expansion into both secluded and urban locations and an unusual openness, which has attracted many non-Buddhist visitors with a wide range of activities. However, as we shall see, it also retains many traditional elements of Tibetan Buddhism.

Tibetan meditation and devotion

Tibetan Buddhist practice is combined at Samye Ling with Akong Rinpoche's broad vision for the centre and activities include 'meditation, personal advice, study or therapy', depending on people's individual needs (*25 Years of Samyé*

Ling, 1993: 4). Meditation, devotional activities, and retreats and courses are often overlapping rather than separate activities, with no standard path for all to follow.

Lama Yeshe (2004) explained that meditation and devotional practice may well vary from that in Tibet, not through any conscious adaptation but simply because each lama teaches in his own way, helping individuals to find the best method of taming their own minds. Similarly, Trungpa (1996: 75) insisted that meditation can hardly be learnt from a book or even in a class, but only through 'a personal relationship between teacher and pupil'. Initial meditation instruction emphasizes correct posture – especially keeping the spine straight – to direct the flow of energy within the body, and so start to transform negative emotions, the 'five poisons' of jealousy, anger, ignorance, desire and pride (Yeshe Losal, 2001: 100).

Students begin traditional Kagyu practice with the Four Ordinary Foundations, meditating in turn on the preciousness of human life, death and impermanence, karma, and existence in *saṃsāra* (Yeshe Losal, 1997: 169). Such basic meditations are said to loosen the grasp on material things and to purify defilements. Next come the Four Special Foundations or *ngōndro* practices. Taking refuge and making prostrations while visualizing the lineage tree helps to reduce the grasping ego, reciting the 'hundred-syllable mantra' while visualizing Dorjé Sempa (Vajrasattva) helps to transform negative attitudes and purify one's karma; 'making a mandala offering ... to the Buddhas and bodhisattvas' develops generosity and generates merit, and 'Guru Yoga' develops a devotion to the guru as 'inseparable from the Buddha' (Yeshe Losal, 1998: 232). All four practices are repeated 110,000 times, often taking many years.

These practices can lead either to lengthy retreats and complex visualization practices, or to the more accessible path of using *shinay* (Tib.: Skt *śamatha*) meditation to reach a calm state, followed by *lhakthong* (Tib.: Skt. *vipaśyana*), where both 'penetrating insight and intuitive wisdom' are gained (Nydahl and Aronoff, 1989: 10). The distinctions between preparatory and advanced practices are not always clear-cut, again depending on individual needs. Shanks (2002) explained that the *ngōndro* practices 'develop your familiarity with visualization' as part of the Kagyu *Mahāmudrā* tradition. This eventually involves tantric practice where students are 'totally involved in the energy system of that particular deity', learning various practices before developing a single practice appropriate to their needs. However, while *Mahāmudrā* deity visualizations and mantras may be seen as 'the deepest and the highest' practices, when their function is fulfilled, 'you are still resting in *śamatha* with the insight and clarity ... of the *vipaśyana*'.

Gelongma Kunzang (2002) described the *Mahāmudrā* course at Samyé Ling as a 'progressive structure of *shinay* and *lhakthong* meditation' with people at various stages over several years. These *śamatha* and *vipaśyana* methods – often focussing on the breath or a physical object – will not always involve visualizing deities; different practices are used as appropriate for the individual, guided by a meditation master. Lama Yeshe (2001: 27–8) explained that although *Mahāmudrā* may be seen as 'the highest meditation practice', its essence is 'just to learn to accept everything the way it is'. Until one can follow such simple yet profound instructions, lamas prescribe 'complicated visualizations to channel your strong mind energy'.

As well as meditation periods, the daily schedule at Samye Ling includes three *pūjās* dedicated to specific deities or bodhisattvas. Morning prayers are dedicated to Green Tārā, 'the female aspect of the Buddha's wisdom and compassion', and also to ask for the blessing of the whole Kagyu lineage; afternoon prayers are dedicated to Mahākāla, 'the Protector of the Kagyu Lineage', and evening prayers to Chenrezig (Avalokiteśvara), the 'Lord of Compassion' (Kagyu Samye Ling, n.d.: n.p.). There are also long-life prayers for Lama Yeshe, Akong Rinpoche, the Dalai Lama and the seventeenth Karmapa.

These *pūjās* often follow a common format, from the preliminary practice of taking refuge to the Mahāyāna practice of reciting the *bodhicitta* prayer (asking that all beings may be free from suffering) and the Vajrayāna practice of deity visualizations. The specific deity is invited, various prayers are offered, and a mantra is repeated while practitioners visualize themselves as identified with the deity or engage with their personal visualization practice. A further prayer is recited to purify mistakes or distractions, and the visualization is then gradually dissolved into emptiness, where the practitioner rests. After a final prayer for good fortune, merit is dedicated to all beings (Kunzang, 2002).

The visualization process develops over time. Beginners may try hard to create a mental image of a statue or painting they have seen, but when they relax the mind and allow an image to form naturally, what appears is no longer a solid object, but transparent and insubstantial, 'like a rainbow, or like the moon's reflection in water' (Kunzang, 2002).

The central Chenrezig practice follows the same pattern: Chenrezig is visualized emitting rays of purifying light and the practitioner 'becomes one with Chenresig and recites the mantra *oṃ maṇi padme hūṃ*' many times' (Waterhouse, 1997: 194). When the visualization dissolves, all beings are seen as Chenrezig, and all sounds are heard as the mantra. In a seven-branch prayer, practitioners pay homage and make offerings, confess their faults and rejoice in the virtue of all beings, asking that both Dharma and Chenrezig's compassion will continue, that any merit may be for all beings, and that all suffering beings may be reborn in the presence of Chenrezig, the 'loving Protector' and compassionate Buddha who is their only refuge ('Chenrezig Prayers', 1979). Practitioners also visualize *themselves* as Chenrezig, recognizing that his compassion and wisdom also exist within their own minds. This practice gradually permeates the practitioner's daily life, so that eating, walking or speaking may be seen as 'an offering to the deity' for the benefit of all beings (Yeshe Losal, 2001: 118).

Each practice requires the empowerment or 'transmission of the lineage', giving permission to practice the visualizations; the 'scriptural transmission', giving permission to read the text, and instructions on how to recite and perform the *pūjā* itself (Kunzang, 2002). Initial group instruction may be followed by individual guidance when the practice has deepened. Such initiation is not seen as a magical transmission of wisdom, but rather a 'pouring' of wise teaching from one open mind to another (Trungpa, 1987: 55).

Prayers are transcribed into roman script, with English versions printed beside them, but chanting remains in Tibetan, as the ancient blessings in the words themselves might be lost in translation (Kunzang, 2002). Tibetan chanting is seen as preserving the lineage transmission of highly realized teachers. One group who tried chanting in English found it 'boring and meaningless' and returned to the beauty and poetry of the Tibetan: when Westerners begin to attain high levels of realization, then 'chanting will be poetic in English' and it will be time to change (Yeshe Losal, 2004).

As well as chanting, prayers and visualizations, *pūjās* include offerings, prostrations, *mudrās* (symbolic hand gestures) and music – all used as 'skilful means' to develop and gather the merit of 'positive tendencies in the mind', and to enable practitioners to see their Buddha Nature more clearly. Offerings of flowers, lights, incense and cake are made and then visualized as 'limitless, absolutely inexhaustible', not to please the Buddha, but to symbolize and encourage generosity (Kunzang, 2002). Prostrations are recommended 'to loosen the grip of egoism', especially for Westerners, whose intellectual minds often produce excuses to avoid spiritual practice, or to give up when they experience problems (Yeshe Losal, 1997: 170). Finally, the pleasant music of drums, bells and cymbals is used to invite the deity 'to come into the space in front of you', or to accompany prayers for good fortune, though it may sometimes be louder and more forceful, accompanying wrathful images when 'we need something stronger to move obstacles' (Kunzang, 2002).

The year-round programme at Samye Ling includes introductory meditation courses and further weekends on the Four Ordinary Foundations, tranquillity and insight meditation (*śamatha* and *vipaśyana*), the six *pāramitās* or perfections, compassion and mindfulness, and the 'four limitless meditations' of loving-kindness, compassion, sympathetic joy and equanimity (Kagyu Samye Ling, 2004). As well as lamas, monks and nuns, experienced lay people have begun to lead these courses. A typical introductory weekend will focus mainly on *śamatha* meditation, with instruction and practice on posture, awareness of the body, and focussing on the breathing, but also simple visualization of light and colour, and slow walking meditation around the outside of the temple.

There are also retreat weekends for practitioners on specific practices or *sādhanas*, including those of Chenrezig, Tārā, and Guru Rinpoche or Padmasambhava (who is traditionally said to have brought Buddhism to Tibet). In each case the text is explained and 'guidance given on chanting, visualization and mantra' (Kagyu Samye Ling, 2004), and students may receive authorization from Akong Rinpoche or Lama Yeshe to practise the *sādhana*. These courses are led by experienced monks or nuns.

Students may attend week-long guided meditation retreats at the nearby Purelands Retreat Centre, where teaching sessions may include 'relaxation, visualization, walking meditation and mindfulness', using *śamatha* or *vipaśyana*

THE KARMA KAGYU TRADITION

techniques (Kagyu Samye Ling, 2004). Further week-long retreats have focussed on compassion and insight, developing loving-kindness, Mahāyāna philosophy, the theory and practice of Tibetan Buddhism, and Buddhist practice in daily life, with longer retreats on the Four Special Foundations and on *Mahāmudrā* practice.

As a Retreat Master who spent 12 years in strict retreat himself, Lama Yeshe (2004) underlined a flexible approach here, with retreats lasting a weekend, a week, a month, 3 months or a year, to suit the time people have available. Students on the full 4-year retreat live as monks and nuns in separate isolated centres, spending 18 hours each day in prayer and meditation (*25 Years of Samyé Ling*, 1993: 8), sleeping upright in a wooden box 'to keep the spine straight and the body's energies flowing' (Quirke, 1992: 14). They are thus able to learn 'all the main practices of the Karma Kagyu lineage', as part of a longer programme including summer schools on 'the fundamental theory of Buddhism and the Kagyu tradition' (Holmes, 1989: 223).

Akong Rinpoche has also developed visualization exercises for group or individual use, dealing with the wildness of the mind. Thoughts, feelings and sensations are first imagined as transformed 'into universal compassion in the form of golden light' which radiates to all beings. Exercises focus on impermanence and compassion, inhaling others' suffering into one's own heart and breathing out towards them 'all goodness, virtue and happiness' (Akong, 1994: 118, 160). The boundary between therapeutic and spiritual exercises is blurred here: students are invited to share each session with all beings, wishing them freedom from suffering, and the 'sphere of golden light' is said to be 'the symbol of the awakened state of mind' (Akong, 1994: 139). There have also been weekend workshops on complementary therapies and activities such as yoga, Tibetan medicine, aromatherapy, stress and relaxation, and broader subjects such as feng shui, drawing, *thangka* painting and Tibetan art. They are usually led by Western lay people, who may not be Tibetan Buddhist practitioners.

These activities are symptomatic of an imaginative and wide-ranging approach at Samye Ling, linking therapeutic or recreational courses with spiritual activities or fundraising. However, even traditional meditation and devotional activities are very varied, inviting the individual to choose what is most appropriate for them, guided by a meditation master.

Tibetan teachings for Western individuals

Kagyu teachings are said to be based on 'those common to all forms of Buddhism: purity of conduct, non-aggression and self-mastery through meditation' (*25 Years of Samyé Ling*, 1993: 19), as well as developing compassion for all beings, and working to remove their suffering. Lama Yeshe (2001: 120) explained that the Kagyu school is known as the 'practice lineage', and so stresses 'meditation, diligence, belief, trust and faith', which enable students to make spiritual progress quickly.

Mahāmudrā teachings are described as 'direct indications about the very character of mind itself', which experienced teachers can use to help students reach 'the very heart of the Buddha's message in the quickest possible way' (*25 Years of Samyé Ling*, 1993: 19). After becoming systematized by Gampopa, *Mahāmudrā* became 'one of the core elements of the Kagyü school', with its emphasis on recognizing the unity of compassion and insight and 'the identity of emptiness (śūnyatā) and samsāra' (Keown, 2003: 164).

Gampopa's *Gems of Dharma, Jewels of Freedom* (1995) is studied in detail at Samye Ling by students preparing for the long retreat (Holmes, 1995: vi). Gampopa deals in turn with the following: the potential for enlightenment, precious human existence and 'the good mentor', impermanence, suffering, karma, loving-kindness and compassion, taking refuge and developing *bodhicitta*, the bodhisattva vow, the six *pāramitās* or perfections (generosity, morality, patience, effort, meditation and wisdom), the bodhisattva path and the enlightened activity of Buddhahood.

Many of these teachings are included in writings and activities associated with Samye Ling. Trungpa's *Meditation in Action*, published in 1969, emphasized the role of the guru, and the importance of the six perfections, and lectures published in 1973 include surrendering to the guru, the Four Noble Truths, the bodhisattva path, *śunyatā* or emptiness, wisdom and compassion (Trungpa, 1996, 1987). Akong Rinpoche stressed right motivation, a positive attitude, right conduct, compassion and mindfulness in *Taming the Tiger* (1994), and we have seen Lama Yeshe's emphasis on the Four Ordinary and Four Special Foundations (Yeshe Losal, 1997, 1998). His more recent *Living Dharma* (2001) included discussion of Buddha Nature, taming the body, speech and mind, developing *bodhicitta* and loving-kindness, and impermanence. Courses at Samye Ling have included many of these elements and interviewees confirmed their relevance, underlining the importance of taking refuge, the bodhisattva vow and the development of compassion, with particular emphasis on the role of the guru as refuge, and the importance of practising for the sake of all beings. If this seems a formidable body of teachings, Lama Yeshe (2001: 43) reminded readers more simply to 'remember this loving kindness and develop Bodhicitta, the motivation to work for the benefit of all sentient beings'.

Batchelor (1994: 116) emphasized the 'key role of the spiritual teacher' in the Kagyu and other Tibetan traditions, with the 'direct compassionate assistance' of the lama seen as vital for spiritual progress. Although teachings are accessed gradually through the daily activities of meditation, study and work, one cannot get far without a qualified teacher 'to transmit the material to you in such a way that there is no misunderstanding' (Shanks, 2002). As we have seen, students need to receive empowerment and instructions from a teacher before beginning specific practices. Both Akong Rinpoche and Lama Yeshe often speak informally and explain the teaching in a practical rather than theoretical way, so that students can integrate it into their daily lives (Lamzang, 2002).

With the stress on practice, there is seldom a formal structure for study. Occasionally Akong Rinpoche will ask the monks and nuns to study particular aspects of the ritual together, for example, with an experienced teacher, and

Westerners are gradually beginning to take on these roles. Otherwise students are expected to read, listen to teachers or attend courses as appropriate, on their own initiative (Dechi, 2002).

It might be thought that such complex teachings would need simplifying or adapting for a Western audience, and Trungpa (1987: 13ff.) coined the phrase 'spiritual materialism' to warn his Western students against accumulating religious knowledge – or worse still, using spiritual techniques to reinforce egocentricity – rather than engaging genuinely with spiritual development. However, the Kagyu school also emphasizes its lineage of traditional teachings. Holmes (1995: x) complained that the Western attempt to 'window-dress Buddhism' – by reinterpreting awkward elements such as the hell realms as symbolic rather than 'nightmare states that can really happen after death' – may appear convenient 'but it corrupts the tradition'.

Akong Rinpoche and Lama Yeshe are keen to preserve the pure transmission of the teachings, ensuring that ideas are correctly communicated in translation from Tibetan into English. However, Westerners sometimes have 'more paranoid neuroses' than Tibetans and more 'problems with their hope and fear' (Dechi, 2002) which may need an emphasis on different aspects of the teachings. Rather than ignoring, minimizing or withholding traditional teachings, lamas are seen as skilfully seeking 'the most appropriate sequence with which to familiarize the Western mind with Dharma' (Shanks, 2002), bearing in mind that many concepts are initially unfamiliar, and that individuals are only gradually capable of understanding the teachings they need to develop their spiritual lives.

Lama Yeshe (2004) confirmed that while no teachings are seen as unsuitable for Westerners, there are certain 'higher levels of practice' for which people must be properly prepared, through 'many years of retreat', as in Tibet. Tibetan Buddhism is very new in Europe and 'you can't expect everything to come straightaway'. He explained that Samye Ling offers different paths to suit different temperaments, including those who may benefit either from studying Buddhist philosophy or from intense meditation practice. This choice in itself is part of traditional Tibetan Buddhism, and it is this flexibility which has helped the tradition to develop so quickly in Europe.

Kagyu lineage masters

The Kagyu tradition traces its teachings back to the Buddha, but tends to look to the founders of its own lineage as exemplars, as well as the Karmapa in his successive incarnations (*25 Years of Samyé Ling*, 1993: 18–19). Founders include the Indian teachers Tilopa (989–1069) and Naropa (1016–100) as well as the Tibetans Marpa and Milarepa. These 'four main saints or realized people in the lineage' are seen to exemplify different paths to enlightenment, by living as 'a meditator and hermit' (Tilopa), 'a scholar and monk' (Naropa), 'a householder with a wife and children' (Marpa) and 'a wild crazy yogi' (Milarepa) (Dechi, 2002).

Narratives of these Kagyu teachers are widely used and respected. Trungpa (1987: 31f.) included stories of Marpa and Milarepa in his lectures, and Lama Yeshe (2001: 92–3) used the narrative of Milarepa's death as an example of forgiveness. Different temperaments are perhaps drawn to different figures, each revealing their Buddha Nature in a different way (Shanks, 2002). Interviewees particularly mentioned being inspired by Milarepa, whose independent spirit, austere lifestyle and miraculous powers have made him a popular figure throughout Tibetan Buddhism.

These narratives must be transmitted from teacher to student within the Kagyu lineage for them to remain authentic; little attention is given to the academic evidence of historical records, and even the written texts within a lineage need to be 'interpreted accurately by the holder of that lineage' (Shanks, 2002). In this way there are seen to be lineages going back to the Buddha himself, though these are particularly complex in Tibetan Buddhism, sometimes involving incarnation lineages as well as initiation and the transmission of teachings.

Material from the Tibetan scriptures and commentaries is widely used, though often accessed through the teachings of a master who has studied it, rather than studied directly by each practitioner (Lamzang, 2002). Gampopa's *Jewel Ornament of Liberation* was also described as the 'complete authentic record of the whole of the *Buddhadharma*', acting as a reservoir of knowledge for the preservation of the Tibetan Kagyu tradition (Shanks, 2002).

The Kagyu lineage is seen as extremely important to preserve the purity of the teaching and its continued transmission. Empowerments for different practices may be received from various lineage holders, but eventually there is 'one particular teacher who shows you the nature of your mind' and so becomes the practitioner's 'root guru', inspiring their practice as a whole (Shanks, 2002).

Several contemporary figures are also looked on as living exemplars. The Dalai Lama (who is a Gelugpa monk) is greatly respected as both the incarnation of Chenrezig and the spiritual leader of Tibet. The head of the Kagyu tradition, the seventeenth Karmapa, is venerated as the reincarnation of the sixteenth Karmapa, who helped bring Tibetan Buddhism to the West. Interviewees spoke warmly of their personal regard for Akong Rinpoche and Lama Yeshe as both lineage masters and exemplars, while recognizing that this aspect might be rather less emphasized now in the West than was traditionally the case in Tibet.

Faith, devotion and transforming emotions

We have already seen evidence of the experiential dimension of the Karma Kagyu tradition. Lama Yeshe (2001: 81f., 100, 120) has explained the emphasis on 'belief, trust and faith' in making spiritual progress: *vipaśyana* or insight meditation is used to confront and dismantle emotional obstacles, and even correct meditation posture helps to transform negative emotions. He stressed the importance of faith, warning students against doubt, since 'Mahamudra is all about knowing, deep down in our mind, that our Buddha nature is pure and perfect'

(Yeshe Losal, 2001: 138). Interviewees confirmed that intense faith and devotion – especially towards the guru – are an essential part of the Kagyu tradition, both as prerequisites for calming the mind and as the means of achieving great spiritual progress.

Compassion and loving-kindness are also frequently emphasized. Trungpa (1987: 99) described compassion as the 'environmental generosity, without direction', which no longer distinguishes between oneself and others, and Lama Yeshe (2001: 134) pointed out that even Milarepa could not subdue the demons which attacked him, 'but when he showed them loving kindness, they dissolved'.

Lama Yeshe (2001: 31, 53) suggested that 'letting go of our emotions', instead of rejecting them or following them blindly, will allow much of our suffering to fall away. He explained, however, that Vajrayāna Buddhism does not attempt to 'by-pass our emotional turmoil' to find peace and quiet, but aims instead 'to get rid of the root of our sufferings...[and] to deal with the poisons' (Yeshe Losal, 2001: 38). One week-long retreat in 2004 focused on these 'five mind poisons' of ignorance, anger, desire, pride and jealousy. When they are recognized as distortions of 'primordial wisdom', they can be purified and eventually transformed back into their natural state of 'enlightened energy' (Kagyu Samye Ling, 2004).

Interviewees confirmed the importance of transforming emotions rather than suppressing or abandoning them. Powerful feelings may need first to be calmed to gain some objectivity but then with faith and openness their negative energy can be changed into positive emotions: a powerful anger, for example, might eventually change into 'incredible strong joy' (Dechi, 2002 interview). One interviewee described how the loneliness of monastic life – if not denied or indulged as self-pity – could be transformed into a more confident sense of independence. Another pointed out that while happiness and joy are common in deep meditation, even these positive emotions should be used to benefit others, rather than merely enjoyed or indulged. Students are encouraged to recognize anger and other powerful emotions as temporary feelings and to avoid hurting others (and damaging their own karma) by acting on them.

Lama Yeshe (2004) described Tibet before the Chinese invasion as 'a very stress-free country', where people's minds could be at peace, in contrast to the mental turmoil of Western materialism. Thus he felt the techniques of Tibetan Buddhism – particularly the meditation and the understanding of impermanence – were well suited to helping Westerners overcome their unhappiness. This may not be an adaptation of Tibetan Buddhism to bring mental peace to Westerners, but rather a skilful choice of existing methods to deal with rather different emotional problems.

The Five Golden Rules and the monastic code

Ethical behaviour in the Karma Kagyu tradition is guided by the 'Five Golden Rules', a positive rewording and slight reordering of the Five Precepts. As well as refraining from killing, stealing, lying, intoxicants and sexual misconduct, practitioners are expected 'to protect life . . . to protect others' property . . . to speak the truth . . . to encourage health . . . [and] to respect others' (Yeshe Losal, n.d.: n.p.). Lama Yeshe added that following these rules would 'keep Kagyu Samye Ling a pure and special place for ourselves and others', emphasizing that moral behaviour affects the community as well as the individual. Shanks (2002) explained that one hopes to move from not harming to actually helping, quoting Akong Rinpoche's succinct advice: 'Develop your compassion, and enlightenment takes care of itself'.

All the food served at Samye Ling is vegetarian, as part of keeping the first precept of not harming living beings. This appears as stricter than Buddhist practice in Tibet, where vegetarianism is more difficult because of the climate. Booking forms ask visitors to note that 'Samye Ling is not a drink or drug rehabilitation centre' and that 'smoking, alcohol, drugs . . . and fishing are not permitted'. As well as being a reminder to newcomers, this may reflect the memory of the centre's early years before following the Five Golden Rules became the norm.

There is an elaborate monastic code based on the Five Golden Rules but with the additional practice of complete celibacy. Monks and nuns have similar vows, taking 35 vows on ordination and a further 200 or more on higher ordination later on if they wish. All these minor vows are elaborations of the five main root vows, again based on the Five Golden Rules. If a monastic deliberately breaks one of the five root vows, he or she is 'no longer a nun or a monk' and would have to ask to reordain, while breaking a minor vow would entail confession and purification (Dechi, 2002). Lama Yeshe (2001: 50) is very practical here: seeing one's wrong action, one performs prostrations, asks for forgiveness, makes reparation if possible, and then 'it's your duty to get over feelings of guilt'.

While monks and nuns keep their main vows strictly, a flexible approach allows them to handle money and to own their own clothes and modest possessions, in contrast to the *Vinaya* rules followed by Forest Sangha monastics. This is 'based on the motivation behind behaviour' rather than the letter of the law (Lamzang, 2002). Even the Five Golden Rules may very occasionally be broken, where compassion may override preceptual behaviour. Perhaps with the right motivation, one might harm someone to prevent them from harming others, though it requires considerable realization to act skilfully here (Dechi, 2002).

The minor monastic rules are seen as less relevant in the modern Western context and subject always to a compassionate approach (perhaps eating an evening meal when visiting one's mother, for example, to avoiding upsetting her). Keeping the five vows and remaining celibate is what is expected of a monk or nun. Lama Yeshe (2004) drew a contrast between this flexible approach and strict *Vinaya* observance: if monks insist on not eating after midday or not allowing women to drive them around, fewer Westerners will be drawn towards Buddhism, as they cannot understand such restrictions.

Although the monastic rules are the same here as in Tibet, the tradition itself is perhaps more flexible than others. Lay people may also find that keeping the

Five Golden Rules is all that can be practically achieved in Western secular life, and so Lama Yeshe (2004) emphasizes 'taming the mind, taming the body, taming the speech' rather than insisting on keeping many rules. These broad ethical guidelines seem to represent the greater flexibility of Buddhism in Tibet, rather than a Western adaptation of Tibetan Buddhism.

Tradition and adaptation in a Buddhist community

Samye Ling is not only a Buddhist community and a centre for Buddhist teaching and practice, but also 'a spiritual base and place of regeneration for some 5,000 or so people, of all walks and beliefs', which aims to preserve Tibetan culture and to support a range of humanitarian, therapeutic and interfaith activities (*25 Years of Samyé Ling*, 1993: 5). Lama Yeshe (2004) explained that the centre's broad and flexible approach reflects the fact that the Buddha taught in many different ways. Even on yoga weekends people often attend meditation and 'talk about dharma' and so may gain benefit from the Buddha's teaching.

The monastic community is at the heart of Samye Ling. Lama Yeshe is unusual in having no monastic responsibilities in Tibet, so is able to concentrate fully on 'establishing the Sangha and continuing the lineage in the West' (Yeshe Losal, 2001: xix). Seniority in the community (shown by where an individual sits in the temple) depends more on retreat practice and level of realization than on length and level of ordination and may change as some individuals progress more quickly than others (Dechi, 2002).

While Samye Ling might appear traditional, Waterhouse (1997: 183) pointed out that Lama Yeshe has introduced 'new ideas into monastic training' with the approval of the Tibetan authorities. Having seen Westerners take life vows which they could not fulfil, he invited them instead to ordain first as novices for a year (Yeshe Losal, 2001: xix). Lama Yeshe (2004) confirmed that this is 'something unique to the West' in Tibetan Buddhism: within the Kagyu lineage, he is free to make his own decisions and felt that this gradual approach would be more successful. He first gives lay people the five root vows, to be kept for at least 6 months, or until he is happy with their progress. Then they may ordain for one year, and if they wish to continue, for a second and third year. Only then are they allowed to take lifetime vows. These 'young monks' or 'young nuns' as they are called, wear a red shirt for their first year, orange for the next 2 years, and then yellow for life. This process has similarities with the innovative roles of *anagārika* in the Forest Sangha and postulant in the OBC, though both these are temporary roles undertaken *before* ordination, rather than temporary ordination.

In 1998 Lama Yeshe took 11 of the Western nuns to Bodh Gaya for them to 'receive the full Bhikkuni or Gelongma vows' and so to allow 'full ordination of nuns within the Tibetan tradition' (Yeshe Losal, 2001: xxii). This took place with the help of Chinese nuns, there being no Tibetan ordination line, and so was more an innovation than a reconnection with Tibetan tradition. Rawlinson (1997: 11) pointed out that in Western Tibetan Buddhism, women are 'far more significant' than in Tibet, with a combination of traditional and innovative roles.

The role of teachers is particularly important in Tibetan Buddhism. They are often recognized by their practice and level of realization, rather than any outer status: although Akong Tulku was known as a *rinpoche* (a title of respect given to reincarnate lamas), what drew people to him was 'his wisdom and compassion in his daily actions' and his continuing ability to help people (Dechi, 2002). Teachers may also be formally recognized by the Karmapa or senior lamas as a 'realized' person. Akong Rinpoche and Lama Yeshe are seen as the main teachers at Samye Ling, and individuals may ask for guidance from them whenever they wish. While they are seen as authoritative figures whose instructions would normally be followed, they are also open to question and discussion if people feel their advice is inappropriate.

Teachers look at practitioners closely, perhaps over a long period, before accepting them formally as students (Lamzang, 2002). Individuals may receive meditation instruction and spiritual guidance from several teachers within the lineage, but they will only have a single 'root guru' who remains their main teacher (Dechi, 2002). Trungpa (1987: 28) described the importance of 'surrendering' to the guru – with an open mind rather than wishing to get something from him – as 'the necessary preparation for working with a spiritual friend'. The guru may also be visualized as 'a manifestation of the ultimate Buddha mind', or even as a Buddha or a deity (Shanks, 2002), though this is clearly a symbolic practice, and very different from actually worshipping the guru.

Teaching often takes place in classes and courses rather than through personal interviews. Sometimes students only meet their guru rarely, maintaining the spiritual relationship through their devotion and practice rather than regular face-to-face contact. Senior teachers are still almost all Tibetan, since 12 years of retreat are needed to become a Kagyu lama. Only three Westerners have been granted this title, including the Danish-born nun Lama Zangmo, who leads Kagyu Samye Dzong London. As Lama Yeshe (2004) pointed out, there is no point in demanding European teachers before they are ready: if Westerners 'practise in the retreats... [and] gain a certain realization' then Tibetan Buddhism in Europe will become 'very alive, very powerful, and the teachers will be Europeans'.

The Samye Ling community includes about 100 people living at the centre and another 100 or so in the surrounding area. Small informal groups help to run the centre, with occasional meetings of the whole community. Community members may feel some tension between their spiritual practice and work duties but not usually between lay people and monastics, as 'we accept that we live in slightly different worlds' (Dechi, 2002). Lay people also visit Samye Ling and its associated centres throughout the year.

Unlike Amaravati or Throssel Hole, this is very much a Buddhist *centre* rather than a Buddhist monastery. The large Samye Ling shop and general stores offers books on Theravāda and Zen as well as Tibetan Buddhism, statues, *thangkas*, incense, posters, T-shirts and Tibetan craftwork. In the nearby Tibetan Tea Rooms, monastics and lay people chat with some of the thousands of annual visitors, with gentle pop music in the background. Online bookings, credit card payment, fixed charges for accommodation and meals, and a purpose-built visitors' accommodation block can make Samye Ling appear a little like a Buddhist hotel, and booking forms still remind visitors that the centre cannot offer 'free board and lodgings in exchange for work'.

Humanitarian, therapeutic and environmental activities deserve special mention here. The Rokpa (Tib. 'help') movement, founded by Akong Rinpoche to support Tibetan refugees in India and Nepal, has expanded to support homeless, sick and elderly people in 19 countries (*25 Years of Samyé Ling*, 1993: 10), as well as educational, medical and environmental projects in Tibet itself. In Scotland Rokpa Glasgow combines charity, Dharma and therapy by running a soup kitchen and offering yoga, massage, psychotherapy and meditation classes. Zen and Theravāda groups also meet there. Rokpa Dundee offers similar activities, including outreach yoga and meditation classes from Fort William to Thurso.

Akong Rinpoche, who is fully trained in traditional Tibetan medicine, founded Tara Rokpa Medical College to teach these skills to Western students. He saw that Eastern and Western traditions might complement each other here, and so places were made available in the community for 'those recovering from severe mental distress' (*25 Years of Samyé Ling*, 1993: 15). He has developed therapeutic techniques to help people 'to mature and develop their own understanding and universal compassion' (Akong, 1994: 192), whether or not they are interested in Buddhism, and a year-long training programme is available for therapists. Lama Yeshe (2004) also sees therapeutic and spiritual approaches as complementary, as so many people have the 'mind problems' which Buddhism addresses.

The development of Holy Island near Arran is an ambitious project combining environmental conservation with a concern for world peace, physical and mental health, and cooperation between faith communities. A sixth-century Christian hermit lived on the island, which Lama Yeshe described as 'sanctified by the intense prayer and contemplation carried out there' (Quirke, 1992: 15). Early in a 10-year renovation and building programme, several young men previously involved with drugs were ordained for a year to work as volunteers (Levine, 1993: 32). The Centre for World Peace and Health, which opened in 2003 with accommodation for 60 people, is used for interfaith meetings, therapeutic workshops and meditation retreats. The larger Monastic Retreat Centre will provide long-term retreat facilities for Tibetan Buddhist practitioners. It has been designed throughout with radical 'ecological strategies for energy, food, water and waste management' (www.samye.org.uk: see 'Combining Technology and Nature on Holy Island', 1996: 32–8).

Substantial funding has been raised by special appeals for both Holy Island and the temple at Samye Ling, where the new south wing – including large kitchen and dining areas, visiting teachers' apartment and copper roof – is set to cost £1 million. Pilgrimage treks to Tibet and Nepal have also generated income both to restore historical and sacred sites in Tibet and to complete the *stūpa* at Samye

Ling. All courses, accommodation and meals are charged for to cover running costs. In 1992 the 4-year retreat cost £8000, and Quirke (1992: 15) reported that the resident community met about half the centre's running costs, paying 'according to their means' rather than on a flat monthly rate. The shop and tea rooms also generate substantial income for the centre.

Holmes (1982: 92) reported that there was initially 'considerable wariness and even some hostility from the local community', though a more positive relationship has gradually developed: Samye Ling's presence has kept the primary school open and helped to provide work locally. Barwick (1988: 13) found that there was still some resentment, not towards monks and nuns, but towards what one woman called 'the hangers-on' spreading through the small Eskdalemuir valley, but this feeling seems to have faded again in recent years.

Samye Ling has a reputation for openness towards other spiritual traditions, based on its aim to 'help bring mental and spiritual well-being to both Buddhists and non-Buddhists alike' ('Karma Kagyu Samye-Ling Tibetan Centre', 1979: 236). Lama Yeshe (2001: 144) is particularly keen 'to develop harmony and good communications within the Buddhist community': he has good friends in the Theravāda and Zen communities, including Ajahn Sumedho, and emphasizes that 'we are all following Buddha, Dharma and Sangha'. However, Samye Ling has little contact with the newer forms of Buddhism in Britain: Lama Yeshe (2004) has some misgivings about transplanting Buddhism wholesale into European culture and suggested that a tradition can only survive with a continuous lineage of realized teachers. He has built up close contacts with Christian leaders in Anglican, Catholic and Church of Scotland communities and worked with Jews, Muslims, Hindus and Sikhs on interfaith projects: he spoke of his respect for all faiths which can bring 'satisfaction and benefit' to humanity (Yeshe Losal, 2004).

There is a complex mixture here. The monastic community and the role of the teacher and guru appear traditional, though temporary ordination and the enhanced role for nuns and lay people are Western adaptations. A Buddhist centre in Scotland with such a wide range of activities, thousands of visitors, and a businesslike approach to funding, is certainly different from a monastery in Tibet, though the very flexibility to adapt to the needs of people in different situations is a traditional feature of Tibetan Buddhism.

Preserving Tibetan culture

Samye Ling has built up a strong arts and crafts tradition, with 'painting, printing, statue-casting and wood-carving' (Holmes, 1982: 91), and more recently pottery, weaving and photography. Each of these has contributed to the rich physical surroundings of the centre, often in traditional Tibetan style.

The massive Samye temple, designed by Akong Rinpoche and the resident Tibetan master artist Sherab Palden Beru, is seen as both the 'spiritual heart' of the centre and 'a place of prayer and inspiration for many thousands of Buddhists and non-Buddhists alike' (www.samye.org.uk). It has been described as 'the largest Tibetan style temple in Europe' (*25 Years of Samyé Ling*, 1993: 12), standing four storeys high, with its golden roof shining above the mature trees. The ground floor interior, 40 m by 12, will hold 1,000 people, but is usually partitioned into three areas to accommodate prayers and courses simultaneously. The whole area is covered with Tibetan iconography in the form of 'paintings, statues, wood carvings, silk-screen prints, [and] hand-woven carpets' (*25 Years of Samyé Ling*, 1993: 12).

The shrine room has a large golden Buddha in the earth-touching posture (representing the victory over Māra just before his enlightenment), and 1,000 further golden Buddhas in red and gold cases around three walls. Gold symbolizes wealth, encouraging generosity by making the best possible offering, and the further colours of yellow, blue, red, green and white correspond to the five elements of earth, water, fire, wind and space respectively (Dechi, 2002). The temple is seen as a visual reminder of the wisdom and compassion which is both the Buddha's achievement and 'our own potential': temple dragons, for example, holding jewels representing the six *pāramitās*, are auspicious symbols of the bodhisattva's spiritual power and freedom (Lamzang, 2002).

Much of the interior is covered with wall paintings or traditional *thangkas* (painted hanging scrolls), depicting either saints of the Kagyu lineage or deities, which are used to help the visualization practice. Like medieval Christian iconography, they provide visual rather than verbal links into spiritual narratives. However, this cannot easily be westernized, as the meanings are very profound and artists themselves need 'enough realization to transform the style of the paintings' (Dechi, 2002).

Sherab Palden is responsible for many of the paintings and is training students in traditional *thangka* painting. A large *thangka* may take 2 years to complete, its creation being seen as a spiritual practice rather than merely decorating the temple. Both *thangkas* and statues are completed by 'opening the eyes', painting them in and bringing the image to life. When blessed and placed on the shrine with prostrations and offerings, 'you really feel they are Buddha and then the blessing is there' (Kunzang, 2002).

Outside the temple, the next phase of the Samye Project will eventually form a huge quadrangle, with kitchen, dining and accommodation facilities, teaching and library areas, audio-visual facilities and a museum. A large *stūpa* for healing and world peace stands opposite the original Johnstone House, and a similar one is planned for Holy Island. Work on the island has included planting 35,000 native trees, restoring the lighthouse and cottages as retreat houses, and rock paintings in various places depicting Marpa, Milarepa, Gampopa, the first Karmapa and Gautama Buddha.

In an interesting mixture of Christian heritage and Buddhist symbolism, a stained glass workshop on Holy Island has produced glass panels of the 'Eight Auspicious Symbols' for the Retreat Master's house and a 'Knot of Eternity' window for the converted farmhouse which has become part of the Centre for World Peace and Health. However, the content and symbolism of this important dimension seems to have remained traditionally Tibetan.

Conclusion

The emphasis throughout on traditional elements underlines the importance placed on preserving the purity of the Karma Kagyu lineage. Complex meditation techniques and devotional practices are taught with great care within a framework of existing Kagyu teachings, maintaining the traditional and highly important role of the teacher and guru. The traditional practice of 4-year retreat is well established. Narratives continue to centre on the inspirational Kagyu lineage masters, including contemporary figures. The experiential dimension still centres on the importance of faith and devotion and the necessity of transforming rather than subduing the emotions. The Five Golden Rules remain as broad ethical guidelines for lay people and as root vows for monastics, and the monastic sangha is still at the heart of Samye Ling. Traditional Tibetan arts and crafts, from weaving to temple-building, are preserved and passed on to Westerners.

However, there are also many aspects which appear as non-traditional elements, if not conscious adaptation to the Western environment. The history of Samye Ling, born in the 1960s counterculture, is inevitably very different from that of a monastery in Tibet. Its current programme includes courses with little obvious connection with Buddhism, blurring the boundaries between spiritual, therapeutic and recreational activities. Teachers seem to choose those teachings which they feel are most appropriate for individuals, rather than copying a standard traditional path, though this may not be different from practice in Tibet. Individuals are encouraged to choose for themselves which narratives they find meaningful or inspiring, and what form of emotional development and transformation is relevant to them. There may be a more flexible approach to ethical behaviour, though (unlike Tibet) vegetarianism is practised and encouraged.

The organizational and social dimension in particular includes a number of innovative elements to accommodate Westerners such as temporary ordination, full ordination for nuns, the development of a partially secularized Buddhist centre which attracts many visitors, humanitarian, therapeutic, environmental and interfaith activities, and a businesslike approach to funding.

It is not sufficient to weigh these traditional and non-traditional elements against each other to see whether preservation or adaptation is the dominant feature here. The flexibility that seeks to accommodate the temperament of the individual, and so may appear as a concession to the Western psyche, is itself an important traditional feature of Tibetan Buddhism. In Lhasa or Eskdalemuir, the lama will direct and guide each student as an individual, whether in practising appropriate meditation techniques and devotional activities or in therapeutic activities less directly connected with Buddhism. The practice of presenting teachings in the most appropriate way is also traditional in Tibet: they may be taught rather differently at Samye Ling to suit Westerners, but still within the traditional pattern of Kagyu lineage masters. Similarly with ethical guidelines, a more flexible approach reflects rather than contrasts with Tibetan practice.

The Holy Island project presents an interesting final example. In seeking to provide both secluded long-term retreat facilities and an interfaith world peace centre, Samye Ling seems to be combining traditional contemplative practice with an openness which is particularly appealing to Westerners. The Karma Kagyu tradition is simply flexible enough to incorporate a wide variety of activities, without losing contact with its traditional Tibetan teaching and practice.

8

THE NEW KADAMPA
TRADITION (NKT)

Historical background

Formed in 1991, the New Kadampa Tradition (NKT) is the newest of the seven organizations under consideration, though it has an important background in Tibetan Buddhism, both in Tibet itself and in Britain. The movement describes itself as 'an entirely independent Buddhist tradition' inspired and guided by 'the ancient Kadampa Buddhist Masters and their teachings, as presented by Geshe Kelsang Gyatso' (Kelsang, 2001: 398). The NKT has expanded more rapidly than any other Buddhist tradition in Britain. Like SGI-UK, it has sometimes been portrayed as a controversial organization, described by Bunting (1996a: 1) as a rich and expansionist 'sect' which aims to become the largest Western Buddhist movement and by a former follower as 'a fundamentalist movement' which removes members' personal choice (Kay, 2004: 110). Again a balanced approach is needed here: the practitioner's confident belief may appear as dogmatism to an unsympathetic observer.

The Gelug teachers Lama Thubten Yeshe (1935–84) and Lama Zopa Rinpoche (b. 1946) taught Westerners in Nepal and visited Europe in 1974. Centres began to emerge with Tibetan teachers appointed by Lama Yeshe, who established the Foundation for the Preservation of the Mahāyāna Tradition (FPMT) in 1975 to coordinate their activities. The two lamas visited Britain in 1975, where growing support enabled Conishead Priory – a sadly neglected Victorian mansion in Cumbria – to be purchased in 1976. The Manjushri Institute was established there with Lama Yeshe as Spiritual Director, and 12 of the 70 students on an initial meditation course remained as a new spiritual community. Restoration work began with income raised from small businesses and renting areas for alternative therapy workshops (Kay, 2004: 55).

Lama Yeshe and Geshe Kelsang (b. 1931) had been classmates, and he asked their teacher Trijang Rinpoche (1901–81) to invite Geshe Kelsang to become the resident teacher at Manjushri (Belither, 1997: 6). He arrived in 1977, after many years in retreat since leaving Tibet in 1959, and under his direction the centre expanded, with a growing community of monastics and lay people, aiming to create 'a residential college for Buddhist studies' with 200 students ('Manjushri

Institute', 1978: 171). A Geshe Studies programme was established, lamas visited to teach and Wisdom Publications moved from Delhi to Manjushri: Kay (2004: 56) felt that 'Lama Yeshe's vision of Manjushri Institute as the spiritual and educational hub of the FPMT had crystalised'.

However, there were tensions under the surface. Geshe Kelsang developed a close relationship with his students, while the FPMT directed Manjushri remotely from Kathmandu (Batchelor, 1994: 202). In 1979 Geshe Kelsang opened the Madhyamaka Centre in Yorkshire without FMPT approval: Lama Yeshe asked him to resign, but his students petitioned him to remain, and a struggle ensued for control of Manjushri Institute, which eventually withdrew from the FPMT. As Kay (2004: 61f.) reported, this was a difficult period, with divided loyalties and a reluctance to acknowledge the conflict between respected lamas.

During the early 1980s the community expanded to almost 80 people – including 16 ordained Westerners – combining spiritual training with restoration, fundraising and residential courses on Buddhism. Weekend workshops on alternative therapies continued, and 6,000 tourists visited the Priory in 1982 (Church, 1982: 149f.).

Early in 1987 Geshe Kelsang began a 3-year retreat in Scotland, writing extensively and designing the training programmes which were to become 'the core of the New Kadampa Tradition' (Belither, 1997: 10). His centres still received visiting Gelug teachers, but there was also 'a growing pool of Western ordained and lay teachers' ('Manjushri Institute', 1988: 183).

The Madhyamaka Centre moved to a mansion outside York in 1986, where highly committed young followers – led by Geshe Kelsang's senior disciple, Gen Thubten Gyatso (Neil Elliot) – studied on teaching programmes as large as those at Manjushri (Kay, 2004: 69). By 1989 there were 23 students on the new Teacher Training Programme at Manjushri and the Madhyamaka Centre had 30 residents and 11 further branches.

On returning from retreat in 1990, Geshe Kelsang introduced what Kay (2004: 76) described as 'new and radically exclusive policies', insisting that students follow his own programmes rather than Geshe Studies, relying on him alone rather than other teachers or authors. He had become highly critical of what he saw as Gelug Buddhism's 'degenerate' inclusivism (Kay, 2004: 88) and a Gelugpa hierarchy which, according to Belither (2004), attempted to prevent him from passing on teachings received from Trijang Rinpoche concerning the protector deity Dorje Shugden.

The Manjushri Centre in London, established by Lama Yeshe in 1980, became increasingly remote from Geshe Kelsang, and in 1990 changed its name to Jamyang Meditation Centre, emphasizing its FPMT credentials, and appointing a new Director ('Jamyang Meditation Centre', 1990: 179).

The NKT was formally created in 1991 in what Kay (2004: 88) described as 'a schismatic event', separating Geshe Kelsang's centres from mainstream Gelug Buddhism. It emphasized three new study programmes, said to embody the 'pure tradition' from Tsongkhapa (1357–1419), the founder of the Gelug school. Manjushri Institute became Manjushri Mahayana Buddhist Centre, and Geshe

Kelsang invited centres and branches under his direction (almost 30 in all) to join the NKT and accept him as Spiritual Director. Despite some resistance, most students felt that this new emphasis brought further 'energy and focus' to the movement (Kay, 2004: 79).

Extensive *Middle Way* advertisements appeared for Geshe Kelsang and his centres, courses and publications. While claiming an ancient Tibetan lineage, the NKT described itself as 'a recent development', responding to 'the needs of the contemporary practitioner' by enabling Westerners 'to engage in systematic study and practice of Buddhadharma' ('Heruka Buddhist Centre', 1991: 184).

The new movement expanded rapidly at Manjushri, Madhyamaka and elsewhere, with 48 British centres (and 14 abroad) in 1992 ('The Sixty-two Centres of the NKT Mandala', 1992: 42). There were 103 centres and groups by 1993 (though some were simply rooms hired for meetings), while NKT advertising claimed there were 'around 4000 people involved at various levels' (Scott, 1995: 8). In 1996 Bunting (1996a: 1; 1996b: 26) described the NKT as Britain's largest Buddhist organization, with about 3,000 members and over 200 centres, including 21 residential centres with about 400 residents. However, Kay (2004: 97) reported that there were no more than 3,000 regular NKT members worldwide in 1996, despite the growth of centres in many countries. Fluctuating number of overall members may reflect different levels of involvement.

The most controversial episode in the NKT's history centres on the worship of the protector deity Dorje Shugden. Originally seen as a worldly spirit, Dorje Shugden was promoted by Trijang Rinpoche's teacher as 'a guardian of *Gelug* orthodoxy and exclusivism', according to Kay (2004: 48), so that 'a formerly marginal practice became a central element'. Trijang Rinpoche became the Dalai Lama's junior tutor, continuing to promote Dorje Shugden as an enlightened Buddha and the supreme protector of the Gelug tradition.

The Dalai Lama had earlier consulted Dorje Shugden himself, but 'gradually came to view the practice as not only unhelpful but also harmful' (Waterhouse, 1997: 159). In the early 1980s the Dalai Lama restricted reliance on Dorje Shugden to private rather than public practice. The tension this caused within the Gelug and wider Tibetan community may reflect some opposition to his ecumenical approach, according to Kay (2004: 49–51). While the FPMT followed the Dalai Lama's advice, Geshe Kelsang began instead to expand Dorje Shugden practice from a private *pūjā* for monastics to the whole Manjushri community and in 1986 gave a series of public Dorje Shugden initiations. The Dalai Lama's office wrote to warn him, but this information was not passed on to students (Kay, 2004: 70–2).

In 1996 Dorje Shugden supporters organized demonstrations against the Dalai Lama in London. Geshe Kelsang supported these demonstrations and gave interviews strongly criticizing the Dalai Lama (Kay, 2004: 104). This provoked hostile media coverage: Bunting (1996a: 1) referred to 'an aggressive international smear campaign' organized by 'a British-based Buddhist sect', and Brown (1996: 2) quoted Geshe Kelsang as saying that many years of practice would be wasted if the Dalai Lama's view prevailed. The real issue may not have been religious freedom but, as Williams (1996: 130–1) suggested, a conflict between a sectarian Gelug conservatism and the Dalai Lama's modernizing and inclusive approach. This would explain why Geshe Kelsang's monastery in India formally expelled him for his opposition to the Dalai Lama (Lopez, 1998: 195).

Following such criticism, the NKT soon withdrew from the campaign. Some members were distressed by the controversy and left the movement, though most supported Geshe Kelsang's view. Belither (2004) reported that the issue was widely discussed within the NKT, but many members 'found the accusations against Dorje Shugden practice absurd' and continued as before. Belither saw this as an unpleasant episode, with hostility towards the NKT from other Tibetan traditions who would have rejected similar restrictions on their own practices. The argument here was perhaps about authority and independence, as well as spiritual practice and an inclusive or exclusive Gelug Buddhism. Geshe Kelsang's disciples again followed the teacher they knew rather than a remote authority, even that of the Dalai Lama.

Meanwhile, Geshe Kelsang's senior disciple Gen Thubten Gyatso was 'disrobed and banned' from the NKT, ostensibly because of 'a breach of his monastic vows' (Bunting, 1996c: 9), though there is some confusion here. A large new temple opened at Manjushri in 1997, and in 1998 the NKT joined the Network of Buddhist Organisations (NBO), partly to improve its public image, but also perhaps because NKT leaders realize 'that separation from wider Buddhist currents may create more problems than it solves' (Kay, 2004: 214).

The movement continues to expand, with about 250 monks and nuns, 267 UK centres and branches in 2003 and further centres and groups in North America, Europe and elsewhere, making over 500 in all (Waterhouse, 2001: 139; *Directory of Kadampa Buddhist Centres and Branches*, 2003). The Manjushri Centre has about 90 residents, including 20 nuns and 10 monks and can accommodate a further 100 visitors for weekend courses (Pagpa, 2004). Other substantial residential centres include the Tara Centre in Derbyshire, with nearly 40 residents. Kay (2004: 25) estimated that there were up to 3,000 active members in all.

There is still disagreement about how to interpret NKT history. The New Kadampa Tradition is said to have been established by Tsongkhapa in fifteenth-century Tibet and 'introduced into the West in 1977' by Geshe Kelsang (Kelsang, 1992: 139; www.manjushri.org.uk), but is also described as being 'established as a distinct tradition in 1991' (Belither, 1997: 1). There seems to be some difficulty in reconciling an ancient lineage with a recent schism.

Kay (2004: 83–4) felt the movement's own account has shifted considerably, playing down conflict in 'an overarching narrative of continuity' which may need to be challenged. He found FPMT students who view Geshe Kelsang as a 'rogue geshe', seizing control of Manjushri Institute, manipulating students and developing a personality cult around himself, and new disciples were often unaware of the NKT's background, due to the policy of 'consciously forgetting its FPMT roots'. An alternative view is that FPMT teachers became increasingly remote, with Geshe Kelsang's single-minded approach and personal example inspiring many students. The FPMT background is not emphasized in current NKT literature, though Belither's *Modern Day Kadampas* (1997: 6) acknowledges Lama Yeshe's role in setting up Manjushri Institute and establishing Geshe Kelsang as its teacher.

Tibetan *Lamrim* meditation and *sādhanas*

Daily practice at Manjushri Centre includes communal prayers and meditation, work periods and a substantial study commitment. The regime is relaxed rather than austere, with personal practice left to the individual. Lay people with work or family commitments may perform *pūjās* in private when they cannot attend prayers in the temple. There are similar activities at smaller centres. Individual NKT members may have a less formal practice but still follow this pattern of devotional prayers, meditation and study.

Geshe Kelsang (2001: 299–300) describes two phases of meditation, first contemplating a specific oral or written 'spiritual instruction' (analytical meditation) and then focussing on the 'virtuous state of mind' that arises (placement meditation). These are seen as interdependent and appear similar to traditional *vipaśyana* and *śamatha* meditation in other Tibetan schools.

NKT meditation is explained in detail in the *New Meditation Handbook*, which offers 'many different levels of meditation practice' and invites readers to begin wherever they 'feel most comfortable' (Kelsang, 2003: 4). Specific meditations include the following: precious human life, death and rebirth, karma and *saṃsāra*, and taking refuge; the development of equanimity, kindness and compassion towards all beings, and *bodhicitta*; understanding emptiness and relying on a spiritual guide. For each subject, readers are asked to recite *Prayers for Meditation*, contemplate a brief text, hold an object in the mind, dedicate the merit towards the specific realization and the happiness of all beings, and assimilate the practice into their daily life. An appendix offers a week's retreat schedule covering the whole sequence, with particular emphasis on renunciation, 'tranquil abiding', emptiness and the spiritual guide (Kelsang, 2003: 154–5).

Although these are traditional subjects, it is unusual to see such detailed instructions accessed primarily through the printed word, implying that one can learn a series of complex meditations – and even undertake meditation retreats – without the personal guidance of a teacher. This seems to prescribe a single path for all, rather than the individual approach of traditional Tibetan Buddhism, taking account of different temperaments, though interviewees suggested that readers would usually visit an NKT centre for further guidance. The sequence of meditations is based on the *Lamrim* or 'stages of the path' practice: practitioners often take a new topic each day or each week, focussing on these in their personal meditation, during the 15-minute 'meditation break' in devotional prayers and in daily life activities (Namgyal, 2004; Pagpa, 2004).

Introductory meditation weekends are designed to be as accessible as possible, with brief talks, simple body relaxation and short meditation sessions. An initial breathing meditation from the *Handbook* is introduced to calm the mind: students are asked to imagine exhaling problems and negative thoughts as if they were black smoke and inhaling blessings and positive thoughts 'in the form of pure, white light' (Kelsang, 2003: 132). This is similar to practice at Samye Ling, and interviewees emphasized that all NKT meditation is firmly based on traditional sources, and 'presented in a way that's accessible for Westerners', rather than consciously adapted or changed (Namgyal, 2004).

A section on 'Taking and Giving' in *Transform Your Life* helps to explain the connection between meditation and devotional activities. Geshe Kelsang claimed that disciples who visualize taking on the sufferings of others and giving them happiness will 'gradually develop the actual power to do so', in a process 'similar to the Tantric practice of bringing the result into the path' (Kelsang, 2001: 219). Thus those who visualize themselves as 'a wish-fulfilling jewel' will be able to radiate light through the universe, bringing 'the supreme happiness of permanent inner peace' to all living beings (Kelsang, 2001: 222). This underlines the importance of visualization for both meditation and devotional practice.

Interviewees confirmed that all NKT centres perform the same prayers and ritual practices. Chanting is used to prepare for meditation, 'to increase our merit and positive energy', and to receive blessings 'from enlightened beings, from the gurus of our lineage' (Prasad, 2004). Individuals may use specific practices at different times, typically combining the *Lamrim* meditations with a particular tantric deity practice, such as Vajrayoginī, but 'within the context of the *Heart Jewel*, and Je Tsongkhapa and Dorje Shugden' (Jenkins, 2004).

Perhaps the most important adaptation within the NKT is the translation of all Tibetan texts and prayers into English for Western disciples, and the modernized musical style of the *sādhanas*. The translations all come from Geshe Kelsang himself, helped by a few disciples, though his English is less than fluent, and they often have little Tibetan; so it is hard to see whether translations reflect the spirit of traditional Tibetan texts and prayers. Most *sādhanas* have also been simplified, though it is traditional for lamas to add or remove prayers as they see fit.

'Prayers for Meditation' are often chanted at NKT meetings, using a CD with two singers, guitar and flute, in a rather New Age musical style. They follow a traditional Tibetan format used in other *sādhanas*, and described in the *New Meditation Handbook* (Kelsang, 2003: 133–9). This consists of the following: going for refuge; generating *bodhicitta* and the 'four immeasurables' of boundless love, compassion, sympathetic joy and equanimity; imagining the Buddhas and bodhisattvas as physically present; a seven-limbed prayer of prostration, offerings, confession, rejoicing in virtue, asking holy beings to remain, requesting Dharma teachings and dedicating merit; offering the mandala (seeing the universe as a Pure Land of happiness); asking for and receiving blessings (becoming filled with 'rays of light and nectar' from the Buddha's heart); following specific meditation instructions; and dedicating the accumulated merit for the happiness of all beings.

Interviewees confirmed that 'Wishfulfilling Jewel' and the shorter 'Heart Jewel' were the most frequently used *sādhanas*, as Waterhouse (1997: 167) had found. They combine the 'Guru Yoga of Tsongkhapa' with the 'Dharma Protector' or Dorje Shugden practice, described in Geshe Kelsang's *Heart Jewel* (1997: viii), where they are said to have been 'revealed by Manjushri, the Wisdom Buddha', and to form 'the essential practices of the New Kadampa Tradition'.

Visualizing and meditating on Tsongkhapa is said to bring 'the blessings of all the Buddhas' (through a lineage from the historical Buddha to Geshe Kelsang), to reduce negative karma and 'increase our merit, life span, and Dharma realisations' (Kelsang, 1997: 6, 14). As Tsongkhapa is identified with Avalokiteśvara, Mañjuśrī, and Vajrapāṇi, requests made to him will bring the disciple 'great compassion... stainless wisdom... and great power in destroying obstacles' (Kelsang, 1997: 51).

Dharma Protectors are described as emanations of Buddhas or bodhisattvas who protect practitioners from obstacles to their spiritual practice, the main protector of Tsongkhapa's lineage being seen as Dorje Shugden, who has appeared in many different forms since the Buddha's time. He is said to care for devotees 'like a father caring for his children', bringing protection, blessings, guidance and success to all living beings; indeed, he must be relied on as 'the embodiment of the Three Jewels' (Kelsang, 1997: 92, 95).

The texts of the *sādhanas* are given as appendices. The pattern follows that of 'Prayers for Meditation', and is similar to that used at Samye Ling, though the contents focus on Tsongkhapa and Dorje Shugden rather than Chenrezig or Tārā. Interviewees confirmed that although the Dorje Shugden practice was still central to the NKT, the Guru Yoga prayers were equally important (Namgyal, 2004).

While the 'Wishfulfilling Jewel' is performed daily, several further *sādhanas* are also used. These include prayers to Avalokiteśvara, Heruka, Vajrayoginī, Tārā, Mañjuśrī, Amitāyus and the Medicine Buddha, recited on successive Sunday mornings, and a longer 'Offering to the Spiritual Guide', performed each fortnight (Namgyal, 2004; Pagpa, 2004). Individuals may recite specific *sādhanas* in their personal practice, perhaps using the Tārā practice for protection or the Avalokiteśvara prayers to develop compassion, as 'ways of visualizing and relating to particular aspects of the enlightened mind' (Jenkins, 2004). There are also prayers for the long life of Geshe Kelsang, reflecting the traditional veneration towards senior teachers.

All these *sādhanas* have either been 'compiled from traditional sources' by Geshe Kelsang (1997: 122) or translated under his supervision. They are available as booklets, rather like the chanting sheets at Samye Ling, though here the texts are all in English, and some are available on CD to aid communal or individual chanting.

Each *sādhana* requires both the 'formal initiation' of the appropriate empowerment and 'a commitment to perform it regularly', according to Waterhouse (1997: 168–9), though she found that such empowerments were 'usually given en masse' to anyone who could attend and pay the fee, rather than within the traditional teacher–pupil relationship. Geshe Kelsang has given Dorje Shugden, Vajrayoginī or Vajrasattva empowerments to groups of over a hundred people ('Manjushri Institute', 1986: 207; 1987: 134; Waterhouse, 1997: 158). Originally he performed all empowerments himself, maintaining that they may only be given by 'an authentic Tantric Vajra Master' ('Empowerment', 1992: 2) but this became impractical as the movement grew and spread, and current publicity shows that local teachers in large British centres regularly offer such initiations. Geshe Kelsang has claimed that even those with 'little previous experience of Dharma in this life' have potential through 'the imprints of former Tantric Teachings', and so should receive empowerments repeatedly to renew commitments and establish a relationship where the 'Vajra Master becomes like a mother or father' to recipients ('Empowerment', 1992: 2).

Although these meditations and *sādhanas* are seen as continuing the tradition of Atiśa and Tsongkhapa, they are now presented in a Western context, detached from the complexities of Tibetan Buddhism: 'we have taken the core practices ... and the important deity practices, and made it a little simpler' (Belither, 2004). While Geshe Kelsang's early works emphasized technical tantric practice, more recent books are broader and more accessible, again reflecting a move towards greater simplicity.

The NKT also offers courses and retreats for both the general public and committed members. One-day courses at Manjushri during 2004 included inner peace, loving-kindness, concentration, the *Heart Sūtra* and following a spiritual guide. Weekend courses included meditation retreats, compassion, freedom from fear and *thangka* painting, as well as the Four Noble Truths, Tsongkhapa empowerment and Vajrasattva empowerment. There are further week-long retreats as well. A similar range of therapeutic courses, meditation classes and specific empowerments is also available in other larger centres.

Two annual festivals allow many followers to come to Manjushri to receive empowerments and teachings from Geshe Kelsang in person. Recent 3-day Spring Festivals have centred on the Avalokiteśvara empowerment and commentary, or the Medicine Buddha empowerment and healing practices, while 2-week Summer Festivals have included teachings on *Mahāmudrā* practice or the Buddha Amitāyus empowerment, followed by further teachings from Geshe Kelsang's books.

Tibetan teachings and systematic study

Geshe Kelsang has frequently emphasized the lineage of the teachings which inform NKT practice and which derive from 'the ancient Kadampa Buddhist Masters' (Kelsang, 2001: 398). Prasad (2004) explained how Atiśa condensed earlier practices into the pattern of *Lamrim* teachings, which was later clarified by Tsongkhapa, 'the founder of New Kadampa Buddhism', and is now presented by Geshe Kelsang.

Geshe Kelsang's *Introduction to Buddhism* (1992) gives an initial idea of which specific teachings are seen as important. The nature of the mind, karma and reincarnation, the preciousness of human life, the role of meditation, death, and the commitments of going for refuge are all covered in the first section on 'Basic Buddhism'. Second, the 'Path to Liberation' includes understanding the Four Noble Truths, developing renunciation, and the training of moral discipline, concentration and wisdom. Third, the 'Path to Enlightenment' involves becoming a compassionate bodhisattva (by developing *bodhicitta* and the six perfections), understanding the ultimate truth of emptiness and finally attaining Buddhahood. Interviewees confirmed the nature and progression of these traditional teachings.

Geshe Kelsang's *Transform Your Life* (2001) is seen as the most comprehensive and current explanation of NKT teachings. The first section, 'Foundation', deals with inner peace, the mind, reincarnation, death, karma and rebirth, human suffering and adopting a daily spiritual practice. Developing inner peace through transforming negative mental states is said to lead towards the lasting peace of Nirvana. The mind is seen as a separate entity which moves to the next life when we die, so that understanding reincarnation is vital to ensure future happiness. Meditating on death will prompt the search for protection to avoid dying unprepared. Karma is explained in detail, with heaven and hell realms taken literally as places of possible rebirth; and contemplating human suffering will bring the motivation to abandon the round of rebirth. The daily practice recommended involves 'faith, sense of shame, consideration for others, non-hatred, and effort' (Kelsang, 2001: 79).

The second section, 'Progress', builds on earlier understanding and practice. Learning to cherish all living beings is seen as the ultimate way of both solving problems and granting wishes. This involves giving up the deluded and selfish view of one's own importance, developing compassion by wishing all beings to be free from their suffering, and eventually developing the ability to take on their suffering oneself and so bring them happiness. *Bodhicitta* or the 'supreme good heart' combines the wish for enlightenment with deep compassion for others, and is seen as 'the very essence of the Bodhisattva's training' (Kelsang, 2001: 232). Finally one comes to the ultimate truth of emptiness, where suffering and disease dissolve into the eternal happiness of enlightenment. Although sometimes expressed idiosyncratically, there is little contrast here with traditional Tibetan Buddhism.

Like other traditions, the NKT emphasizes going for refuge to the Three Jewels, though the 'twelve special commitments' are more detailed than we have seen previously. Followers promise to take refuge repeatedly, 'always to encourage others to go for refuge', to avoid 'teachers who contradict Buddha's view' and the influence of 'people who reject Buddha's teaching', to see any scripture as 'the actual Dharma Jewel' (respecting 'every letter of the scriptures and every letter of explanation of Buddha's teaching') and to see any ordained person as 'an actual Sangha Jewel' (Kelsang, 2003: 160–4). Such commitments may encourage proselytizing and an exclusive and literalistic approach, but they also imply a deep respect for all scriptures and other monastic traditions.

As with other Tibetan traditions, there is a strong emphasis on relying on a spiritual guide, which Geshe Kelsang (2003: 113) claims will enable his followers to overcome confusion, develop wisdom and 'receive the powerful blessings of all enlightened beings'. The Buddha is said to have described such reliance as 'the root of the spiritual path', bringing benefits which include protection from harm and lower rebirth, and the fulfilment of current and future wishes.

Waterhouse (1997: 152f.) found NKT teachings very similar to traditional Gelug Buddhism, though the emphasis on exclusively pure lineage and practice contrasts with the Dalai Lama's inclusive approach. Kay (2004: 57) agreed, pointing to a 'doctrinally conservative' approach where Geshe Kelsang sees 'the faithful transmission and continuation of the tradition' as being 'more important than adapting the teachings or innovating new ones for westerners'. Interviewees confirmed that Geshe Kelsang's teachings are seen as completely traditional, though their presentation might be unfamiliar to a Tibetan Buddhist, as NKT is 'putting them into a Western context, allowing that transition to take place' (Belither, 2004). Teachings were not 'watered down nor spiced up for the Western mind', but skilfully re-presented in an appropriate way (Jenkins, 2004).

Geshe Kelsang's books are claimed as 'the most comprehensive presentation of the Buddhist path to enlightenment available in any western language' ('Buddhism: The New Kadampa Tradition', n.d.). No other texts are available in Manjushri's bookshop or library, reflecting what was described as the traditional practice of being 'encouraged to stick to your own tradition . . . to avoid confusion' (Pagpa, 2004). The three most popular works – *Introduction to Buddhism*, *The New Meditation Handbook* and *Transform Your Life* – have sold 165,000 copies between them, showing their appeal far beyond the movement itself.

All the books are commentaries on Tsongkhapa's teachings. Geshe Kelsang sees them as transmitted to him as if he were 'a tape recorder into which the Wisdom Buddha, the Dharma Protector Dorje Shugden, has placed the cassette of Je Tsongkhapa's teachings' (Belither, 1997: 8). Thus he encourages readers of *Transform Your Life* to develop faith in 'a book that reveals the spiritual path', by contemplating the book itself as a light to dispel ignorance and '*the supreme Spiritual Guide from whom I can receive the most profound and liberating advice*' (Kelsang, 2001: 83). This seems to elevate the status of Geshe Kelsang's own works, and indeed they are displayed in the Manjushri temple shrine cabinet next to Dorje Shugden, with two volumes enshrined in the lantern above. Interviewees confirmed that practitioners rely solely on Geshe Kelsang's books, making no distinction between them and the teachings and scriptures on which they were based.

Sections of Geshe Kelsang's core teachings (on the mind, reincarnation, karma, cherishing others, compassion, *bodhicitta* and emptiness) are often copied from one work to another, but there is an important shift in emphasis from tantric meditation manuals towards more accessible works such as *Transform Your Life* and the *New Meditation Handbook*. Interviewees confirmed that early texts were mainly for internal study, while more recent books are intended 'for a general everyday audience' (Pagpa, 2004). There may be tensions between preserving an ancient tradition and appealing to a Western audience: Geshe Kelsang's interpretation of Tsongkhapa's version of Atiśa's teachings is presented not as one strand within Gelug or Tibetan Buddhism, but as a comprehensive version which needs no outside comparisons.

The role of study is considerably more prominent in the NKT than the other six traditions. The three programmes devised by Geshe Kelsang are said to 'form the core of the New Kadampa Tradition', as they encourage 'systematic study and practice' in a contemporary Western context (Belither, 1997: 10). This is said to be 'what distinguishes the NKT from other Buddhist traditions' ('Buddhism: The New Kadampa Tradition', n.d.).

The General Programme is described as 'a basic introduction to Buddhist teachings and meditation that is suitable for beginners', but which also 'includes advanced teachings and practices from both Sutra and Tantra' (www.manjushri.org.uk). A specific introduction to NKT teaching and practice is presented here as a general introduction to Buddhism. These sessions are taught in many centres, with teachers often basing lectures and discussion exclusively on Geshe Kelsang's books, sidestepping questions where he has given no specific answer, according to Waterhouse (1997: 164). Prasad (2004) confirmed that new teachers may rely on a text such as *Transform Your Life* but will gradually draw on their own experience as well.

The Foundation Programme involves systematic study of five of Geshe Kelsang's books, covering the *Lamrim* instructions, the development of compassion, the *Heart Sūtra*, Shantideva's *Guide to the Bodhisattva's Way of Life* and the nature of the mind (Kelsang, 2001: 399). This programme is taught mainly in residential centres, requiring strong commitment over 4 years, with students working through each text with a teacher and individually, tested by examination. Waterhouse (2001: 141) found that Geshe Kelsang's books were learnt by heart and accepted with no critical interpretation.

The Teacher Training Programme, lasting up to 7 years, includes the study of seven further books by Geshe Kelsang. Students are often ordained, and usually residents at centres, studying four mornings each week, again reading and memorizing texts for examination, with regular meditation retreats and appropriate behavioural commitments. Waterhouse (1997: 166) reported that Geshe Kelsang saw this programme as 'a western equivalent to the traditional Tibetan Geshe degree', and said that a single qualified teacher is more important to him than a thousand students, even if a hundred of them become enlightened.

All residents at NKT centres are enrolled on one of these study programmes, with most of the Manjushri community following the Teacher Training Programme (Pagpa, 2004). The three programmes may not always form a single progressive path for individuals to follow. Instead they reflect 'three types of Kadampa practitioner', according to Prasad (2004), the General Programme focussing on daily life, the Foundation Programme on meditation practice and the Teacher Training Programme on 'the entirety of the different teachings'.

The study programmes have been widely criticized as rote learning. Waterhouse (1977: 166) found disciples in Bath were expected to memorize texts in full and were invited to teach on their 'ability to function as a channel' for

Geshe Kelsang, rather than the extent of their knowledge. Kay (2004: 94, 110) felt Geshe Kelsang's books are used as a substitute for the 'direct and personal contact' seen in other Tibetan traditions, with a 'narrow, simplified and literalised reading of the Tibetan *Gelug* tradition' being taught across the movement. Bunting (1996b: 26) quoted from an NKT teaching skills handbook advising students to 'internalise' Geshe Kelsang's books so that they can be quoted 'word for word': this handbook insisted that all teachers 'must give exactly the same explanation, otherwise the NKT will disintegrate' (quoted in Kay, 2004: 95).

Interviewees described a very different picture. The handbook was written without Geshe Kelsang's approval, by the subsequently discredited Gen Thubten Gyatso, and was little used, remaining 'unknown to most NKT students or teachers' (Belither, 2004). Study programmes were said to adopt a critical approach, with students encouraged to ask questions and explore difficulties (Namgyal, 2004). They were designed in response to students' needs, rather than imposed by Geshe Kelsang: like other study programmes, there are outlines to memorize, but these are to support spiritual practice, and even examinations centre on practitioners' experience rather than learning texts by heart (Jenkins, 2004). Moreover, memorizing is 'entirely traditional' in Tibetan Buddhism, since monks often use chanting and other means to assimilate and internalize teachings. Far from expecting 'blind faith', study sessions rely firmly on explanation and sometimes lively discussion (Belither, 2004).

Perhaps the defining element here is not the teachings themselves, but the systematic way in which they are studied and passed on. The strong emphasis on assimilating Geshe Kelsang's works means that talks may come from memorized texts rather than personal understanding. There does appear to be a faith-based rather than a critical approach to teachings, rather like that in Sōka Gakkai International-UK (SGI-UK). We may choose to view this as what Titmuss (1999: 91) called the 'dogmatic or superior viewpoint' of expansionist organizations, or as what Barker (1999: 20) described as 'the unambiguous clarity and certainty' of New Religious Movements (NRMs).

Kadampa lineage masters and Geshe Kelsang

Geshe Kelsang (2003: 134) describes the figure of Śākyamuni Buddha as 'our main object of visualization', seated at the centre of a great gathering of holy beings, Buddhas and bodhisattvas 'like the full moon surrounded by stars'. Interviewees confirmed that the story of Śākyamuni is highly treasured in the NKT, and this is reflected at the Summer Festival, where a play showing his life is staged each year. He is seen as 'the Buddha of our time', whose image is central in the temple, and whose story is 'central to our faith' (Jenkins, 2004). We have also seen that Dorje Shugden, Avalokiteśvara, Mañjuśrī and others are prominent in NKT *sādhana* practice.

The NKT frequently refers to its pure lineage, passing from Śākyamuni to Mañjuśrī and Maitreya (both mythical rather than historical figures) and 'further

Indian Buddhist Masters', before Atiśa (982–1054) brought their teachings together and 're-introduced them into Tibet'. They were then passed down to Tsongkhapa, who with 'special instructions received directly from Manjushri, established the Kadam Dharma' and with it the New Kadampa lineage, which was passed down through the Gelugpa lineage to Geshe Kelsang (Belither, 1997: 2f.). These Kadampa teachers are described as being not only 'great scholars' but also 'spiritual practitioners of immense purity and sincerity', so that the authenticity of the tradition is maintained by 'an unbroken lineage of realized practitioners' (Kelsang, 2001: 397).

Tsongkhapa has a special place in the NKT narrative. He is said to have 'single-handedly revitalised Buddhism in Tibet', being seen by all Tibetan Buddhists 'as the second Buddha' ('Buddhism: The New Kadampa Tradition', n.d.). Kay (2004: 89) described how the NKT has presented itself as 'the guardian and custodian of the pure tradition of *Tsong Khapa* in the modern world', with Geshe Kelsang revising the lineage tree in later editions of his books, deleting dedications to the Dalai Lama, distancing himself from contemporary Gelug leaders and 'promoting himself as the principle authentic disciple and direct lineage descendent'. However, Belither (2004) explained that one of two existing lineages was removed to avoid possible confusion.

Geshe Kelsang (1992: 117) claims that while Buddhas may appear in any form, their most important role is 'emanating as a Spiritual Guide', to lead disciples towards liberation by their teachings and example. Whoever encounters 'a qualified Mahayana Spiritual Guide' and follows their teachings will 'definitely attain full enlightenment and become a Conqueror Buddha'. Like other Tibetan teachers, he has encouraged his own followers to 'rely on the holy Spiritual Guide' and 'always practise in accordance with what your Spiritual guide says' (Kelsang, 2001: 371–2). While these statements appear as commentaries on Tsongkhapa's teachings, they are also used to underline the author's own status, as the primary spiritual guide for NKT members is Geshe Kelsang himself.

Bunting (1996b: 26) presents an extraordinary picture of Geshe Kelsang as a reclusive figure, seen by his followers as omniscient and omnipotent, with no need to eat, sleep or breathe: she claimed that the traditional Tibetan Buddhist view of the teacher as 'Buddha-like' has been 'conflated with Western theism so that Kelsang becomes a sort of god'. Interviewees found this description ridiculously exaggerated, as Bunting had simply not checked the facts: perhaps even journalists may accept mythical narratives uncritically.

Faith in Geshe Kelsang is certainly a prominent feature of the NKT. Waterhouse (1997: 181–2) described it as the movement's 'foundation', allowing him to select, adapt and present teachings and practices for westerners. His authority stems from being seen as 'a fully enlightened being', from an authentic lineage, who 'has studied the sutras and tantras', and all three reasons are 'traditional in terms of Tibetan Buddhism'. Followers were taught to see Geshe Kelsang 'as a representative of the Buddha', then with Buddha-like qualities, 'and finally as a Buddha, and thus as someone with the authority to adapt Buddhism for a western audience' (Waterhouse, 2001: 139). While this is in keeping with Tibetan tradition, Geshe Kelsang's current authority does not come from the Gelug school but from his Western followers.

Kay (2004: 76) suggested that Geshe Kelsang's increasingly 'exclusive approach to practice' is linked to his unquestioned authority. He originally encouraged a critical and enquiring attitude, but has more recently emphasized the development of 'unwavering faith and confidence' in a single teacher, introducing non-traditional teaching which amounts to 'an injunction to study only under Geshe Kelsang and teachers who have trained under him' (Kay, 2004: 92). However, interviewees insisted that Geshe Kelsang's role is consistent with both traditional teaching and different levels of belief. Jenkins (2004) described reliance on the *guru* as the core of her practice, though she was aware that her faith in Geshe Kelsang as someone who 'performs the function of a Buddha for me' might be misunderstood by outsiders. Belither (2004) explained that viewing Geshe Kelsang as an enlightened Buddha is still 'an expression of personal devotion' rather than a requirement of belief.

Geshe Kelsang (1997: 6–11, 16) uses several examples of paranormal powers in his books, describing miracles associated with statues of Tsongkhapa and ritual healing practices to bring rain, cure diseases and disabilities, and offer protection against thieves and enemies. He claimed to have found his mother's reincarnation through dreams and divination, and to have recovered from serious illness after being blessed with a *mala* supposedly 'blessed by the Wisdom Buddha Manjushri' (Kelsang, 2001: 25f., 217). However, he also pointed out that Tsongkhapa's pure life and teachings were far more important than his clairvoyance, and that the motivation of *bodhicitta* and compassion is what makes miracles possible (Kelsang, 1997: 5; 2001: 217). Interviewees confirmed that such narratives are used to illustrate the power of faith or the reality of rebirth, rather than to emphasize magical powers (Namgyal, 2004).

A final important narrative concerns the presentation of Western Buddhism. The NKT describes its purpose as preserving and promoting 'the essence of Buddha's teachings in a form that is suited to the western mind and way of life' and claims that only Geshe Kelsang has achieved this ('Buddhism: The New Kadampa Tradition', n.d.). Waterhouse (1997: 177, 180) was told that Geshe Kelsang had been able to 'extract Buddhism from the east' and to 're-present it in a form that is suitable and accessible' to Westerners, so that both the 'essence... [and] the essential practices' are retained, but no longer 'mixed with the eastern culture'. However, as she pointed out, Geshe Kelsang is teaching practices 'which depend upon very complex ideas about Tibetan deity practice', and although this is not explained to NKT followers, these are 'concepts which characterise Tibetan Buddhism and give it its identity'.

There is a genuine paradox in claiming that NKT teaching and practice are both entirely traditional yet no longer part of Tibetan Buddhism, and thus fully accessible to the West. Followers may be unaware that the movement retains teachings, practices, terminology and iconography which are woven into the fabric of Tibetan Buddhism. The NKT's attempt to maintain the essential features of an ancient and pure lineage, while distancing itself from contemporary Gelug Buddhism, has to be seen as part of the narrative of establishing a new Buddhist movement.

Faith, devotion and *bodhicitta*

Geshe Kelsang (2001: 79–80) has firmly encouraged faith and devotion in his followers, describing faith as 'the root of all virtuous qualities and spiritual realizations', adding that faith may be directed towards 'enlightened beings, spiritual teachings, spiritual realizations, and Spiritual Teachers and friends'. Kay (2004: 93) argued that NKT members are urged to adopt 'wholehearted faith and commitment' rather than an attitude of 'critical enquiry', but Waterhouse (1997: 181) found that practitioners often relied on 'their own experience that the teachings are true' as well as their faith in Geshe Kelsang. Interviewees reported that members were encouraged to investigate doubts rather than ignore them, so that the faith which then develops is based on experience (Namgyal, 2004).

Like the Karma Kagyu tradition, there is also an emphasis on 'inner peace'. Geshe Kelsang (2001: 7) described the need 'to develop and maintain a special experience of inner peace' to promote 'lasting happiness', replacing negative mental states with positive ones. Interviewees confirmed that faith, devotion and the calm of inner peace were equally important to them. Devotional practice was said to move the mind closer to the wisdom and compassion of more realized practitioners and so to prepare for the inner peace which will be experienced (Jenkins, 2004).

The practice of compassion and generosity is repeatedly emphasized by Geshe Kelsang, encouraging followers to develop compassion for all beings and to take on their sufferings oneself: wishing others to be happy will enable practitioners 'to be reborn as a human or a god, to have a beautiful body in the future, and to be loved and respected by many people' (Kelsang, 2001: 211, 190). While this may be traditional within Tibetan Buddhism, its presentational tone suggests that emotional responses are encouraged out of enlightened self-interest as well as for those who are suffering.

Perhaps the most potent emotional response is the conscious development of the 'supreme good heart' of *bodhicitta*, the wish to attain enlightenment out of 'compassion for all living beings' (Kelsang, 2001: 231). Those who develop *bodhicitta* will find virtues perfected, problems solved and wishes fulfilled; they will be freed from all negative mental states; and will act only for the benefit of others. Practitioners are encouraged to develop the 'four immeasurables' of love, compassion, sympathetic joy and equanimity to support *bodhicitta*, wishing all beings happiness, freedom from suffering and attachment, and the 'joy of liberation' (Kelsang, 2003: 133).

Geshe Kelsang (2003: 133) described how 'fear of the sufferings of samsara... and of rebirth in the lower realms' can bring the motivation to take refuge in the Three Jewels. Waterhouse (1997: 173) also reported that teaching on the hell realms was used to encourage followers 'not to break their commitments for fear of future suffering'. Although familiar in Tibetan Buddhism, this is rarely mentioned in Britain outside the NKT. Interviewees spoke of various ways of dealing with negative emotions, depending on one's ability and stage in the practice. Delusions such as anger should not be either denied or indulged, but allowed to pass and so gradually uprooted from the mind (Jenkins, 2004). Similarly the development of compassion may be used to counteract a negative emotion such as strong anxiety (Pagpa, 2004).

Moral discipline for monastics and lay disciples

The emphasis on ethical behaviour is perhaps not as prominent in NKT literature as in some other traditions, perhaps because it is widely understood among followers. Geshe Kelsang (2001: 43, 79, 85) has described moral discipline as 'the foundation for the spiritual life', and encouraged practitioners to avoid the ten non-virtuous actions of 'killing, stealing, sexual misconduct, lying, divisive speech, hurtful speech, idle chatter, covetousness, malice and wrong views'. Instead they should 'create virtuous and positive actions', through practising 'faith... non-hatred, and effort' and more specifically a 'sense of shame and consideration for others', which are said to be 'the foundations of moral discipline'. Even those practising moral discipline may still be 'contaminated' by the deluded grasping at 'an inherently existing I or self who is acting in a moral way': this needs to be countered by 'exchanging self with others', cherishing only others rather than the deluded view of the self and by developing compassion and *bodhicitta*, working for the well-being and happiness of all beings, rather than following selfish wishes (Kelsang, 2001: 56, 164).

The ten ordination vows summarize the monastic code. These are to 'abandon killing, stealing, sexual conduct, lying and taking intoxicants', and instead to 'practise contentment, reduce my desire for worldly pleasures, abandon engaging in meaningless activities, maintain the commitments of refuge, and practise the three trainings of pure moral discipline, concentration and wisdom' (quoted in Waterhouse, 1997: 174). A further vow not to eat after midday has now been dropped. A monk or nun who broke these vows would be expelled for at least a year, and would have to ask permission to reordain.

Lay people will often take the *prātimokṣa* vows, identical to the Five Precepts, and similar to the first five monastic vows, but avoiding sexual misconduct rather than adopting complete celibacy. As in the Karma Kagyu and SRM traditions, monastics and lay people practice moral discipline in broadly similar ways. They will both often take the bodhisattva vow to gain enlightenment for the sake of all beings: Kelsang Namgyal (2004) explained that the different vows overlap and build on each other, the bodhisattva vow in particular reflecting 'the bodhisattva mind of not wanting to hurt other people', emphasizing the more positive ethical aspects by 'trying to benefit others all the time'. The bodhisattva vows have specific 'downfalls' which have the force of additional ethical precepts. These include 'Praising oneself and scorning others', 'Not giving wealth or Dharma', 'Not accepting others' apologies' and 'Holding wrong views' (*The Vows and Commitments of Kadampa Buddhism*, 2002: 8), all of which have echoes of Zen's Ten Great Precepts.

The bodhisattva vow encourages the practice of renunciation for both monastics and lay people (Namgyal 2004), emphasizing that there is less distance between them in the NKT than in some other traditions. Perhaps the difference is more between ordinary NKT members and community residents, monastic or lay, who will be expected to show an even higher standard of moral discipline.

A 'post-Tibetan' Western organization?

NKT centres are described as 'legally and financially independent', bound together by devotion to Geshe Kelsang, rather than 'organizational or financial structures' ('Over the Moon', 1992: 46). However, the NKT constitution – designed to 'protect the Centres from corruption and degeneration' – firmly restricts them to 'protecting and promoting the pure tradition of Je Tsongkhapa' and determines their management structure, with separate spiritual and secular roles ('A Healthy Constitution', 1992: 36). These include a resident teacher, an education programme coordinator, and an administrative director. Each centre must also follow a consistent pattern of teaching content and method, and Kay's description of the NKT as 'uniform and centrally administered' (2004: 85) may not be unfair.

Apart from Geshe Kelsang, there are no ethnic Tibetans in the NKT, and no remaining links with the rest of Tibetan Buddhism. Belither (2004) described the NKT as 'a Mahāyāna Buddhist tradition with historical connections with Tibet', rather than a Tibetan tradition, and he explained that Geshe Kelsang wishes his followers always 'to present Dharma in a way appropriate to their own culture and society without the need to adopt Tibetan culture and customs' (Belither, 1997: 7–8). However, there remains an apparent contradiction between claiming a pure Tibetan lineage and complete separation from contemporary Tibetan religion, culture and politics.

While Geshe Kelsang's role as spiritual guide is crucially important, there is no 'hard line' enforcing his instructions and individuals may regard him as an authoritative teacher or a spiritual friend offering advice (Namgyal, 2004). However, Kay (2004: 94) found the role of NKT teacher described as a 'channel' for transmitting Geshe Kelsang's teachings 'without colouring them with their own personal ideas', and one saw himself as 'a talking book' where 'Geshe-la's teachings come through your mouth'.

Until recently Geshe Kelsang himself has 'always been available for private consultations' to support students with any difficulties, though he has recently moved from Manjushri to a secret retreat house in the United States to 'regain his strength for his teaching commitments and his writing', and to allow other teachers to take on more responsibility (Belither, 2004). His senior disciple Gen-la Samden is now resident teacher at Manjushri, and continues to offer individual advice to community members on their practice.

Waterhouse (1997: 139–40) found that while ordination is often 'the normal progression for unmarried members', there is also considerable emphasis on lay practice, in contrast to Tsongkhapa's 'strict monastic rule' in Tibet, where tantric practice was restricted to experienced monks. Unlike the Karma Kagyu tradition, full ordination is not available, and those who do ordain remain as novices, though again this is common in Tibet. Namgyal (2004) explained that NKT monks and nuns are simply described as 'ordained', and usually take the name 'Kelsang' from Geshe Kelsang, who still ordains all monastics personally. NKT ordination vows have been slightly modified to be 'more appropriate for westerners' (Waterhouse, 2001: 139): vows are always taken for life, though some monastics have disrobed over the years.

There is less separation between monastics and lay people than in some other traditions. Geshe Kelsang (1997: 169) defines Sangha traditionally as 'four or more fully ordained monks or nuns' but adds that this may also include 'ordained or lay people who take Bodhisattva vows or Tantric vows'. Monastics no longer sit in the traditional order of precedence, which was seen as peripheral, and Geshe Kelsang has encouraged 'more integration' between monastics and lay people (Pagpa, 2004), which may begin to blur the distinction between them.

Most teachers are appointed to centres by Geshe Kelsang before they have completed the Teaching Training Programme and continue studying by correspondence, with an intensive study programme at Manjushri each summer. After 4 years as a resident teacher, monastics take the title 'Gen' and lay teachers become 'Kadam' (Namgyal, 2004). Most resident teachers are ordained, with only a few centres having a lay teacher, though local branch classes are often taught by lay students (Prasad, 2004). Kay (2004: 85) found that lay people were almost as likely as monastics to be given teaching and leadership roles; and he sees this as an important Western adaptation of Gelug Buddhism, again because this includes tantric practices which Tsongkhapa restricted to those with 'a solid grounding of academic study and celibate monastic discipline'.

The image of the family is widely used in NKT literature. Kay (2004: 111) described how Manjushri is called the movement's 'mother centre', with festivals as 'family reunions', and followers as 'the sons and daughters of the same father [Geshe Kelsang]'. This 'primary metaphor' is used, he suggests, to support group commitment and to evoke 'the traditional qualities that are considered lacking within modern society'.

Waterhouse (1997: 175f.) found no discrimination between monks and nuns, with 'many well-respected nuns who play leading roles', although one woman was 'uneasy about having to remain a ten-precept nun' and was unaware of the wider debate about women's ordination in Buddhism. The ordination of Kelsang Rigma, a married woman with five children, who lived with her family as the resident teacher at the Hull centre, showed that the NKT 'values not only the contribution which women can make but also the parental role'. Kay (2004: 85) also found men and women acting equally as teachers and leaders, partly due to the emphasis on the bodhisattva vows, which 'cut across the traditional hierarchies – including gender-based distinctions – that are considered irrelevant to Buddhist practice in the West'.

Soon after its formation the NKT became a registered charity to help raise and distribute funds. Fees are charged for meetings, payable at the door or by a monthly 'Centre Card' covering all local classes (Waterhouse, 1997: 144). The Manjushri Spring and Summer Festivals generate considerable income from the 2,000 or more lay and monastic guests. Like Samye Ling there are fixed charges for accommodation and courses, and a large shop and general stores sells Geshe Kelsang's books, CDs of *sādhanas* and statues.

More controversially, Bunting (1996b: 26; 1996c: 9) claimed that monastics changed out of their robes to sign for state benefits, residents financed NKT centre mortgages with their housing benefit, some members were pressurized into donating money through covenants or loans and the movement had acquired large properties including 'several stately homes'. Waterhouse (1997: 144) reported properties being bought and renovated as local centres, with set board and lodging fees for residents who were often on state benefits, and she questioned whether those on the Teacher Training Programme were genuinely available for work.

All such accusations of wrongdoing were vigorously denied by interviewees, who explained that using housing benefit to support mortgages is wholly legitimate and that monastics often have part-time work and may wear ordinary clothes if this is more convenient (Namgyal, 2004). While smaller centres may struggle financially, donations were always voluntary. Manjushri's large community and popular courses make it financially secure, a few people are sponsored because of their NKT work but others are on 'extended working visits' or work locally, and some are legitimately on employment benefit (Belither, 2004). However, while individual rule-bending has never been sanctioned, it may sometimes have been knowingly ignored, at least in the past.

Kay (2004: 60) described how the Manjushri Institute bookshop originally stocked a wide range of material, and Geshe Kelsang's early books included references to other Tibetan, Theravāda and Zen authors. He argued that an increasingly exclusive approach discouraged students from reading books by other teachers: they are often largely unaware of other Buddhist traditions, and some members even 'consider that the NKT is now the only pure tradition of Buddhism in the world' (Kay, 2004: 90). However, Belither (2004) explained that although only Geshe Kelsang's books are studied at centres, there is 'no rule against NKT students reading books from other traditions', as this is a matter of personal choice.

Bunting (1996b: 26) also claimed that the NKT excluded a family for questioning 'the total dependence on Kelsang', expelled one member for praising the Dalai Lama and threatened another with legal action if he published his concerns about the movement. She concluded that the movement's response to criticism is 'to exonerate the organization and throw the blame back on to the dissenting individual'. Again interviewees strenuously rejected such claims, which they saw as coming from disgruntled ex-disciples whose evidence is biased. This is certainly sometimes the case, but there is also a continued unwillingness to acknowledge that the movement itself may have made mistakes.

Waterhouse (1997: 147) reported that the NKT initially avoided contact with other Buddhist groups to preserve 'the purity of their lineage'. However, 2 years after the Dorje Shugden controversy, the movement applied to join the NBO and was accepted, prompting several Tibetan groups loyal to the Dalai Lama to leave. Kay (2004: 214) suggested that the NKT joined the NBO simply to 'reduce the potential for future misunderstanding and misrepresentation', rather than from a genuine wish for cooperation, but at least it is now prepared to have a 'working relationship' with other Buddhist traditions in Britain.

Interviewees may have unwittingly supported Kay's view, by confirming that it was hostility from other Buddhist groups, and wild suggestions about NKT practice, which prompted them to join the NBO. They felt that there was limited benefit in contacts and meetings with other Buddhist organizations. There was a certain wariness here, as if members wished to improve the NKT's image without engaging too closely with other Buddhists.

Kay (2004: 84) argued that NKT literature has concentrated on recent developments and ignores the FPMT. Some interviewees seemed unsure about the movement's background, and those who have joined more recently may be unaware of its controversial origins. Scott (1995: 9) found the Dorje Shugden practice 'somewhat downplayed in public NKT materials' even before the controversy, and hostile media coverage has made the movement sensitive to criticism. Recent NKT publicity sometimes minimizes or even omits the movement's name: leaflets offer retreats at 'a thriving Buddhist community' or work at a centre which 'caters for all levels of interest in meditation and Buddhism' without mentioning the NKT ('Weekend Meditation Retreats', 2003; 'Working Visits at Manjushri Buddhist Centre', n.d.). An organization which appears reluctant to display its own title may continue to be regarded with suspicion.

An article in *Full Moon* argued that the NKT brings 'the prospect of Buddhism becoming a global religion' ('Over the Moon', 1992: 46). Bunting (1996b: 26) described the movement's aim as opening 'a centre in every major UK town' and becoming 'the biggest umbrella Buddhist organisation in the West'. Waterhouse (1997: 143) found that 'casual attenders' were 'encouraged in enthusiastic terms to attend further courses', and often felt this was an evangelical approach. According to Kay (2004: 96), the NKT aims to spread worldwide, but it is sensitive to accusations of 'empire-building' and claims that expansion 'stems from a pure motivation to help others'. Interviewees reflected this view: Belither (2004) explained that the movement's aim was 'simply to present the Buddhism of our tradition to as many people as possible who might be interested'.

One of the 'twelve commitments' of going for refuge within the NKT is 'always to encourage others to go for refuge': Geshe Kelsang (2003: 164) advised followers to speak skilfully to people to help them develop 'fear of suffering and faith in the three Jewels'. Belither (1997: 13) confirmed that all NKT centres 'should have as their goal the establishing of new centres in order to help the people in that locality'. Interviewees claimed the movement's expansion was led by local demand rather than central control, as more people start groups because of their faith in Geshe Kelsang and his teachings (Jenkins, 2004). As Kelsang Namgyal (2004) explained, 'we would like everyone to have inner peace...so we are trying to give it to as many people as possible'.

With no remaining Tibetan links, central control of teaching, little contact with other schools, an expanding programme of residential centres, widespread if selective publicity and overt proselytizing, the NKT as an organization is far removed from the mainstream of traditional Tibetan Buddhism.

A Westernized Tibetan iconography

Like the Kagyu tradition, the NKT has an important and complex iconography. Much of this is exemplified by the new temple at Manjushri Centre, whose three-tier design consists of a square main hall which can seat 700 people, an octagonal clerestory and a tall lantern. The exterior has large wooden doors on all four sides, surmounted by golden deer and Dharma wheels and a repeated frieze of traditional Tibetan 'eight auspicious signs' in local limestone.

The interior is carpeted throughout, with rows of chairs and only a few meditation cushions. Three walls are mainly of glass, with rows of offering goddesses (bare-breasted musicians and dancers) in pastel-coloured relief plasterwork above. The fourth wall is almost filled by a huge shrine cabinet, with three glass cases housing statues mostly clothed in gold brocade garments. The central figure is of Śākyamuni Buddha (flanked by Mañjuśrī and Maitreya), with large statues of Tsongkhapa and Dorje Shugden and Geshe Kelsang's raised seat and photograph placed prominently in front of these images. Here we see the founder, reformer, protector and spiritual guide of the tradition portrayed together in a visual summary of the NKT's lineage and deity practice. There are also finely bound copies of Geshe Kelsang's works, one of them prominently displayed in the traditional Kanjur cabinet, which contains 100 volumes of scriptures in Tibetan.

There are also huge *thangkas* representing Vajrayoginī, Heruka, Dorje Shugden, and the Indian and Tibetan lineage masters. All these statues and paintings (and the images of Buddhas, bodhisattvas and deities available in the shop) still appear as strongly Tibetan, though the NKT now has qualified Western artists, whose work may be seen increasingly as more generalised Buddhist images, not linked to Tibetan culture, according to Kelsang Namgyal (2004).

Geshe Kelsang (2003: 131) encourages his followers to make offerings to Buddha images as if they were 'actually in the presence of the living Buddha', including bowls of water or 'flowers, incense, candles, honey, cakes, chocolate, or fruit'. Many such offerings are placed in front of the shrine cabinets. Local centres frequently copy this pattern of shrine cabinets, offerings and photographs on a more modest scale, though still often occupying a whole wall of their shrine room.

While the iconography of the NKT remains clearly Tibetan to an observer, Belither (2004) argued that the symbolism 'would be recognised across traditions', and Kelsang Namgyal (2004) confirmed that there is no attempt to preserve a Tibetan style, which is to do with 'another country's culture' rather than the essence of Buddhism. There may be an ambivalence here, reflecting the NKT's unusual relationship with traditional Tibetan Buddhism, but the prominent images of Śākyamuni, Tsongkhapa, Dorje Shugden and Geshe Kelsang himself, whatever their style, indicate the veneration with which these four figures are regarded.

Conclusion

Waterhouse (1997: 178) argued that the NKT is based so firmly on Geshe Kelsang and his texts and *sādhanas* that the so-called 'essential Buddhism' which he presents for Westerners 'must be an essential *Tibetan* Buddhism'. Yet while the NKT strongly emphasizes its pure unbroken Tibetan lineage, it has no Tibetan followers and claims to stand outside current Tibetan Buddhism. This means that comparisons with the parent Gelug tradition will have different values for NKT members and for observers of the movement.

Certainly the NKT has expanded very rapidly in a short time, and its historical background remains problematical. Complex meditations and *sādhanas* – including the controversial Dorje Shugden practice – have been translated into English and simplified, but are still firmly based on Tibetan practice. Teachings are also similar to traditional Tibetan Buddhism, though the distinctive study programmes may present a relatively narrow interpretation. Important narratives include historical and mythical Buddhas and bodhisattvas, the role of lineage, the identi-fication of Geshe Kelsang as an important spiritual guide and the presentation of a pure Buddhism to the West. There is an emphasis on strong faith, inner peace, the development of compassion and *bodhicitta* to overcome negative emotions and on traditional moral discipline, with relatively little difference between monastic and lay ethical codes (unlike Tsongkhapa). A highly centralized organi-zation includes lay and monastic teachers, little or no gender bias, an ambivalent relationship with other Buddhist groups and a strong wish to expand through residential centres, publicity and proselytising. The movement's complex iconography is said to represent Buddhism as a whole but still appears very similar to that of Tibetan Buddhism.

The NKT could be viewed from outside as a movement aiming at what Titmuss (1999: 91) called 'conversion and empire-building', with a dogmatic and superior viewpoint, 'narrow-minded claims to historical significance', intolerance of other traditions and 'strong identification with the leader or a book'. A more scholarly external view might emphasize instead the enthusiasm, firm beliefs, urgent message and 'charismatic leadership' which Barker (1999: 20) saw as characteristic of many NRMs. An alternative picture from inside the movement would include a wish to bring inner peace to more people, based on a pure lineage of teaching and practice, with faith and confidence in an authentic spiritual guide. Our choice of interpretation may depend on how we engage with the other viewpoint, as well as the evidence itself, and until recently the NKT's supporters and critics have largely ignored each other.

Experienced disciples suggested to Kay (2004: 112) that the NKT's appeal was due to a combination of Geshe Kelsang's 'very conservative and traditional presentation of Buddhism' and Westerners' wish for 'a meaningful alternative to spiritual pluralism'. The NKT may represent a form of 'evangelical Buddhism', with a powerful appeal to those seeking certainty and an unquestioning faith in a living person and his writings, but this interpretation tends to ignore the movement's context. The NKT was born into a very different atmosphere from that of the 1960s, and Geshe Kelsang's 'conservative and traditional' approach may have inadvertently struck a chord with young people in the more austere 1980s and 1990s. Perhaps Buddhism cannot be separated from its cultural setting as easily as some have claimed.

A movement only formed in 1991 may still be in a relatively early phase of activity, sometimes characterized by rapid expansion, enthusiastic and single-minded practice, firm (perhaps even narrow-minded) adherence to particular teachings and the confidence to ignore outsiders. It may well be that the NKT continues in this mode for some time, though it has already shown itself as sensitive to criticism, and may soon be more willing to engage with other Buddhist traditions in Britain.

9

FRIENDS OF THE WESTERN
BUDDHIST ORDER (FWBO)

Historical background

Each of the traditions considered so far has sprung from a single Asian Buddhist tradition – whether Theravāda, Tibetan or Japanese – with varying degrees of adaptation to a new context in Britain. The Friends of the Western Buddhist Order (FWBO) does not fit into this pattern but consciously draws on and adapts a range of Buddhist teachings and practices from several schools. It is an unusual movement which, like SGI-UK and the NKT, is often seen as controversial, and again it is important to steer a middle course between promotion and prejudice here.

The FWBO's background is closely linked to that of its founder Sangharakshita (Dennis Lingwood, b. 1925). He began to read Buddhist texts as a teenager, practised meditation during wartime army service in India and spent two further years there 'as a freelance wandering ascetic', begging food and meditating, but with 'no contact with Buddhists of any kind' (Sangharakshita, 1993: 13; 1988a: 28). In 1949 he was ordained as a *sāmaṇera* in Kushinara and given the name Sangharakshita. During his *bhikkhu* ordination at Sarnath in 1950 he had a strong sense of his identity as a Buddhist being 'recognized and appreciated by other Buddhists' (Sangharakshita, 1993: 7, 13), though he did not join a monastic community to train as a monk.

He briefly studied Pali texts at Benares Hindu University and began to learn about Vajrayāna from Lama Govinda (the German-born Tibetan Buddhist teacher). However, according to Subhuti (1995a: 68), he met nobody 'whose penetration of the Dharma was greater than his own' and so relied on scriptures, ancient Buddhist writers and 'his own reflections and insights'. By 1955 he was looking for 'an inner guru', feeling that Vajrayāna initiation could establish an 'essential connection with a higher reality'. The following year he received Green Tārā initiation from a Tibetan lama, and this meditation practice (with others from later initiations) brought 'the inner guidance which he had so long desired' (Subhuti, 1995a: 69–70).

Sangharakshita established the Triyāna ('three-vehicle') Vihara in 1957 in Kalimpong, as a 'non-sectarian' centre for Buddhist study. He received initiations and teachings from prominent Tibetan lamas such as Dhardo Rinpoche, Jamyang Khyentse Rinpoche and Dilgo Khyentse Rinpoche, while the Chinese yogi C.M. Chen guided his meditation and introduced him to Ch'an Buddhism (Subhuti, 1995a: 78–85). However, none of these became 'a real spiritual guide': he still relied on his own understanding of the Dharma and 'the higher spiritual energies embodied in the Buddhas and Bodhisattvas' (Subhuti, 1995a: 76). This unusual background raises questions of tradition and lineage within the FWBO.

In 1963 the English Sangha Trust (EST) invited Sangharakshita to become head of the Hampstead Vihara. With 14 years as a monk, his own *vihāra*, wide knowledge of Buddhist teachings and 'ordination and initiation into all three *yanas*', he could claim to have 'the experience, understanding and authority to unite and lead the Buddhists of Britain', according to Subhuti (1995a: 97).

He threw himself into this new role, giving meditation classes and lectures, editing the Vihara's journal, and forming a 'Sangha Council' to maintain monastic discipline and guide lay Buddhists. He surprised lay people at the 1964 Buddhist Society Summer School by eating informally with them and suggesting a devotional *pūjā* – perhaps the first for Western British Buddhists – which the majority attended and enjoyed (Sangharakshita, 1988a: 75–6; Subhuti, 1994: 214). Sangharakshita included material from different schools in his lectures, advocating a partial merging of lay and monastic roles and an English Buddhism independent from Asian traditions, 'with an attitude and outlook of its own' (Sangharakshita, 1965a: 30; 1965b: 141). He also stopped the teaching of *vipassanā* meditation at the Vihara, feeling it might cause mental disturbance (Subhuti, 1994: 181). This approach clearly upset more traditional EST members.

While visiting India in 1966, Sangharakshita received a letter dismissing him from the Hampstead Vihara. According to Subhuti (1995a: 107), the trustees failed to give any reasons, and Sangharakshita had simply offended them by ignoring some of the minor rules. EST sources insisted that reasons *were* given ('The Ven. Sthavira Sangharakshita: A Statement', 1967: 13), and Walshe (1967: 11) added oblique comments about 'the purity of the Sangha and the exemplary conduct of its members'. The allegations hidden here would become explicit much later.

Sangharakshita's immediate decision to start 'a new Buddhist movement' was supported by Dhardo Rinpoche and Dilgo Khyentse Rinpoche, according to Subhuti (1995a: 108–9): returning to England free from official British Buddhism and 'the petty restrictions of monastic formalism', he grew his hair long and wore robes only for formal occasions. The FWBO began in London in 1967 with weekly public meditation classes and study groups for more committed members, 12 of whom were ordained into a new 'Western Buddhist Order' (WBO) by Sangharakshita in 1968 (Subhuti, 1988: 31). Grades of ordination were originally envisaged, from '*upāsaka/upāsikā*' (lay brother/sister) to '*bhikkhu/bhikkhunī*' (monk/nun), but these were later replaced by a single 'Dharmachari' ('Dharma-farer') ordination (Subhuti, 1994: 125–6), where Order members were given a new Sanskrit or Pali name.

Most of the original Order members left to practise in other traditions, but a core of disciples formed under Sangharakshita's guidance for meditation, lectures and seminars. Early retreats fostered both heightened states of consciousness and 'a constant tendency towards hedonistic indulgence': Sangharakshita's own exploration of the 1960s counterculture included rock concerts, taking marijuana and LSD (Subhuti, 1995a: 118, 110) and what he later described as a period of 'sexual experimentation' ('Buddhism, Sex and the Spiritual Life', 1987: 12). While such behaviour certainly attracted young people, it also meant that Sangharakshita was 'largely shunned by what we might see as the then UK Buddhist establishment' (Waterhouse, 2001: 146).

The new movement was experimental, partly because Sangharakshita had 'never participated in a broader spiritual community' (Subhuti, 1994: 124), and a pattern of urban centres, single-sex communities and Right Livelihood businesses only emerged gradually. The first FWBO community, at Sarum House in Purley, found problems when members of a Zen group were included, and the movement decided to minimize contacts with other traditions to 'develop its unique approach undiluted and unmarred by the sectarianism and confusion of much modern Buddhism' (Subhuti, 1988: 32). A mutual hostility between the movement and other Buddhist organizations may explain why the *Middle Way* gives no information on the early years of the FWBO.

There were soon 30 Order members, though many subsequently left, unable to sustain the strong commitment needed. A centre was established in Highgate in 1971, where the movement attempted to create an 'alternative society, free from economic necessities and social expectations', with Order members and others squatting in derelict houses (Subhuti, 1988: 35). Despite further ordinations, Sangharakshita saw most FWBO members as 'lukewarm in their commitment to the Three Jewels and lax in their practice of the Path' (Subhuti, 1995a: 127). He took a sabbatical in 1973, partly to encourage others to take more responsibility, and in 1976 moved to Padmaloka, a large house in Norfolk which became the movement's headquarters and a men's community and retreat centre. Bethnal Green fire station was converted and opened in 1978 as the London Buddhist Centre, with meditation, study and yoga classes, a cooperative which involved 'printing, building and decorating, wholefood distribution and catering', and a residential community for 25 men. ('Sukhavati is...', 1978: 149). Subhuti (1988: 38) claimed that further communities, shops and businesses nearby made this 'the nucleus of a small Buddhist neighbourhood'.

In 1980 the movement had seven centres in Britain, but still remained wary of 'official' Buddhism. An FWBO advertisement at the end of one *Middle Way* issue cheekily invited: 'You've had the theory, now try the Practice' ('Friends of the Western Buddhist Order', 1980: 145). Mindful of their controversial reputation, publicity sometimes played down or omitted the FWBO name, yet by 1981 there were 21 groups and Church (1982: 165) fairly described the movement as 'probably the largest single Buddhist organization in Britain'.

The movement celebrated Sangharakshita's sixtieth birthday in 1985 by collecting £150,000 to buy a mountain valley in southern Spain to provide 'a secluded vihara' for him (Subhuti, 1995a: 171). He became a patron of Angulimala, the Buddhist Prison Chaplaincy Organization, in which some Order members were working in cooperation with other Buddhists (Subhuti, 1988: 192).

By the mid-1980s there were 20 communities, 9 urban centres and 3 retreat centres (Bell, 1991: 115). In 1986 half the 300 Order members lived in communities, and some of them joined Tibetan, Nichiren and Theravāda Buddhists at Amaravati to celebrate Buddha Day ('Padmaloka Notebook', 1986: 26). Subhuti (1988: 186–202) described 5 years of developments up to 1988, with new centres and businesses, greater emphasis on meditation and study, an expanding women's wing and growing numbers of Order members. Sangharakshita was gradually delegating responsibility, while his television appearances, interviews and public talks had brought 'growing recognition and influence outside the Movement'. The movement had also expanded in India, where it was claimed to be 'a major social force' among ex-untouchables (Subhuti, 1988: 200, 194).

There were 20 UK centres by the early 1990s, with classes and courses running in 30 towns and cities ('FWBO Report', 1992: 67; 1993; 114). Sangharakshita continued to devolve his responsibilities as head of the Order, reflecting the growth of the movement, which had become so large that most members had 'little or no personal contact with its founder' (Subhuti, 1994: 26). By 1994 a 'College of Public Preceptors' was formed, with responsibility for ordinations: based at Madhyamaloka, a new main centre in Birmingham, their responsibilities grew considerably in the next few years (Vishvapani, 2004).

The number of UK Order members doubled during the 1990s, from about 250 to about 500, with more women than men seeking ordination for the first time (Vishvapani, 2002). A women's retreat centre opened in Wales in 1994, and Dharma Life magazine was launched in 1996, aimed at Buddhists from all traditions. A large new Manchester Centre included 'a natural health centre and yoga studio' ('FWBO Report', 1996: 206) as well as Clear Vision Education, producing internal FWBO videos and teaching material on Buddhism for UK schools ('Friends of the Western Buddhist Order', 1997: 61).

Subhuti (1995a: 174) admitted that in 1988 there were 'some serious difficulties in the movement in Britain', and two attacks on the FWBO brought renewed controversy. In the *Guardian*, Bunting (1997: 2) made detailed allegations of 'sexual manipulation and oppressive authoritarian cult behaviour', sometimes involving Sangharakshita, and characterized the movement as misogynistic and anti-family, promoting homosexuality and casual sex. Kulananda (1997a: 18) responded that isolated incidents should not implicate the whole movement, which is based on traditional ethical precepts, and Vishvapani (1997: 21) criticized Bunting for sensationalism, arguing that the FWBO had learned from such problems.

The *Guardian* correspondence was followed in 1998 by the persecuting zeal of *The FWBO Files*, a lengthy but anonymous online document from a British ex-monk 'with twenty years training in an orthodox tradition', repeating the allegations of homosexual behaviour and abuse, and claiming that the FWBO condoned benefit fraud, indoctrinated children, attacked women and the family, encouraged intolerance and aimed 'to become the only form of Buddhism in the West' (www.ex-cult.org/fwbo/fwbofiles). The FWBO response dealt with each charge in detail, dismissing most of the homosexual allegations as rumour, and finding other claims unfounded, exaggerated or absurd: *The FWBO Files* was dismissed as an intolerant and 'sectarian attack' (FWBO, 1998: 18–20, 48).

In 2000 Sangharakshita passed the headship of the Order to the Preceptors College, appointing Subhuti as its first Chairman. The last few years have seen dramatic changes within the FWBO, including more overt criticism of Sangharakshita, emphasizing the existence of both different voices within the movement and different phases in its development. The number of Order members continues to rise, with 677 in the United Kingdom in 2004 (Vishvapani, 2004) and a higher proportion of women ordained in recent years. With almost 80 groups and centres in the United Kingdom, an estimated 'core membership' of around 2,000, and about 5,000 people with 'regular involvement with the movement' (Waterhouse, 2001: 147), the FWBO is one of the three largest Buddhist traditions in Britain.

Multi-tradition meditation and devotion

The FWBO teaches two forms of meditation for beginners, with further techniques for 'more advanced practitioners': these initial methods are seen as 'psychological exercises', which do not involve specifically Buddhist teaching (Subhuti, 1988: 50, 52). Beginners classes use a centre's shrine room, but with no devotional activity, an Order member guiding the class in practice for 25 minutes, using the two techniques on alternate weeks.

Mindfulness of breathing (*ānāpānasati*) is taught to develop concentration and calmness. The breath is observed rather than controlled, first counting each exhalation and inhalation, and as concentration develops, feeling the breath in the lungs and then in the nostrils. By this method it is claimed that the 'four stages of integration, inspiration, permeation, and radiation, known as the four *dhyanas*' may be achieved (Subhuti, 1988: 54–5). The other method taught is *mettābhāvanā* or development of loving-kindness. *Mettā* is described very positively as 'an ardent urge to act for the welfare of others'. Beginners are taught to develop *mettā* in five traditional stages, first for oneself, then for a friend, a neutral person, an enemy and finally for all of them, and indeed for all beings (Subhuti, 1988: 55–6).

These are both traditional Theravāda forms of *samatha* meditation, and more experienced meditators will be encouraged to add further *samatha* practices, perhaps including the other *brahma-vihāra* practices with the *mettābhāvanā* (Vajragupta, 2002). The Zen practice of 'just sitting', without observing the breath or directing the mind, is also recommended to prevent meditation from becoming forced and to facilitate 'a natural and balanced progress' (Subhuti, 1988: 60).

Bell (1991: 210) found that meditators were only introduced to *vipassanā* or to Mahāyāna and Vajrayāna meditation techniques after extensive preparatory work. Sangharakshita always discouraged beginners from practising *vipassanā* meditation and it is not taught or practised at public centres, though it may be learnt at retreat centres by Friends or Mitras (Dharmaghosha, 2002). (A 'Friend' is anyone who attends meetings: a 'Mitra' (Skt. 'friend') is a more committed FWBO member.) More recently, however, *vipassanā* has sometimes been introduced earlier on, partly because the ordination process now takes longer, but also because the technique is beginning to be seen as safe and beneficial even for fairly new meditators (Vishvapani, 2002).

Mitras who are accepted for ordination will attend training retreats, where they begin the 'Going For Refuge' practice which involves visualizations and Tibetan-style prostrations and prayers (Vajragupta, 2002). In the pre-ordination period a 'Six Elements' practice is used, reflecting in turn on 'earth, water, fire, air, space and consciousness' and gradually detaching from identification with them (Vishvapani, 2002).

At their ordination candidates are formally given the Three Refuges and Ten Precepts, with a 'mantra and visualization-meditation practice' taught them by their preceptor (Subhuti, 1988: 142). A white silk scarf or *kesa* (borrowed from the Zen tradition) is placed round the new Order member's neck as a symbolic robe and worn for meditation, *pūjās* and classes. Order members take on the specific visualization practice or *sādhana* as their main practice, visualizing a particular Buddha or bodhisattva and reciting the appropriate mantra. Although these come from the Tibetan tantric tradition, they are not seen as tantric practices within the FWBO, but simply as 'expressions of Going for Refuge in relation to the Buddhas and bodhisattvas', according to Vishvapani (2002), emphasizing that 'you are in communication with some embodiment of enlightenment'.

As well as regular meditation on the figure given them at ordination, Order members may take on additional figures later if they wish. These figures together form a kind of FWBO 'pantheon', based originally on those Sangharakshita was introduced to in India, but also with others which have 'emerged out of people's personal spiritual practice'. However, *sādhana* practice is not the same as worship, since these figures are not 'objective existent beings' but rather they are 'symbols, qualities and attributes that one can cultivate in oneself' (Sanghadevi, 2002).

Order members may still practice the mindfulness of breathing and *mettābhāvanā* as well as their specific *sādhana* practice and will join in a simultaneous *mettābhāvanā* meditation once a month, directing 'feelings of *mettā* towards the whole Order' (Subhuti, 1988: 135). They may receive informal guidance from their preceptor or while on retreats, but are expected to become independent, building up their own meditation practice as appropriate (Vajragupta, 2002).

While beginners classes concentrate on meditation and Buddhist teachings, devotional elements are gradually introduced. The *pūjās* in FWBO communities, retreats and meetings include bowing to the Buddha image, offering flowers, candles and incense, chanting in Pali or English and reciting devotional verses

(Subhuti, 1994: 65–7). A short *pūjā* devised by Sangharakshita may be used, and eventually – in meetings with regular members rather than beginners – a 'Sevenfold Puja' adapted from Shantideva, which includes an emphasis on Going for Refuge, as well as scripture readings, chanting mantras, and reciting the *Heart Sūtra*. The Sevenfold Puja includes verses or chants described as 'Worship... Salutation... Going for Refuge... Confession of Faults... Rejoicing in Merits... Entreaty and Supplication... [and] Transference of Merit and Self Surrender' (Subhuti, 1988: 68). Most of the verses are in English, though specific mantras are chanted in Sanskrit (*FWBO Puja Book*, 1995). The Sevenfold Puja is usually performed communally at centres or retreats, though individual Order members may also use this practice when on solitary retreat, or as part of their Tibetan-based *sādhana* practice of visualizing particular deities or bodhisattvas (Sanghadevi, 2002).

'Essential Buddhism' from several schools

The FWBO practice of consciously drawing on several Buddhist schools is seen most clearly in its teachings. Rawlinson (1997: 503) describes the movement as essentially 'non-denominational, both doctrinally and as an institution', though it could be seen instead as a new denomination with unusually complex origins. It combines teachings selected and adapted from traditional sources with new ideas of its own, and it is sometimes difficult to distinguish between them.

Sangharakshita has borrowed the phrase 'Basic Buddhism' from Christmas Humphreys to describe 'a core of common material' in the scriptures of all schools, including the Four Noble Truths and the Noble Eightfold Path, which 'provides the *doctrinal* unity of Buddhism' (Subhuti, 1994: 41). He argued that this unified Basic Buddhism has gradually acquired 'layers of culture which are superimposed upon it' so that modern Western Buddhists often encounter only a national or regional sub-tradition rather than Buddhism as a whole (Sangharakshita, 1990a: 59, 58). Thus they often 'identify Buddhism with one or other of its specific forms', believing that Theravāda or Tibetan or Zen Buddhism is the only real form of Buddhism (Sangharakshita, 1996b: 10).

It is therefore vital for Western Buddhists to distinguish between 'what is really Buddhism' and what is the culture of various Asian countries, according to Sangharakshita (1990a: 60). The FWBO has assumed that the essential and the peripheral can and must be separated, relying on Sangharakshita's authority to determine what is really necessary. Bell (1991: 370) explained that while the FWBO draws on all Buddhists schools, 'it does not accept the institutional forms or practices of any', developing instead suitable Western forms to express the 'essence' of Buddhism. This might be seen as an attempt to return to an 'original Buddhism', rather like Protestant attempts to rediscover an 'original Christianity' in the Gospels. However, Vishvapani (2004) argued that the FWBO is drawing on the whole Buddhist tradition, engaging with core teachings shared by all schools, rather than simply seeking out the most ancient of them.

Sangharakshita (1959: 99, 104) originally described the 'three *yānas*' (Hinayāna, Mahāyāna and Vajrayāna) in Tibetan terms as 'three progressive stages of spiritual ascent', though he argued that improved communication and new translations will eventually bring 'a World Buddhism which accepts the basic authenticity of the whole Buddhist tradition'. Returning to England from India, he was 'determined that British Buddhism should not fall into a narrow sectarianism but should be a Triyana Buddhism', according to Subhuti (1995a: 97). Perhaps the conservativism of British Theravāda Buddhism suggested to him that these were the only two options. Sangharakshita now 'values all three historical *yānas* equally', according to Subhuti (1994: 48), as there are advanced teachings in the Pali canon and elementary ones in Tibetan Buddhism. Vishvapani (2002) confirmed that the FWBO does not teach Triyāna Buddhism as a progression from one *yāna* to another, quoting Sangharakshita as saying 'there are no higher teachings, only deeper realizations'.

Sangharakshita (1990a: 63–4) maintains that the FWBO neither promotes nor rejects any single Buddhist school, but instead draws on each of them for what is relevant in the West, including Theravāda meditation, Mahāyāna *pūjās*, Tibetan mantras and the Zen emphasis on work. He argued that Western Buddhists must choose between following 'an existing Eastern Buddhist tradition' and selecting and combining elements to create a new Buddhist tradition, as the FWBO has done (Sangharakshita, 1992a: 56). The selection of FWBO teachings may simply represent elements which appealed to Sangharakshita: however, Sanghadevi (2002) argued that they all focus the value of Going for Refuge, and Vishvapani (2002) confirmed that any personal preferences are based on Sangharakshita's wish to 'draw on those things that are relevant to our spiritual lives'.

Subhuti (1994: 56) argued that even with this selective approach, the FWBO has remained an orthodox movement whose teachings are always consistent with Basic Buddhism: while the movement 'did not adhere to any traditional school of Buddhism, Sangharakshita ensured that it was entirely traditional'. This is an unusual claim. Individual elements of FWBO teaching may be traditional within their various schools, but the process of selecting and combining teachings from different Buddhist schools has rarely been attempted in such a conscious way and can hardly be described as traditional.

Sangharakshita (1985: 274) has argued that Buddhist scriptures, rather than current Asian Buddhist practice, are 'our most reliable guide to the true nature of Buddhism'. This is reminiscent of Victorian scholars looking for the 'essence' of Buddhism in Pali texts: it is again an essentially Protestant approach, identifying correct practice with scripture rather than tradition and ignoring the development of Asian Buddhism. Sangharakshita (1985: 276) claimed that as Pali, Sanskrit, Chinese and Tibetan texts are all translated into English, Western Buddhists will inevitably 'derive inspiration and spiritual guidance from the whole of the canonical literature of Buddhism', rather than being 'limited to any one form of Eastern Buddhism'. However, the availability of texts does not make them compulsory: it seems far more likely that most British Buddhists will continue to practise within different traditions, each using its own scriptures.

Subhuti (1988: 111–24) explained how texts chosen by Sangharakshita have helped to shape FWBO teaching and practice. The *Udana* (Theravāda) shows that the essential difference is between 'the committed and the uncommitted', rather than between monks and lay people, a principle taken up in the WBO. *Dhyāna for Beginners* (Chinese) is a meditation manual by Chi-I (539–97), the founder of T'ien t'ai Buddhism, and the FWBO uses the same principle of stages of meditation. *The Tibetan Book of the Dead* is ascribed to Padmasambhava, founder of the Nyingma school (to which most of Sangharakshita's Tibetan teachers belonged), who is seen as a kind of spiritual ancestor of the FWBO. Śāntideva's *Bodhicaryāvatāra* (Indian) has an important position in the movement because of its 'emotional intensity' and deep wisdom, and some of it verses are used in the FWBO Sevenfold Puja, helping to generate *bodhicitta*, the wish for enlightenment.

There is considerable encouragement to study within the movement. Centres run introductory courses on Buddhism, classes for regular members and study courses for Mitras and those seeking ordination. The 3-year Mitra course involves intensive reading and weekly meetings with Order members for presentations and guided discussion of taped lectures by Sangharakshita (Sanghadevi, 2002). Subhuti (1988: 106) described Sangharakshita's seminars on specific texts as 'the primary source of teachings within the FWBO', claiming this as the traditional method of studying the scriptures 'with a teacher who has himself studied them under the guidance of a teacher'. However, Sangharakshita has usually studied these texts on his own, so the interpretation begins with him, rather than being linked to a traditional lineage.

This should not be seen as an exclusive approach. Waterhouse (2001: 149) described how students are encouraged to use the texts, Sangharakshita's commentaries and modern critical scholarship, including discussion of 'the provenance and status of the text'. Individuals may choose which texts they wish to study, and FWBO centres often have extensive libraries with a wide range of material.

Sangharakshita (1967: ix) originally described the act of 'Going for Refuge' to the Three Jewels as a profoundly transforming 'spiritual rebirth'. He came to see this as the definition of a practising Buddhist – one who accepts the Buddha as the 'ultimate spiritual guide', who works to 'understand, practise and realise' the teaching and who seeks 'inspiration and guidance' from past and present Buddhists (Sangharakshita, 1992b: 17). However, he argued, this 'Going for Refuge' has often been devalued or ignored. None of his teachers emphasized its importance, and he discovered its significance for himself, eventually seeing it as 'the key to everything…[and] the basis of our new Buddhist movement' (Sangharakshita, 1990a: 86).

He developed the idea of five different levels, which Subhuti (1994: 92–4) has explained. 'Cultural Going for Refuge' is a nominal Buddhism including mainly social participation; 'Provisional Going for Refuge' involves 'some definite response to the Three Jewels' and initial meditation and study, perhaps within a Buddhist movement; 'Effective Going for Refuge' implies a 'decisive reorientation', a full commitment corresponding to WBO ordination; 'Real Going for Refuge' implies a 'transforming insight that brings one on to the transcendental path'; and 'Ultimate Going for Refuge' is enlightenment itself, with no distinction between oneself and the refuge.

According to Subhuti (1995a: 173), Sangharakshita's emphasis on the centrality of Going for Refuge also links the founder and the movement: the Order itself 'sprang out of Sangharakshita's own Going for Refuge and therefore, in a sense, rested upon it'. This suggests that each supports and legitimizes the other, so that criticism of Sangharakshita would undermine the movement itself: Vishvapani (2004) confirmed that while such criticism is now 'common currency in the FWBO', it remains a problematic area for some members.

Sangharakshita (1990a: 30–1, 40–1) has argued that in modern society the 'virtually powerless individual' is threatened by the various groups which make up the 'virtually all-powerful state', while Buddhism enables a person to grow into the 'true individual' who has gone beyond 'group consciousness' by developing a higher 'reflexive consciousness'. Similarly Subhuti (1988: 9, 11) described the Dharma as 'the Path of the "Higher Evolution" of the Individual', leading to freedom from group conformity, greater self-awareness and understanding of reality and finally to 'Absolute Consciousness', the enlightenment which is 'the goal of the whole evolutionary process'. The idea of the 'evolution of the true individual' sounds odd to many Buddhists: popular in the FWBO during the 1970s as a metaphor for spiritual progress, it is little used now, according to interviewees. What remains is the contrast between an ego-driven 'individualism' and the genuine self-reliance of 'individuality' (Dharmaghosha, 2002; Sanghadevi, 2002).

The FWBO has strongly criticized Christianity, which Sangharakshita (1990a: 36–9) saw as siding with the group and persecuting the individual. Fear of an omnipotent God who 'enforces group values' is said to bring only guilt, so that Christians are damaged both 'psychologically and spiritually'. Until Christianity abandoned theism and saw Christ 'as a teacher rather than as a Saviour', a new spiritual movement like the FWBO would be needed to protect the individual.

This led Mellor (1991: 73, 77) to suggest that the FWBO was in some sense a 'Protestant Buddhism', as English Buddhists who attack Christianity for being authoritarian, institutionalized and dogmatic are making the same points as Protestant critics of Catholicism. Sangharakshita (1992a: 52) made a lengthy and indignant response in *The FWBO and 'Protestant Buddhism'*, arguing that most British Buddhists still had 'a sentimental attachment to Christianity' which hindered their full commitment to Buddhism. For Sangharakshita (1992a: 86, 54) Christianity means 'traditional, orthodox Christianity, Roman Catholicism', rather than the liberal Protestantism which rejects central doctrines and is only 'Roman Catholicism in dilution'. This extraordinary view of Christianity – in a country which has been Protestant for four centuries – applies exactly the same test of orthodoxy which Sangharakshita explicitly rejects for Buddhism. Perhaps Protestantism does not look like the enemy he wishes to recognize.

Hostility towards Christianity has undoubtedly mellowed, though interviewees suggested that the British Christian background still leaves a residue including both guilt and an uneasiness about sexual desire. Attempts by the Dalai Lama and Thich Nhat Hanh to suggest common ground between the two religions are still viewed with suspicion, as 'the Dharma stands on its own' (Dharmaghosha, 2002).

The uncompromising tone of FWBO teachings, especially in the early years, is unusual: the trenchant criticism of Christianity, traditional Buddhist schools and their British followers sits uneasily with Buddhism's reputation for tolerance. However, as the young idealists of the 1960s counterculture gradually became middle-aged, the tone has softened considerably, and the movement now appears in the context of a very different British Buddhism.

While the FWBO clearly emphasizes a distinctive range of teachings, they are not always radically different from other traditions. The difference between 'essential Buddhism' and 'cultural additions', the role of scriptures and the necessity for personal commitment and spiritual growth, are themes which concern all traditions in their new British context, and even hostility to Christianity is sometimes visible elsewhere. The FWBO's unique doctrinal approach is in advocating the conscious selection and combination of teachings drawn from Theravāda, Mahāyāna and Zen sources. This is something genuinely new in a Buddhist movement.

Sangharakshita and a new Western Buddhism

Traditional Buddhist schools take their existing narratives with them to new countries, emphasizing or downplaying elements as appropriate in their new cultural context. Stories about the Buddha, early disciples, Tibetan teachers and Zen Masters all play their part in contemporary British Buddhism. The FWBO is in different position here: with no lineage to pass down narrative elements, it has chosen them for itself, in a sense creating its own narratives as the movement develops.

The historical Buddha is still seen as extremely important: his life story is often told early on in FWBO courses, emphasizing that there is a real personality behind the teachings (Sanghadevi, 2002). These narratives are used at festivals, with readings from Theravāda or Mahāyāna scriptures and as part of Mitra courses. The statue on the shrine in FWBO centres reminds members of the Buddha's enlightenment and helps 'connect them to the myth of the Buddha', encouraging them to follow him (Vajragupta, 2002).

Order members may also examine and reflect upon the narratives associated with the particular Buddhas or bodhisattvas visualized in their *sādhana* practice. Several of these figures appear on the FWBO 'Refuge Tree', an idea borrowed from Tibetan Buddhism by Sangharakshita for Order members to visualize. Subhuti (1994: 58–9) described the iconography in detail. The historical, past and future Buddhas sit on a central lotus, with teachers from the main Buddhist traditions above them, bodhisattvas including Avalokiteśvara and Mañjuśrī on the left, disciples including Śāriputra and Moggalāna on the right, and scriptures from all Buddhist schools at the rear. Sangharakshita himself sits at the front, surrounded by his Indian teachers from the Theravāda, Ch'an and Tibetan traditions, as 'a recognition that he is the link between Order members and the wider tradition'.

Although Sangharakshita studied only briefly with these teachers, they are pictured as lending authority to the WBO, and Dhardo Rinpoche is said to have regarded Sangharakshita's disciples as his own (Subhuti, 1995a: 148). Interviewees reported that some Order members appreciate knowing their teacher's teachers and may see an important lineage here. For others the FWBO is a new tradition and the Refuge Tree is simply a reminder of where Sangharakshita's teachings come from, illustrating not the movement's authority but his own. It is not clear how far Sangharakshita's teachers supported his approach or the formation of the FWBO.

Sangharakshita's own story is crucial to the movement's identity. He described himself as the founder, preceptor, teacher and friend of the WBO, emphasizing that 'the Dharma studied, practised, and propagated by Order members is the Dharma as elucidated by me' and also 'as translated by me from the terms of Eastern culture into the terms of Western culture' (Sangharakshita, 1990b: 21, 24). FWBO biographical material on Sangharakshita has few external references, and Subhuti (1995a: 12) described his life of Sangharakshita as 'my version of aspects of *his* version of his life'. Sangharakshita is not only the subject of this important narrative, but also ultimately its creator.

One example here is his time in India. Waterhouse (2001: 148) pointed out that although Sangharakshita claimed 'close relationships with his Asian teachers', they were not maintained when he came to England. *The FWBO Files* attempted to show that he invented his Buddhist training in India, and Shukman (1999: 68) wondered whether the story of a 'wandering ascetic, garlanded with honours by religious dignitaries and bringing the Dharma home to the West' was actually true. The FWBO vigorously defends Sangharakshita's account, supported by his fellow monk Khantipalo (2002), though the *significance* of his contacts with teachers in India may be viewed differently from inside and outside the FWBO.

Sangharakshita (1999: 31) rejects any role as a guru, arguing that authority is based on scriptures, understanding and experience, rather than an individual. Subhuti (1994: 26) claimed that while Sangharakshita's 'influence pervades every aspect of the movement', this was no personality cult; though he also described the 'raw power' of Sangharakshita's 'penetrating gaze' at their first meeting and the 'self-possession and grace' which gave him 'a kind of majesty' (Subhuti, 1995a: 10; 1994: 184). Sangharakshita perhaps encouraged such reverence by describing the FWBO as 'an embodiment of some part of me ... whatever is done for the movement ... is in a sense done for me' (Subhuti, 1994: 297). Subhuti (1995a: 11) confirmed that it would be 'hard to disentangle' Sangharakshita from his writings, his disciples and the FWBO itself as 'so much of his own spirit has passed into what he has achieved'. The increasing variety within the WBO has more recently included criticism of Sangharakshita's personal behaviour, though he retains the trust of Order members as their teacher; and 'disentangling Sangharakshita, the teachings and the movement' is currently a major issue (Vishvapani, 2004). Sangharakshita's story remains ambivalent, depending on who is reading it.

The creation of 'a new Buddhist culture in the West' has been described as the 'foundational narrative of the FWBO' (Vishvapani, 2002). The idea of distinguishing between 'Basic Buddhism' and its 'cultural manifestations' is itself a distinctively Western approach, implying that a contemporary synthesis of Buddhist teachings and practices is inherently superior to traditional Asian Buddhism. Subhuti (1988: 5) argued that few Westerners are ready to 'discard their own culture in favour of a Japanese, Tibetan or Thai way of life' and that the Buddhism of 'agrarian monarchies' is often inappropriate in modern Western socio-economic conditions. Instead of allowing change to happen gradually, the FWBO aims for a conscious and swift transition to a Buddhism which reflects Western rather than Asian culture.

The movement draws on some Western figures for inspiration. Subhuti (1988: 181) cited Blake's religious system, Goethe's individuality and Nietzsche's ideas on personal development as examples of 'creative works which can be of great value to the developing individual', though there is no place for the great Christian writers and mystics. While this may be innovative and imaginative, it is difficult to see it as traditional Buddhism.

Subhuti (1986: 3) claimed that Westerners are 'heirs to the entire Buddhist tradition', who thus should not 'follow one branch at the expense of all the rest': he described the WBO as 'international in character and suited to the needs of the current age'. Kulananda (1997b: 180) argued that the separation between Asian Buddhist traditions is breaking down in the West, so that Western Buddhism will eventually be 'much more of a *melange* than some traditionalists would prefer'. The challenge is not to preserve individual traditions, but to ensure that new forms are based on 'genuine spiritual principles and deep spiritual experience'. Again, however, the great majority of British Buddhists continue to practise in specific traditions, each making its own adaptations to Western culture but showing little sign of merging or fading into the background.

'Emotional positivity' and spiritual friendship

We have seen that the *mettābhāvanā* or development of loving-kindness is emphasized from the beginning in the FWBO, and Subhuti (1994: 203) reported that Sangharakshita has placed increasing emphasis on the 'positive emotions' of loving-kindness, compassion, sympathetic joy and equanimity. One of the most evident characteristics of the FWBO is this emphasis on 'emotional positivity', seen as a counterbalance to the early British Theravāda emphasis on suffering.

It includes supporting people through difficult times rather than ignoring negative emotions: members encourage each other to be open about their feelings and 'to take responsibility for their negative mental states' (Sanghadevi, 2002).

Sangharakshita (1990a: 15) has described the importance of 'wholehearted commitment to spiritual friendship', and Subhuti (1988: 85–93) devotes a chapter to the subject, arguing that true friendship, based on mutual respect rather than emotional need, develops best within the context of committed personal development. The FWBO's social network encourages progressively deeper communication, eventually overcoming distinctions between individuals. This spiritual friendship or 'Kalyana Mitra' may exist between those on the same spiritual level, but is more often experienced between Mitras and Order members who can offer guidance. Such friendship is seen as 'the lifeblood of the FWBO', which defines it truly as 'a Spiritual Movement' (Subhuti, 1988: 93).

Subhuti (1988: 67) also argued that spiritual growth is impossible without 'strong feelings of attraction and desire' for enlightenment. Bowing to a Buddha image expresses and cultivates devotion: offering flowers, candles and incense express gratitude, and chanting Pali or English verses expresses reverence to the Three Jewels. Each section of the Sevenfold Puja is said to evoke 'a different mood of devotion': *Worship* venerates the ideal of enlightenment, *Salutation* acknowledges the distance of the goal, *Going for Refuge* makes a commitment to reduce this distance, *Confession of Faults* acknowledges 'failings and weaknesses', *Rejoicing in Merits* follows to avoid 'a mood of depression and guilt', *Entreaty and Supplication* evokes 'receptivity and openness to the Dharma' and *Transference of Merit and Self Surrender* dedicates the benefit for all beings (Subhuti, 1988: 68).

Both the act of 'Going for Refuge' and ordination into the WBO are frequently described as profound experiences of 'spiritual rebirth'. Ordination retreats involve 'a very deep and intensive experience of the Dharma', and after appropriate training each new Order member becomes a 'well integrated, emotionally positive, capable individual' (Subhuti, 1988: 139, 141). Interviewees described how 'your old self is dying away and you are becoming a new person' at ordination (Vajragupta, 2002). This may appear to echo Protestant theological language, but is actually a common image in religious traditions, and in Buddhism represents the change from an ordinary person to a 'noble one' who has glimpsed Nirvana. The idea of spiritual rebirth is perhaps less emphasized in the FWBO now and used as an image rather than a doctrine (Vishvapani, 2002).

Buddhism is often praised for its tolerance towards other religions, and the different schools have often coexisted fairly well. However, the tone of FWBO attacks on both Christianity and other forms of Buddhism can appear extremely intolerant. Subhuti (1988: 102) referred to Christianity's 'tyrannical deity, its mythology dressed up as history, and its deplorable record of hypocrisy, bloodshed and bigotry'. Worse still, the sense of sin and guilt may be so ingrained that ex-Christians 'may need to blaspheme, to openly and freely ridicule and revile the God who has so distorted and tyrannised their psyches' (Subhuti, 1988: 180).

Belief in God leads only to insecurity, fear and blind obedience without ethical judgement, where anyone who acts well 'is either not a true Christian or is doing the right thing for the wrong reason' (Subhuti, 1988: 179). This is a Buddhist copy of Protestant justification by faith: only *our* good actions are genuine, only *our* compassion is real.

Sangharakshita has sometimes shown hostility to other forms of Buddhism. He is particularly critical of Nichiren Buddhism, with its fundamentalist views and 'an intolerant and dismissive attitude towards other forms of Buddhism' (Sangharakshita, 1996b: 10). This may be fair comment, but he himself refers to 'that spirit of bigotry, exclusiveness and dogmatic authoritarianism for which some modern Theravādins are notorious' (Sangharakshita, 1985: 4), and he feels duty-bound to point out the failings, confusions and distortions in 'many modern Buddhist groups' (Subhuti, 1994: 57). His view of the Theravāda is coloured by personal feelings and contrasts strongly with the Buddhist ideal of tolerant compassion.

These views may not be typical of the movement as a whole and may reflect an earlier period when the FWBO was creating its own identity. Younger members may have a more secular background, and hostility towards Christianity is rarely seen in the movement now, according to Vishvapani (2002). However, the contrast remains between spiritual friendship and an antipathy towards other religious traditions, and it is surely the former rather than the latter which has been a major factor in attracting new members.

Precepts and permissiveness

The traditional Five Precepts, chanted in Pali during FWBO *pūjās*, are taken as the basis for moral behaviour, but seen as guidelines rather than moral absolutes, and also expressed as 'positive precepts' in English. Subhuti (1988: 76–7) explained that the first precept encourages vegetarianism and avoiding activities which harm living creatures, but also involves *mettā* in supporting other people. The second precept encourages generosity instead of greed, including ethical economic relationships and the wise use of natural resources.

The FWBO interpretation of the third precept is highly controversial. Subhuti (1988: 78–9) claimed that repressing sexual desire is as bad as indulging it, and that 'heterosexuality, homosexuality, and masturbation are all potentially healthy means of gaining sexual satisfaction'. While the overall aim is 'freedom from craving', the sexual urge is so strong that 'a period of chastity may be a useful discipline in the development of contentment'.

The fourth precept implies both truthfulness and being open with others. The interpretation of the fifth precept is again unusual. Subhuti (1988: 80) claims that while drink and drugs 'dull or distort consciousness', alcohol may help to 'loosen inhibitions', and recreational drugs may 'offer some people some insights' (though regular drug use is seen as dangerous and hindering spiritual development). Liberal interpretations of the third and fifth precepts may reflect the movement's 1960s origins and a reluctance to proscribe the behaviour sometimes followed by Sangharakshita.

More recently Abhaya (1996) gave an updated FWBO interpretation of the Five Precepts, which appears more traditional, looking at skilful and unskilful actions and emphasizing loving-kindness, generosity, simplicity and contentment, truthful communication and mindfulness, rather than simply abstaining from killing, stealing, sexual misconduct, false speech and intoxicants. The tone here is one of compassion and self-awareness, rather than determining which specific acts are allowable.

In *The Ten Pillars of Buddhism* (1984) Sangharakshita set out the Ten Precepts or 'ten ethical principles' received by Order members at ordination. These are the first four of the Five Precepts and further undertakings to refrain from harsh, frivolous and slanderous speech, and covetousness, hatred and false views. The corresponding 'Positive Precepts' encourage the practice of loving-kindness, generosity and contentment, truthfulness, kindly, meaningful and harmonious speech, and tranquillity, compassion and wisdom. For example, the first precept implies opposition to abortion and nuclear weapons, the second aims at a generosity where giver, gift and recipient become indistinguishable and the third points towards a reduced identification with male or female which brings contentment (Sangharakshita, 1984: 55, 58, 65).

To demonstrate that Order members follow traditional moral guidance taught by the Buddha, Sangharakshita (1984: 13–24) gave detailed references to Theravāda and Mahāyāna scriptural sources for the Ten Precepts. They are very similar to Zen's Ten Great Precepts, but different from the Ten Precepts taken by Theravāda novices (and Forest Sangha *sīladhara* nuns), which include renunciation precepts as well as ethical principles. Sangharakshita (1984: 36–7) argued that monastic precepts are only elaborations of the Five Precepts and that the adoption of different precepts by monastics and lay people has been divisive. *Vinaya* texts and tradition are rejected as emphasizing the monastic lifestyle rather than spiritual commitment: his neat phrase occurs repeatedly in FWBO literature – 'Commitment is primary, lifestyle secondary' (Sangharakshita, 1984: 44).

He argued that Going for Refuge and the Ten Precepts are the best basis for 'unity among Buddhists', who should follow the WBO's example and emphasize 'common and fundamental factors', rather than the 'divisive and superficial' (Sangharakshita, 1984: 40). However, the idea that the WBO has 'given a lead to the rest of the Buddhist world' here sounds like the tail wagging the dog: most Asian and Western Buddhists are quite relaxed about the development of different Buddhist traditions in various countries.

A great deal of attention is paid to sexual behaviour in FWBO writings. A movement of predominantly young people reflected the permissive attitudes of the 1960s, and there has always been 'a broad attitude' towards sex (Sanghadevi, 2002). Sangharakshita (1992a: 17) argued that sexual relationships become less important as followers gradually move towards celibacy, but he saw no need to proscribe particular forms of behaviour, so long as ethical principles are upheld (Subhuti, 1994: 172). Kulananda (1997b: 100) went further, suggesting that Western Buddhists may be 'heterosexual, homosexual, onanistic, transvestite or celibate' and may practise 'monogamy, serial monogamy, polygamy, polyandry or, within limits, promiscuity'. Leaving aside legal restrictions, it is difficult to see how masturbation or promiscuity would pacify rather than stimulate the fires of greed, hate and delusion.

This permissive approach to sexual behaviour has prompted both veiled and overt criticism of Sangharakshita and the FWBO. Walshe (1992: 255) warned of immorality amongst Western Buddhist leaders, arguing that sexual intercourse has always merited '*irrevocable expulsion* from the Sangha', that promiscuity would never be tolerated by 'any legitimate Buddhist school' and that 'sexual relations between teacher and pupil would be regarded with horror'. *The FWBO Files* (1988) was much more explicit, alleging that Sangharakshita was dismissed from the Hampstead Vihara for homosexual behaviour, that two of his disciples committed suicide, that homosexual abuse at the Croydon centre caused another suicide, and that the FWBO actively promotes homosexuality between Order members and their disciples. The FWBO's response dismissed most of the allegations as rumour (and unconnected with the suicides), but admitted that Sangharakshita was sexually active for some years after the formation of the FWBO, and had a 2-year affair with a male disciple in the mid-1970s, only becoming celibate again in the 1980s (FWBO, 1998: 18–20, 34, 36).

These are highly damaging admissions, particularly as Sangharakshita continued to use his monastic title into the 1980s, claimed to have lived as a monk for 'the greater part of my adult life', and argued that chastity 'really defines a monk...if one is not chaste one is not a monk' (Sangharakshita, 1993: 42–3). It appears that Sangharakshita had a series of sexual relationships over many years, while still claiming to be a monk. Although there has been considerable criticism of his behaviour from individuals within the FWBO, the movement has been unwilling to condemn its founder and leader publicly.

Outside the FWBO, it is agreed throughout British Buddhism that sexual relationships between teachers and pupils are an abuse of power. Order members and Mitras may be seen as spiritual friends, rather than teacher and pupil, though this hardly applies to Sangharakshita and his disciples. Vishvapani (2002) explained that sex between Order members and Mitras has never been recommended by Sangharakshita or Subhuti, though it has been discussed, has sometimes happened, and has sometimes helped to develop spiritual friendship.

Interviewees reported that most FWBO members are now in long-term relationships, there is little promiscuity and sexual activity is always regulated by the Ten Precepts, so that manipulative behaviour is never condoned (Dharmaghosha, 2002; Sanghadevi, 2002). However, it is still 'the degree of attachment and addiction' which makes sexual behaviour skilful or unskilful, rather than 'what form of sex you partake in' (Vajragupta, 2002). Finally, Abhaya

(1996: 29) warns against over-dependence on sexual relationships and suggests developing emotional satisfaction through artistic activity and appreciation, communicating with friends and meditation.

While monastic orders have detailed rules for dealing with wrongdoing, Bell (1991: 373) found little regulation within the WBO, conduct being controlled only by 'individual conscience', with no provision for expulsion even for serious offences. When the head of the Croydon Centre was found to be abusing members there in 1988, there was no mechanism to remove him, and such regulations still do not exist.

However, any violent or threatening behaviour will bring suspension, and the need for both confession and reconciliation within the Chapter (the local group of Order members). There are no other formal sanctions, though interviewees explained that Order members can bring peer pressure on individuals who were not following the precepts, and a Chapter might prevent an Order member from taking a class if they were behaving inappropriately (Vajragupta, 2002). Centres tend to work in teams, rather than setting up individual teachers, so that difficulties can usually be dealt with by consensus.

A new society?

Sangharakshita has encouraged disciples to form 'new societies in miniature', where single-sex communities, Right Livelihood businesses and Dharma centres provide 'a radical alternative' to the family, work and leisure (Subhuti, 1994: 221, 233). These most distinctive aspects of the FWBO will be considered here, together with attitudes to the family, women's spirituality, categories of membership, Sangharakshita's role as teacher and relationships with other Buddhists and society as a whole.

FWBO centres, usually in urban locations, are seen as the main way of spreading the Dharma to others (Subhuti, 1988: 148). They are widely publicized to attract people to initial meditation classes, while regular Friends, Mitras and Order members have their own classes and meetings. Titles such as 'Manchester Buddhist Centre' may imply they are the main Buddhist presence in a city, though Vishvapani (2004) maintained that centres make no such claim. There are also several rural centres running retreats for beginners and established members. Local centres are autonomous charities run by Order members, usually making small charges for introductory classes and courses, and contributing to central FWBO expenses. Order members often move between centres, and while an earlier competitive element has now largely disappeared, there is still an enthusiasm to get more people involved (Vishvapani, 2002).

Activities in and around the London Buddhist Centre give a flavour of the movement as a whole. Mitchison (1988: 9) found about 100 FWBO members living nearby, from a wide range of social backgrounds. As well as offering meditation courses and retreats, the Centre describes itself as part of 'a thriving spiritual community' or 'Buddhist village' with its own health food shop, gift

169

shop, bookshop, vegetarian restaurant and natural health centre ('London Buddhist Centre', 2001: n.p.).

Deeper involvement with centres may lead to full-time work in one of these 'Right Livelihood' businesses, originally cooperatives but now reorganized as charities. Businesses include decorating, renovation work, wholefood shops, restaurants and printers, with profits used to support FWBO centres and other projects (Subhuti, 1988: 159, 163, 186f.).

The largest of these, Windhorse Trading, employed 190 members in 1997 at its Cambridge headquarters and 18 shops. Vajraketu (1997: 24–5) described how half the £1.25 million profit in 1996 was used to support FWBO communities and projects in the United Kingdom and India. Products may only be 'ethically neutral' rather than of intrinsic value, but they reflect fair trade and environmental policies. Another substantial business is Windhorse Publications, producing books mainly on Buddhist subjects by Sangharakshita and other authors. Work is seen as an important part of spiritual practice, using teams for mutual support and starting each working day with devotional chanting.

Financial support for employees is given according to need rather than status, so that those with families receive more. Typically this covers rent, bills and food, a little spending money, and 6 weeks 'retreat allowance' (Vajragupta, 2002). Sangharakshita (1992b: 15) explained that Right Livelihood businesses represent the 'integration of Buddhism into the economic life of Western society', though Baumann (2000: 386) argued instead that the FWBO has shown that 'Western concepts, such as a capitalist work ethic, ecological considerations, and a social-reformist perspective, can be integrated into the Buddhist tradition'. Either way, this seems a remarkable achievement, unique in British Buddhism. Observers might see full-time work for subsistence wages as exploitative, but insiders would claim they are freely committed to working in a supportive environment and developing Western Buddhism. More recently, however, Vishvapani (2002) reported a swing away from working in Right Livelihood business, partly due to a more prosperous economy, and some shops and other businesses have closed.

The third distinctive feature here is the FWBO single-sex community, described by Sangharakshita (1992b: 13) as the 'residential spiritual community, which to some extent replaces the institution of the nuclear family'. The initial impetus often came from men and seemed to exclude women. Subhuti (1988: 35) argued that 'men and women have different spiritual needs' which should be addressed separately: FWBO members usually felt their deepest relationships were same-sex friendships, as between the sexes there is 'a deep and natural incompatibility of aims and interests' (Subhuti, 1994: 165). This has a doctrinaire tone, echoing the early days of the movement, and may represent an 'official' version not necessarily supported by ordinary members. Sangharakshita recommended those working in Right Livelihood businesses to live in communities, where they 'have access to regular spiritual support' (Subhuti, 1994: 244), but such arrangements are often decided by individuals rather than pressure from the movement (Vajragupta, 2002).

A single-sex community which provides friendship and support without sexual tension implies that members are heterosexual, but Vishvapani (2002) felt that such communities work well even where some members are homosexual, perhaps reflecting a widely held view within the movement that 'men are from Mars and women are from Venus'. There is less pressure now to live in communities, with less than half of Order members doing so, and those who remain are there to enable deeper communication rather than to avoid romantic attachment.

The FWBO's attitude towards the family has also been controversial. Subhuti (1988: 167) strongly criticized the nuclear family, and hoped that alternatives might be developed to support children without 'condemning married people to an isolated pairing which stultifies and breeds resentment'. He saw the 'couple' (heterosexual or homosexual) as 'a fragile and unwholesome unit', which involves 'clinging and delusion', and is 'the enemy of the spiritual community' (Subhuti, 1994: 173–4). No evidence is offered for such assertions, which sound more like personal prejudice than Buddhist teaching.

Sangharakshita argued that women FWBO members may have children if they wish, 'without necessarily expecting the father to live with them all the time' (Subhuti, 1994: 176), suggesting that child-rearing is mainly women's work. Bell (1991: 294, 339) found a 'strong anti-family feeling' within the movement during the early 1980s, concluding that the FWBO has 'some of the spirit of Buddhist monasticism' about it, with family relationships subordinated to the interests of Order members.

With increasing numbers of women members, hostility to the family has faded. Many Order members are married, perhaps spending time both with their families and in single-sex communities, developing their relationship within the context of a wider range of spiritual friendship (Vajragupta, 2002). An FWBO marriage ceremony has been proposed, though only between Order members or those approaching ordination (Subhuti, 2000: 16). In 1994 Sangharakshita presented 'guidelines for Buddhist parents', acknowledging their role within the movement (Guhyapati, 1998: 61), and families are encouraged to celebrate festivals together. However, some married people with families may still feel marginalized within the FWBO, with what Vishvapani (2002) called 'a backlog of difficult emotions' still to be overcome.

A further contentious area is the FWBO's attitude to women and spirituality. Subhuti (1994: 167f.) argued that while women have 'the same spiritual potential as men', male assertiveness may make it easier for men 'to make their Going for Refuge effective', and Sangharakshita's experience with female disciples led him to see women as 'at somewhat of a disadvantage, at least at the commencement of spiritual life'. Certainly the men's wing developed faster than the women's, though women's ordination is now fully developed, with a similar training pro-gramme to men, and ordination is to a single mixed Order.

However, Sanghadevi (2002) quoted a notorious aphorism used by Sangharakshita and taken up in a booklet by Subhuti (1995b): 'Angels are to men, as men are to women'. This suggestion of different spiritual levels seems more part of ancient Brahminical India than modern British Buddhism. It reveals an insensitive male attitude which has deeply hurt women within the movement. Vishvapani (2002) reported that Sangharakshita's attitude to women is his personal perception, rather than an FWBO teaching; and it seems to say more about Sangharakshita than it does about women.

Although the views of all members are considered, Subhuti (1994: 249) insisted that the 'spiritual community is hierarchical', as everyone accepts that members are 'at different stages of development'. This is reflected in the three categories of Friend, Mitra and Order member. Anyone who attends a meeting at a local centre is called a Friend. Those who attend regularly and practise meditation may ask to become Mitras, their acceptance being marked during a *pūjā* by offering flowers, candles and incense (Sangharakshita, 1990a: 91). At this stage they formally declare that they are Buddhists, will follow the Five Precepts and will practise in the context of the FWBO (Vishvapani, 2004). Mitras have their own study groups and retreats, and those who eventually express a wish for ordination will ask two senior Order members to become their 'Kalyana Mitras' ('spiritual friends') and to provide guidance and support. Once accepted for ordination, they attend a series of retreats, culminating in a longer ordination retreat.

Order members are not required to be celibate, and are seen as being neither monastics nor lay people, since the Order does not fall into either 'the categories of oriental Buddhism' or 'the religious categories of the West', though it is seen as 'completely faithful to the Buddha's teaching' (Subhuti, 1994: 127; 1995a: 139). Sangharakshita has described the WBO as a middle way between the extremes of 'lax laicism' (where monastics are expected to take all 'spiritual responsibility') and 'rigid, formalistic monasticism' (where lifestyle is wrongly identified with true Buddhist practice) ('FWBO', 1987: 144). However, this polarized rhetoric may not reflect current thinking in the movement, which accepts that there are both highly independent lay people and deeply spiritual monastics in contemporary British Buddhism.

Subhuti (1988: 131f.) described 'a natural spiritual hierarchy' consisting of the 'positive group' (i.e. Friends and Mitras) and the 'spiritual community' of Order members: the latter must retain control of centres, communities and business, as 'by traditional definition, it is only they who are truly Buddhists'. This supports exactly the differential status which Sangharakshita opposes in criticizing traditional monastic attitudes.

The three categories of membership do not necessarily reflect levels of spiritual progress. Interviewees described 'a long process of transforming yourself', where there is no absolute distinction between committed Friends and Mitras and Order members (Sanghadevi, 2002). However, only Order members undertake formal teaching, underlining the idea of development in stages and the principle that 'the most committed person should teach' (Dharmaghosha, 2002).

When the London Buddhist Centre opened in 1978, it was seen as part of an expansion leading towards 'an ideal society' which could influence and change Britain ('Sukhavati is…', 1978: 149), and Sangharakshita (1992b: 11) argued that Western Buddhism must develop to 'change Western society'. Subhuti (1988: 129, 184) has written at length of the 'New Society' whose creation is 'the purpose of the FWBO': it does not require 'anachronistic dress or customs' and 'refuses to be relegated to the status of an interesting hobby'. This coded criticism of British Buddhism in the 1960s appears strangely dated in 1988, perhaps reflecting the movement's isolation from developments in other traditions. Interviewees reported that the New Society concept is less prominent in the movement now, with a greater recognition that Western society is not all bad, and there are other alternatives to be explored (Vajragupta, 2002). Baumann (2000: 373) seems justified in concluding that in this area 'the deliberately revolutionary position of the early FWBO has shifted to one of accommodation and transformation of existing structures'.

As we have seen, Sangharakshita described himself as the founder, preceptor, teacher and friend of the WBO, and his own life and work forms a potent narrative on which much of the FWBO is based. Unlike most Buddhist traditions, the authority for ordination came from Sangharakshita himself, rather than from the *sangha*, though this has now changed with the establishment of the Preceptors College.

Mellor (1991: 84) described the FWBO as based on 'a model of charismatic authority' which accepts Sangharakshita's 'personal authority to be able to distinguish between what is, and what is not, essential Buddhism'. Kulananda (1992b: 103) replied that Sangharakshita 'repudiates charismatic spiritual authoritarianism', which is not quite what Mellor meant. Sangharakshita (1992a: 131) argued that the ability, 'by virtue of study and meditation', to distinguish between the essential and the peripheral, confers 'personal authority', where the teacher can then help people 'to see the difference for themselves'. While FWBO members remain confident in their teacher's judgement, outside observers may feel that Sangharakshita is making decisions on his personal authority and then presenting these as 'essential' Buddhism.

There are varying responses to Sangharakshita within the movement, especially now that many members have little or no connection with him. Vishvapani (2002) suggested that the founding of the Order is based on Sangharakshita's 'ability to inspire and guide others' rather than his authority: the relationship between the WBO and its founder is that 'Sangharakshita founded the movement that the Order created'. Most people continue to feel 'gratitude and devotion to him', according to Vajragupta (2002), though he is not above criticism, and there are questions about his personal practice which some people find difficult to understand (Sanghadevi, 2002). Occasionally, Order members will no longer be able to regard him as their teacher and will resign.

Sangharakshita's roles have changed as he has become less actively involved in the movement. He remains of course as founder, and his written teachings are still seen as highly important, but the roles of 'preceptor, teacher and friend' have largely passed on to others. Movements with charismatic founders often pass through 'interesting times' when the leader retires or dies, as the form of authority and organization inevitably has to change, perhaps with no consensus on how change should be implemented. Vishvapani (2004) commented that it was becoming clearer that 'Sangharakshita does not own the FWBO, and while it is based on his key ideas, he cannot define it any more'.

Batchelor (1994: 337) pointed out that although the FWBO draws teachings from all Buddhist traditions, it is often perceived as 'a self-enclosed organization' with 'limited interaction with the wider Buddhist community'. In *Extending the Hand of Fellowship* Sangharakshita (1996a: 14, 23) set out the principles of 'ecumenity', 'personal contact', and 'orthodoxy' which underlie WBO relations with other Buddhists. Ecumenity, or 'the relation of the Order to the rest of the Buddhist world', is hampered by the latter's division into several 'sectarian Buddhist worlds', often unaware of each other, so that their scriptures provide better guidance than their contemporary practice. He seems to claim a unique perspective which is lacking in all the great Buddhist traditions.

Orthodoxy in Buddhism means accepting the primacy of 'Going for Refuge'; so the Theravāda emphasis on monasticism, the Zen focus on meditation and Tibetan promotion of *bodhicitta* and faith in the guru are all described as unorthodox (Sangharakshita, 1996a: 26–34). Only the FWBO, it seems, has got it right. Leaving aside the interpretation and importance of Going for Refuge in Asian Buddhism, this is again essentially a Protestant position, defined by orthodox *belief*, rather than appropriate *practice*.

Personal contact between individual WBO members and other Buddhists will also be based on 'the level of their Going for Refuge'. If this is shallow, it will be difficult 'to communicate and be friends with them as though they were true Buddhists', and Order members may help them find the importance of Going for Refuge 'by drawing their attention to passages in their own scriptures where this is made clear' (Sangharakshita, 1996a: 42). This is almost the patronizing and self-righteous tone of the born-again Buddhist with whom everyone must agree, to be counted as sheep rather than goats. The exclusive attitude here limits FWBO members' own Going for Refuge, since the *saṅgha* envisaged is neither the historical nor contemporary Buddhist community, but only those whose teaching accords with their own. Again this echoes the narrowness which Sangharakshita criticized in British Buddhism of the 1960s, and it sounds curiously dated in the current climate.

It is hardly surprising that the FWBO has sometimes had difficult relations with other Western Buddhist groups, which Subhuti (1985: 29) described as either 'extensions of Eastern Buddhist culture into the West' or as drawing 'spurious parallels and accommodation with modern thinking'. Friends are free to attend other Buddhist groups, and may be encouraged to visit other traditions, but Mitras have expressed a wish to become more involved, and so are expected to practise only within the FWBO (Dharmaghosha, 2002). Order members often had few contacts outside the movement during the early period, though many of them are now very experienced practitioners, with the confidence to develop links with other teachers and groups, and this has happened increasingly in recent years (Vishvapani, 2004).

A gradual move away from the earlier, more dogmatic approach seen in the literature may reflect the FWBO's growth into a much larger movement, wishing to be seen as part of contemporary Buddhism. It may also reflect Sangharakshita's own position. Subhuti (1995a: 183) argues that the former outsider has now 'become an increasingly respected figure in the Buddhist world', and may be seen as 'one of the elders of Western Buddhism'. Although subjective, this indicates a more outward-looking approach, and Sangharakshita (1996a: 12–13) reflected that in the early 1990s he had 'more personal contact with leading Western Buddhists' than in the previous two decades. Harris (1997: 21) argued that the FWBO's 'hint of disdain' towards contemporary Asian Buddhist practice had prevented the Order from accepting guidance from any tradition: she hoped the movement would realize that Western Buddhist groups need both 'the living tradition of Buddhists in the east and the friendship of other Buddhist groups here'.

The FWBO Files (1998) accuses the movement of being sectarian, aggressively evangelical, encouraging intolerance and aiming 'to become the only form of Buddhism in the West'. This is certainly exaggerated, and relates more to the early period than to the reality of the movement today. While the FWBO is not trying to take over British Buddhism, it (like the NKT) is very visible in urban areas. Instead of aggressive evangelism, Bell (1991: 171) found a consistent effort to promote Buddhism, including advertisements in *The Guardian*, and 'eye-catching and sometimes quirky' publicity for local centre activities, hoping to attract people who may become more deeply involved.

FWBO publications include a video course, *Learning to Meditate* (n.d.), emphasizing mindfulness and 'emotional positivity', and claiming that meditation can bring 'peace and clarity, depth and creativity, confidence and optimism, spontaneity and health'. This tends to present meditation as a self-help panacea, rather than part of Buddhist practice. Clearvision Trust has produced videos and teaching materials on Buddhism designed to be 'suitable for use in schools from reception classes to GCSE' (Waterhouse, 2001: 146) but which may give a westernized view of Asian Buddhist teaching and practice. Bell (1991: 374) commented on the 'confident, uncompromisingly optimistic, visionary tone' of FWBO publications and publicity, though again this has softened in recent years. The FWBO journal *Dharma Life* has presented a much broader picture, expressing a variety of viewpoints, and looking at Buddhism as a whole rather than overtly promoting the movement.

In some ways this is the most important dimension for the FWBO. No other tradition has developed such a distinctive social organization, with its single-sex communities, Right Livelihood businesses and a new Buddhist Order which is neither monastic nor lay. As Vishvapani (2002) pointed out, the FWBO began very much as a *movement*, a radical alternative to normal society, and perhaps the whole idea of movements is waning in contemporary British Buddhism, with people speaking of their *individual* practice rather than belonging to organizations. He suggested that in future the FWBO communities and businesses may not be so central. The unresolved question here is whether these social and spiritual experiments, begun in the heady days of the 1960s, will continue to be relevant in the context of twenty-first century Britain.

A Western Buddhist culture

The FWBO places a particularly high value on the arts, and the rich tradition of Buddhist architecture, sculpture and painting is seen as an important 'focus for devotion and inspiration' (Subhuti, 1988: 96). Sangharakshita (1988b: 93) argued that artistic creation (and even aesthetic appreciation) may inspire individuals to develop spiritually, as a 'conscious surrender to the Beautiful' may help to undermine 'established egocentric patterns of behaviour'. There is also a strong wish 'to create new cultural forms which give expression to the Dharma we practice as Westerners' (Vishvapani, 2002). These ideas are reflected in the widespread use of visual imagery in FWBO centres and publications, often created by practising artists from within the movement, which supports a variety of cultural events.

While in India Sangharakshita came to believe that there was a 'deep inner connection between art and the spiritual life' (Subhuti, 1994: 270). In *The Religion of Art* he argued that much Christian art only 'strengthens the ego-sense', while the genuine 'Religion of Art' sees both 'the creation and enjoyment' of painting, music and poetry as 'primarily a means of liberation from the egoistic life' (Sangharakshita, 1988b: 81, 64). Subhuti (1988: 100) confirmed that artistic appreciation and activities are encouraged in the movement as part of developing the individual: some Order members find that their spiritual commitment 'gives their art a deeper coherence and meaning', and so are able to use their sculpture, painting, music and poetry 'to beautify Centres and shrine rooms...[and] to glorify devotional ceremony'. He felt that Western Buddhist artists, poets and musicians – inspired by images perceived in meditation – will begin to create 'a new Buddhist culture' (Subhuti, 1994: 289).

It is thus no surprise to find FWBO centres, communities and businesses described as 'attempts to create oases of aesthetic harmony amidst the deserts of discord' (Subhuti, 1988: 98), and Bell (1991: 110) referred to the 'uncluttered design, high quality workmanship and restrained colour schemes' often seen at FWBO centres. This emphasis on the arts reflects Sangharakshita's personal interests, in rather the same way that Rev. Master Jiyu's musical interests helped to create the Order of Buddhist Contemplatives (OBC) liturgy. FWBO Buddhist Arts Centres have been established in both London and Brighton, the latter including natural health treatments and yoga classes as well as arts projects and meditation courses (Vajragupta, 2002). The London Buddhist Centre has developed a substantial Arts Centre, and while some activities have had a limited appeal, in 2000 it staged a full-scale oratorio called *Voice of the Buddha*, based on the Buddha's enlightenment, with its own score and lyrics, using a mixture of FWBO performers and professional musicians (Vishvapani, 2002).

A typical FWBO Buddhist Centre, like the one in Newcastle city centre, has a reception room, kitchen and office, and a shrine room with a large statue of the historical Buddha. The central location is often noisy, but convenient and in keeping with a commitment to accessible locations. Larger centres may occupy a whole building, with several shrine rooms and a resident community (Dharmaghosha, 2002). Visual decoration often reflects a mixture of Western and Asian cultures: two large Buddha images made by Chintamani for the London Buddhist Centre have Western faces, but the stylized hair, elongated earlobes, monastic robes and lotus thrones of traditional Asian Buddhas (Subhuti, 1988: plate 7; Kulananda, 1997b: cover). There may be differences between public and private iconography, with the historical Buddha represented in centres, but Order members using statues or pictures of the particular Buddhas or bodhisattvas they wish to visualize (Dharmaghosha, 2002).

The FWBO commitment to the arts is also seen in their books and journals. Windhorse Publications has reprinted Arnold's *The Light of Asia* and produced new poetry by Sangharakshita and others, as well as Sangharakshita's *The Religion of Art*. The symbol of the Windhorse itself is said to show the 'driving energy' of the movement, bearing the Three Jewels on its back 'in loving care to every living creature throughout the universe' (Subhuti, 1988: 72).

The FWBO journal *Dharma Life* is illustrated with images of Asian and Western art, from Buddhist architecture to Renaissance sculpture and has included articles on Western art and literature. However, while Saccanama (1997: 50–3) drew inspiration from Dante and Michelangelo in relating to Vajrasattva, the bodhisattva of purity, most articles on Buddhas and bodhisattvas use traditional Asian images as illustrations, and the *FWBO Puja Book* (1995) has traditional Asian images of the Buddha, Avalokiteśvara and Tārā.

Outside the Tibetan tradition, the FWBO is perhaps the most visually aware of the seven traditions. Following Sangharakshita's example, there is active interest in the arts, both as devotional aids and as a means to spiritual development in their own right. This is an important dimension for the FWBO, though it is not clear from the mixture of Asian and westernized images whether 'a new Buddhist culture' is beginning to emerge.

Conclusion

The FWBO has made the most conspicuous adaptation from traditional Asian Buddhism, drawing on teachings and practice from several schools, while still claiming to be true to 'Basic Buddhism'. This combining of elements is seen not only in their meditation practice, devotional activities and use of scriptures, but also in the multi-tradition context in which teachings, ethical precepts and narrative elements are set, and in their visual iconography. Moreover, the WBO is described as neither monastic nor lay, emphasizing personal commitment rather than lifestyle, as part of a self-conscious attempt to westernize Buddhism, presenting teachings and practices appropriate in modern Britain rather than ancient India.

The FWBO emphasizes both the commitment of Going for Refuge and the emotional positivity of spiritual friendship, but also the importance of scripture study and the need for Right Livelihood. The movement's unusual organization, with centres, Right Livelihood businesses and single-sex communities, forms a spiritual and socio-economic matrix unseen in other traditions. This has had an experimental feel to it and the situation is still changing, with some members reverting to nuclear families and conventional employment.

In contrast to some other traditions, the FWBO firmly emphasizes stages or levels on the spiritual path. This is seen in the categories of membership (Friends, Mitras and Order members), the progressive teaching of different forms of meditation and the progressive experiential commitment of levels of Going for Refuge.

The movement has remained controversial from the time of its origins in the 1960s counterculture, and has been criticized for being eclectic, doctrinaire, intolerant, male-dominated, anti-family and sexually permissive. Much of the criticism is unfair, though its persistence is partly due to the FWBO's self-imposed isolation from other Buddhist organizations. In recent years there has been a willingness to engage with other Buddhists, and this may allay some of the suspicions.

The role of Sangharakshita as founder, teacher and leader has been crucial to the development and character of the movement. In a sense the FWBO rests on his personal experience, teachings and practice of Buddhism. His own choices of Buddhist teachings, of meditational and devotional practice, of ethical precepts and personal behaviour, have become those of Friends, Mitras and Order members since the 1960s. As a new leadership takes over, the emphasis of the movement may change quite rapidly.

Opinions about the FWBO often remain polarized. Observers may perceive an aggressive approach, a distorted Buddhism and personal misconduct, while insiders may experience a confident inspiration, a link with the essential Dharma and deep spiritual friendship. The rather doctrinaire approach seen in the writings of Sangharakshita and Subhuti may no longer be reflected in the attitudes of individual members. According to Waterhouse (2001: 146), the FWBO has overcome its early reputation to become 'a major player in terms of a voice for Buddhism in the UK', and because of its active engagement with the media, it is often found 'acting as an unofficial representative of UK Buddhism'. Vishvapani (2004) argued that people engage with Buddhism in different ways in contemporary Britain, and may well 'draw on the Buddhist tradition as a whole', so that the FWBO may be seen as 'an accommodation between the cultural context and traditionally-derived Buddhist forms'. It remains to be seen whether the FWBO and other Buddhist traditions in Britain can engage with each other on equal terms as spiritual friends.

10

BUDDHISM IN BRITAIN AND BRITISH BUDDHISM

This final chapter will attempt an overview of the subject in four sections. Earlier chapters will be summarized, to draw together information on the historical development of Buddhism in Britain and on the seven largest traditions. Each dimension will be considered in turn, looking at different aspects of teaching and practice to build up a thematic picture of adaptations from Asian Buddhism. The overall extent and diversity of such adaptations will then be assessed. Finally, some comments will be offered about Buddhism in Britain as a whole and whether any distinctive forms of 'British Buddhism' are emerging.

A century of Buddhism in Britain

In Victorian Britain, Christianity became both more diverse and increasingly private, and Buddhism was sometimes viewed as a romantic oriental tradition, whose noble founder and moral precepts had parallels in the New Testament. However, its supposed atheism, lack of an immortal soul and doctrine of rebirth remained problematic, anti-Catholic prejudice fuelled suspicion of monastic ritual and Mahāyāna practices, and there was little understanding of meditation. Even without these difficulties, Victorian conventions meant that 'an overt commitment was socially difficult' (Almond, 1988: 36).

From 1907 the early Buddhist Society was an uneasy mixture of scholars and would-be practitioners, focussing on Theravāda Buddhism with a mainly intellectual or ethical interest. As church attendance declined after the First World War, the number of Buddhists grew slowly, with gradually increasing personal involvement, though the first meditation group was only formed in 1930 and still had an intellectual slant. Even by the Second World War, English Buddhists were usually seen as heathens or eccentrics.

The 1950s saw the first Buddhist Summer Schools, influential books on Buddhism by Humphreys and Conze and several new lay groups. There was increased interest in different schools, and from the 1960s onwards Buddhism expanded rapidly as part of Britain's growing religious pluralism, with monasteries and Buddhist centres in Theravāda, Tibetan, Zen and Western traditions. The Buddhist Society's central role declined as lay groups expanded from a dozen or so in 1961 to almost 1,000 in 2001, in over 30 different sub-traditions, with particularly strong growth from the early 1980s onwards. As well as a deeper commitment to spiritual practice, some lay Buddhists became increasingly involved in the therapeutic and social activities of engaged Buddhism.

Within this complex pattern, the Forest Sangha may appear as a conservative Theravāda monasticism, with traditional teachings, ethics, meditation and devotional practice, rural monasteries with Thai iconography and a social structure little adapted to modern urban Britain. However, there have been significant adaptations, including a new nuns' order, new *anagārika* and *upāsikā* roles as part of enhanced lay participation, chanting in English as well as Pali and an imaginative attempt at British Buddhist architecture; and lesser changes such as the downplaying of cosmological elements, warmer monastic clothing and a simplified etiquette. Monastics and lay people may sometimes have differing perceptions of their respective roles. Adaptations have been made as pragmatic adjustments to life in Britain, rather than conscious attempts at cultural integration and are seen as largely peripheral to the quest for liberation.

Each dimension of the Samatha Trust shows evidence of traditional Theravāda Buddhist teaching and practice, and with Pali chanting, textual study and cosmological elements it may appear even more traditional than the Forest Sangha. However, it is a wholly lay movement with no residential communities and an ethics reflecting mutual trust as well as individual observance. With meditation teachers (often academics or schoolteachers) offering individual guidance in weekly classes, group discussion and imaginative exploration of Buddhist teachings, its flavour is distinctively British.

The Serene Reflection Meditation (SRM) tradition is firmly based in Japanese Sōtō Zen Buddhism, following traditional teachings, *zazen* meditation and monastic ceremonial and social organization. However, there has been a conscious attempt to avoid copying Japanese culture and to establish a British Buddhist identity. This includes English texts and music, a return to traditional celibate monasticism, gender equality, an enhanced role for lay training which emphasizes meditation, and new roles of postulant and lay minister. All these were authorized by Rev. Master Jiyu, whose own influential and sometimes controversial experiences are becoming less prominent.

Sōka Gakkai International-UK (SGI-UK) has been a controversial lay tradition in Britain, where the chanting of *Nam-myōhō-renge-kyō* replaces silent meditation, and the exclusive emphasis on Nichiren's teaching appears to lack a critical approach. With no formal moral code, the legitimation of chanting for personal wishes and complete separation from the Nichiren Shōshū priesthood, this may appear as a highly adapted organization, and its bold, positive and evangelical approach contrasts strongly with more traditional Buddhist movements in Britain. However, SGI-UK is relatively little adapted from its Japanese-based parent movement, whose own adaptation of Nichiren Buddhism is rather beyond our scope. As with other traditions, committed SGI-UK members clearly wish both to transform their own lives and to help others, and any exclusivism may be in the tone rather than the content of the movement's teachings.

The Karma Kagyu school aims to preserve traditional Tibetan teaching, practice and culture, passing on meditation and devotional practices in a monastic context, as well as artistic traditions, under the guidance of ethnic Tibetan teachers. Part of this tradition is a flexible approach to individuals and to new situations, which has led to a number of significant adaptations at Samye Ling. These include temporary ordination for up to 3 years, access to full ordination for nuns, a partially secularized Buddhist centre with lay residents, some Western lay teachers, many visitors and a businesslike approach to funding. As well as meditation retreats, there is a wide range of humanitarian, therapeutic and environmental activities. Presenting teachings in the most appropriate way for Westerners is not seen as an adaptation, as it reflects an individual approach which is traditional in Tibet.

The New Kadampa Tradition (NKT) has attracted both strong support and widespread criticism. It emphasizes an unbroken Tibetan Gelug lineage, yet has no Tibetan followers and claims not to be part of Tibetan Buddhism. Its teachings and practices appear traditional, including the emphasis on Geshe Kelsang as a spiritual guide and the importance of study programmes, though the worship of Dorje Shugden distances it from other schools. Simplified teachings and practices, and English translations, are seen as a skilful re-presentation of traditional elements, rather than a narrowing down or adaptation of the tradition. Like Samye Ling, the Manjushri centre has lay residents, many visitors and businesslike finance, though NKT teachers are almost all ordained. The movement has had a more exclusive, proselytizing and expansionist approach, though it is sensitive to criticism and may be becoming more open to other traditions.

The Friends of the Western Buddhist Order (FWBO) has made a conscious attempt to westernize Buddhism, presenting teachings and practices appropriate for modern Britain. The Order is seen as neither monastic nor lay, emphasizing personal commitment rather than lifestyle, and the pattern of urban centres, right livelihood businesses and single-sex communities is quite unlike more traditional movements. Much of this centres on Sangharakshita as founder, teacher, leader and role model, and the FWBO rests on his personal choice of teachings, practices and lifestyle. He has drawn on various elements from Theravāda and Tibetan teaching and practice, and presented them as an essential Buddhism shorn of cultural accretions. The movement thus claims that its teaching and practice are fully traditional, but of course the conscious choosing and combining of elements from different schools is highly adaptive. Like SGI-UK and the NKT, the FWBO has been a controversial movement, and has been criticized (often unfairly) for being eclectic, doctrinaire, intolerant, male dominated, anti-family and sexually permissive. Aware that its relative isolation has allowed such criticism to persist, the FWBO is beginning to interact more positively with other Buddhist traditions.

Dimensions and adaptation

The individual sections of the last seven chapters could be read horizontally as well as vertically, looking first at the practice dimension of the seven traditions, then the doctrinal dimension and so on. The complex process of adaptation set against the background of different forms of Asian Buddhism may not lend itself to simple conclusions, especially as neither minimal nor complete adaptation is normally found. Moreover, the order in which the seven dimensions have been described broadly reflects their varying significance in British Buddhism, so that relatively small adaptations in an important dimension may be more significant than larger changes in a less prominent area. It may be helpful, however, to summarize adaptation within each dimension, before considering whether an overall pattern may be discerned.

As well as being the most important, the practice dimension is probably the least adapted from Asian forms of Buddhism. Meditation practices appear little altered from their parent traditions: the structured approaches of Samatha Trust and NKT meditation are relatively minor adaptations, and even the FWBO draws on several traditional meditation techniques, though combining them in an adaptive way. The most significant adaptation here is the greater involvement of lay people in meditation. Chanting and devotional activities are sometimes rather more adapted, with four traditions chanting partly or wholly in English, and two of these (the SRM and NKT) adopting Western musical styles. Meditation retreats and courses for lay members could also be seen as a Western adaptation, particularly where the programmes extend to include broader cultural events (SGI-UK and FWBO) or therapeutic courses (Karma Kagyu).

The doctrinal dimension is also relatively little adapted, with traditional teachings frequently emphasized. Changes are usually confined to presentation rather than content, with the Forest Sangha downplaying teachings on cosmology and rebirth, the NKT adopting a more structured approach than traditional Gelug Buddhism and the FWBO again combining elements from several traditions. However, the development of lay study groups in all but the SRM and Karma Kagyu traditions is an important adaptation, particularly the study programmes of the NKT and SGI-UK (though the latter is a Japanese rather than British adaptation).

The narrative dimension is perhaps a little more adapted overall than the practice and doctrinal dimensions. All seven organizations regard traditional narratives about the Buddha as important, and also perhaps further narratives about bodhisattvas and the great teachers of their own tradition. This is often extended to include contemporary figures, whose narratives may sometimes be controversial. The three 'new Buddhist movements' of SGI-UK, the NKT and FWBO also have important newer adaptive narratives concerning the separation from their Asian roots, though again the SGI-UK narrative stems from Japan rather than Britain.

It is almost impossible to discern any meaningful adaptation in the important but problematic experiential dimension, due to its highly personal nature and the wide variety of emotional responses shown by individuals. While people are certainly attracted to different traditions for a variety of reasons, even here there is no clear pattern. Perhaps all one can say is that these responses reflect the experience of those with a British rather than an Asian cultural and psychological background.

The ethical dimension often shows traditional moral codes modified to a greater or lesser extent by Western liberal ideas. The five or ten precepts adopted by all traditions except SGI-UK are usually seen as guidelines rather than specific prohibitions, especially by lay Buddhists, and there is often less distance between the monastic and lay communities in Britain than there is in Asia. Apart from monastic celibacy, there is a common ethical code in the Karma Kagyu, NKT and SRM traditions, and even the conservative Forest Sangha shows some flexibility in interpreting the *Vinaya* rules. Within SRM, the Order of Buddhist Contemplatives (OBC) has reverted to a celibate monasticism no longer practised in Japanese Sōtō Zen, perhaps reflecting Western views. SGI-UK's teaching that chanting and correct understanding of karmic connections lead naturally to compassionate behaviour, without the need for ethical rules, follows that of Sōka Gakkai International (SGI), and so is not a British adaptation. The FWBO's highly flexible interpretation of a traditional moral code reflects the movement's origins in the 1960s counterculture, but its context is seen (at least from within the movement) as one of exercising compassion rather than justifying indulgence.

The most widespread adaptation is seen within the social dimension. All but the Samatha Trust and SGI-UK have Buddhist communities, but with important differences from traditional monasticism. New monastic and lay roles have been established, such as the Forest Sangha's nuns, *anagārikas* and *upāsikās*, OBC postulants and lay ministers, and Karma Kagyu temporary ordination, while FWBO Order members are seen as neither monastic nor lay. The Tibetan traditions and FWBO have developed different forms of residential communities or Buddhist centres where ordained and other committed followers live, work and practise together.

There is relatively little gender bias in much of British Buddhism, with both women and men becoming respected ordained and lay teachers. However, this is some way from the 'post-patriarchal Buddhism' envisaged by Gross (1994: 28). Most senior teachers are still men, and there remains a sense of discrimination against women in both the Forest Sangha and the FWBO, which might be seen as a failure to adapt.

Most traditions have used Western commercial methods to some extent to support their activities, though the Forest Sangha, Samatha Trust and SRM still rely on donations rather than charges for their meditation retreats, and all Forest Sangha literature is distributed free of charge. Unlike the more traditional movements, the three 'new Buddhist movements' of SGI-UK, NKT and FWBO have all used various methods of proselytizing to develop their organizations. Finally, the presence of Theravāda, Tibetan, Zen and other Buddhist groups in Britain brings a new situation of proximity not found in Asian countries, so the way these groups relate to each other – or sometimes fail to relate to each other – could be seen as a further adaptation.

The artistic dimension again shows a range of adaptation. The Karma Kagyu tradition aims to preserve Tibetan culture, arts and crafts, and SGI-UK follows a Japanese iconographical style in the *gohonzon*. The Forest Sangha and Samatha Trust also have a broadly traditional approach, though with some innovation, most visible in the Amaravati temple. SRM uses a mixture of Asian and Western artistic styles, and both the NKT and FWBO are more consciously aiming for a westernized Buddhist iconography, though this is far from fully developed as yet and still relies on many traditional elements.

Looking across the seven traditions, the Forest Sangha and Karma Kagyu appear very close to their Asian parent traditions, though with significant adaptations to their new British context. Although the Samatha Trust is a lay organization founded in Britain, it is often similar to Thai Theravāda Buddhism. The SRM tradition has made a rather more conscious effort to adapt some elements of Japanese Sōtō Zen practice for use in a Western context. SGI-UK, the NKT and FWBO appear to have undergone a more extensive process of adaptation. The substantial differences between these three new Buddhist movements and the other four traditions may suggest a polarization between the more traditional organizations and the three more adapted Buddhist movements which are the largest in Britain today. However, all three retain substantial traditional elements in most or all of the seven dimensions, and in the case of SGI-UK, the adaptation process has taken place mainly in Japan rather than Britain.

The overall pattern here is a highly complex one, and not easily summarized. Batchelor's (1994: 337) idea of a 'spectrum of adaptation' in Western Buddhism, ranging from the minimal change of preserving traditions to the wholesale innovation of abandoning traditions as cultural hindrances, seems at first to apply neatly to Buddhism in Britain. We might conclude that the Forest Sangha has adapted as little as possible, the FWBO has created a genuinely new form of Buddhism, and other movements may be placed somewhere between these two poles. However, Waterhouse (1997: 26) argued that this model oversimplifies the picture by not reflecting the range of adaptation within each tradition. We have seen, for example, that the Forest Sangha has made significant adaptations, including the development of the nuns' order and the use of English chanting, which show a pragmatic attitude to change rather than a wish for minimal adaptation. Similarly, the FWBO has drawn widely on existing Theravāda and Tibetan teaching and meditation practice, and can hardly be said to have abandoned tradition completely.

Perhaps it might be helpful to think instead of a spectrum of adaptation within each dimension. This might run from the Forest Sangha's *Vinaya* ethics to SGI's personalized morality or from Karma Kagyu's preservation of Tibetan culture to the FWBO's westernized iconography. However, each dimension has a different pattern and range of adaptation within it and also a different importance within each tradition. There is the further complication of variable adaptation within a single dimension of a particular tradition. For example, the SRM's practice dimension includes both traditional Sōtō Zen ceremonial and adapted English language and music, the FWBO's doctrinal dimension includes traditional teachings from different schools and the innovative practice of consciously combining them, Forest Sangha ethics include the fixed *Vinaya* rules and a flexible approach to their interpretation, and the NKT's social dimension includes a monastic tradition and enthusiastic proselytizing. The pattern is too complex for the model: even the combination of seven traditions with seven dimensions does not seem to give a fully detailed picture of how Buddhism has adapted in Britain. While the dimensional model has been extremely useful, we need to move beyond it to draw conclusions about British Buddhism as a whole.

Diversity in British Buddhism

Most of the specific questions raised at the beginning of Chapter 1 have been covered during the examination of the seven traditions and brought together by the dimensional analysis in the previous section. The more general question of how far Buddhism in Britain has adapted from its Asian roots – and whether we can see the seeds or shoots of a distinctive 'British Buddhism' – involves moving beyond individual traditions and dimensions to take a broader view. This will include looking at the influence of teachers and other authority sources, lay participation and new Buddhist movements.

Perhaps adaptation might be seen as a process of discarding or downplaying elements and emphases which are felt to be unnecessary. Some British Buddhists, particularly but not exclusively within the FWBO, claim to be able to distinguish between the essential elements of Buddhism and the peripheral elements of Asian culture, so that this 'essential Buddhism' may be separated from its cultural accretions and transplanted into Western society without them.

There are several difficulties here. While there are elements of teaching and practice common to most Buddhist schools, each one also has unique elements it regards as important. Identifying the common elements as 'essential Buddhism' implies that traditions have somehow gone astray, rather than simply developed in different ways. The question of whether the 'essence' of a religion – should such a thing exist – can be extracted from one culture and implanted in another is deeply problematic. Buddhist texts, philosophy and ethics have been unconsciously reinterpreted by supposedly objective scholars, and of course there are many texts, varying philosophical views and even different ethical codes to choose from.

It is difficult to see how the more personal areas of meditation and devotional practice might successfully be separated from the experience of individual Asian Buddhists, who are themselves part of a particular culture. Moreover, those who attempt to define an 'essential Buddhism' are implicitly claiming to be able to set aside their *own* cultural values, in a way which Asian Buddhists have somehow failed to do. Westerners are no more likely than Asians to be able to step out of their background to form disinterested judgements: setting aside one's own cultural values in order to define an 'essential Buddhism' seems almost impossible. There is also a certain irony in looking for an 'essence' in Buddhism, since the Theravāda sees the five *khandhas* or 'factors of personality' as completely 'empty' of a self, while the Mahāyāna describes all phenomena as *śūnya* or 'empty' of essence. Perhaps the real 'essence' of Buddhism is its teaching that there is no 'essence' in anything.

The question of how the authority to distinguish between essential and peripheral elements is acquired and recognized leads into the wider area of authority as a whole. Waterhouse (1997: 219, 237) has identified texts, lineage, teachers and personal experience as four sources of authority in British Buddhism, though she found that different groups acknowledged different sources and related to authority in various ways. Each school acknowledges the authority of their own tradition's texts (with the FWBO drawing on texts from several schools), though they may approach them in different ways, perhaps as devotional scriptures or as practical instructions on behaviour or as documents to be explored critically. A few might take a literalistic interpretation of their scriptures, but most practitioners would be able to make some provisional distinctions between the Buddha's teaching and its Asian context.

Most schools also see lineage as an important source of authority, though again in rather different ways. Monastic traditions usually have authorized ordination lineages, though the Tibetan traditions tend to emphasize their teaching lineages instead, and the OBC has its Zen transmission lineage. Even the lay Samatha Trust and SGI-UK traditions have informal but authorized lineages of teachers or leaders.

Within these various kinds of lineages, teachers are often crucial in deciding on adaptations, particularly where an individual is the only link with the Asian parent religion. Much depends on the nature of the teacher's authority, and the transparency with which adaptations are made. The Forest Sangha remains a branch of Thai monasticism, and Ajahn Sumedho has discussed proposed adaptations with both Thai and Western monastics. The Japanese Sōtō Zen tradition authorized Rōshi Kennett to take the tradition to the West, and her master encouraged her to adapt it to Western culture, though her adaptations were sometimes idiosyncratic and not without controversy. The NKT and FWBO also claim an authentic teaching lineage, though their leaders have become separated from their ordination tradition. Geshe Kelsang's authority to promote a simplified form of Tibetan Buddhism no longer stems from the Gelug school, and Sangharakshita's authority to distinguish between 'essential Buddhism' and its cultural accretions has not been legitimized by the Theravāda tradition. Instead their followers have invested these two leaders with a charismatic *personal* authority to teach, ordain and make adaptations, while still claiming that their teaching and practice is fully traditional.

All traditions acknowledge the authority of personal experience. Waterhouse (1997: 239) found that individuals may feel a tension between this and the 'traditional authorities' of texts, lineage and teachers in their particular school.

Kay (2004: 19) argued that Buddhist groups develop 'consciously worked-out policies and methods' for adaptation, in order to become 'comprehensible and relevant', but this may underestimate the pragmatic or experimental development of most organizations, often responding to members who feel that adaptation is moving too slowly or too fast, or that specific changes conflict with their personal values. There may also be a tension between the level of personal involvement expected by the organization and that which members are prepared to make. Centralized organizations may expect conformity and full commitment, while others may be more accommodating towards different views and levels of practice.

We have seen increased lay participation in every area of Buddhist practice, from meditation retreats and textual study to ethical commitment and new social structures. The Samatha Trust and SGI are completely lay movements, SRM emphasizes monastic and lay training as two equal paths and Samye Ling and Manjushri have mainly lay communities, albeit with a monastic core. Ordination may be seen as the norm for committed followers in the NKT and FWBO, though WBO members are not celibate and are seen as neither monastics nor lay people. The Forest Sangha remains the most traditional, with a clear separation between monastics and lay supporters, though even here the *anāgārika* role and the *upāsikā* movement are important innovations. Smaller groups include both monastic and lay traditions, but the many unaffiliated Buddhists are of course all lay people.

This does not mean, as Coleman (2001: 13) suggests, that 'the fundamental distinction between monk and layperson is swept away': the description by Gross (1994: 24) of Western Buddhism as 'less influenced by the dichotomy between monks and laypeople' (1994: 24) seems closer to the situation in contemporary Britain. The Pali Canon describes prominent and spiritually advanced lay disciples even in the Buddha's lifetime (see Bluck, 2002), and the essential prerequisite for spiritual progress has always been commitment rather than ordination.

*   *   *

Three of our seven traditions have been characterized as 'new Buddhist movements'. Bell (2000: 398) described the FWBO, SGI-UK and the NKT as 'closely bounded, hierarchical organizations' with 'an undisguised commitment to recruitment and expansion' and which point to 'a new direction in British Buddhism'. Kay (2004: 25) refers to them as 'the three main Buddhist movements operating in Britain' whose dominant position has concerned 'members of the wider British Buddhist community'. All three have been seen as controversial, and they have common features which seem to distinguish them from more traditional organizations.

Each of these movements has experienced a crucial separation from its Asian roots. The FWBO was formed in 1967 after Sangharakshita left the Hampstead Vihara and moved away from Theravāda monasticism, though his earlier Triyāna approach meant that the new movement drew on several traditions. Geshe Kelsang has claimed that the NKT continues to represent the pure Kadampa teaching lineage, but its formation in 1991 was a complete separation from its mainstream Gelug roots, and the movement no longer sees itself as part of Tibetan Buddhism. Following disagreements between SGI and the Japanese Nichiren Shōshū priesthood, the worldwide lay membership was expelled in 1991, leading to wholesale reorganization, including the revalidation of *gohonzons* which could no longer be issued by priests.

All three movements have grown rapidly into large organizations: SGI-UK now claims 4,000 active members, with others also attending their 300 groups; the FWBO has more than 650 Order members in Britain, over 2,000 core members and perhaps 5,000 people involved altogether in 80 centres and groups, and the NKT has attracted up to 3,000 active members (again with others also attending) and set up 180 centres and groups. They are certainly the three largest and most publicized Buddhist movements in Britain, but each of these represents less than one-tenth of the total convert Buddhist community, and even the highest combined estimate of 15,000 members is only one quarter of the 60,000 'white Buddhists' in Britain.

These new Buddhist movements have all attracted hostile criticism from the media and are sometimes even referred to as 'cults'. They have been described disparagingly as evangelistic, dogmatic, exclusive and intolerant, though the accuracy of such attacks – and the motivation behind them – is sometimes open to question. Unlike most Buddhist organizations, all three movements aim to attract followers through various forms of proselytizing, though they would certainly characterize this as a wish to share the Dharma rather than 'conversion and empire-building'. They have all sometimes adopted dogmatic views, including claims to represent the true form of Buddhism and a certain intolerance towards other traditions, but these are common features in relatively young religious organizations. It may be more helpful to describe them in Barker's (1999: 20) terms as enthusiastic, with firm beliefs, an urgent message, commitment to a particular lifestyle and perhaps a 'charismatic leadership'. These are all characteristics common to many New Religious Movements (NRMs), and all susceptible to change as the movement grows and matures. Despite some recent attempts to engage in dialogue with others, however, SGI-UK, the NKT and the FWBO may continue to be regarded with some suspicion. A British Buddhism that wishes to appear non-sectarian and tolerant – and indeed has often been so – may still react strongly against any organization accused of being otherwise.

We have seen that all three movements have teachings and practices which other Buddhists would recognize and historical links to traditional Buddhist schools. The enthusiasm and energy of their members shows genuine commitment, and there is no clear dividing line between them and the more traditional Buddhist movements in Britain. If they point to 'a new direction in British Buddhism', they are not alone in doing so.

Conclusions and characteristics

During the twentieth century, Buddhism in Britain grew from a small group of scholars and gentlemen to a substantial community practising Buddhism in many traditions, either in one of a thousand local groups or on their own. While only one in 400 people in Britain call themselves Buddhists, the total of 150,000 is over half the size of the British Jewish community, and while the convert or 'white' Buddhist community of 60,000 represents only 1 person in a 1,000, it is more than twice as large as the Quaker church (Bluck, 2004; www. quaker.org.uk). The wide appeal of books by the Dalai Lama, Thich Nhat Hanh, Sangharakshita, Geshe Kelsang and others shows that Buddhism also has an influence well beyond the community of practising Buddhists.

This expansion has taken place in three overlapping phases, with early academic interest followed by small numbers of lay practitioners and a more rapid growth of monastic and lay centres in different traditions since the 1960s, partly influenced by Asian immigration. As Baumann (2002: 85–93) has shown, this reflects the pattern of Buddhism's development in Germany, France and other European countries, including the arrival of Theravāda, then Zen and finally Tibetan traditions. This is quite different from American Buddhism where Zen came first, followed by Tibetan Buddhism and then Theravāda insight meditation and where convert Buddhists still 'owe an immense debt to Asian-immigrant teachers' (Seager, 2002: 116–17).

Today's global communications and rapid change contrast starkly with traditional societies, and Coleman (2001: 217) may be justified in suggesting that Western Buddhism's story is now 'told in decades, not centuries'. Traditions in Britain have shown different phases of expansion and consolidation, one now appearing more dynamic or more static than another. Many young people who joined new traditions in the 1960s or 1970s are now approaching retirement. Two of the founders or original leaders of those traditions died in the 1990s, and the others are almost all in their seventies. Traditions will soon have to deal with a crucial period where the leadership passes on to younger members, with a different background and fewer personal links to the Asian parent tradition.

Returning to the judgements and predictions of the authors quoted at the beginning, we have seen that Batchelor's 'spectrum of adaptation' is rather too broad a model for British Buddhism. Instead of the single dominant and syncretic 'English form of Buddhism' which Humphreys (1956: 6; 1968: 80) predicted, there seems to be only the 'increasing diversification of the British Buddhist landscape' described by Kay (2004: xiii). The extent and character of adaptations in Buddhist traditions has varied widely, partly due to the 'different authority sources' examined by Waterhouse (1997: 240), and her conclusion that 'for the foreseeable future, no one group or person can represent British Buddhism' seems irrefutable.

Bell (2000: 398–9) concluded that Buddhism in Britain is both 'extremely diverse and prone to sectarianism', though some practitioners have looked beyond introspective meditation groups 'to reach outward to establish their position within the wider religious landscape'. With perhaps 30 monastic or lay traditions (some of them far from monolithic) and many independent practitioners, British Buddhism is certainly diverse. However, this has not usually led to widespread sectarianism, at least not in the bigotry of 'excessive attachment to a particular sect' (*OED*), though the allegiance of some British Buddhists is firmly centred on their own movement. Others are indeed reaching outward, perhaps not to 'establish their position', but rather to bring monastics and lay people together, to forge links with other Buddhists or with Christian monastics, and to participate in the therapeutic, educational or social activities of engaged Buddhism.

The attraction of specific Buddhist movements has already been considered, but the general appeal of Buddhism may be due to broader factors. The emphasis on practice and related experience rather than belief has already been mentioned, and Kay (2004: 5) has referred to Buddhism's contrast with 'those elements of British culture and religion with which people have become disillusioned or dissatisfied'. The decline of mainstream Christian churches during the twentieth century is often associated with their emphasis on correct belief and an institutional inflexibility which made them seem increasingly conservative. Puttick (1992: 6) has described British Buddhists as 'active seekers' who have been 'disappointed by the lack of a living mystical tradition' in Christianity. Of course only a minority of those disappointed with Christianity choose to become Buddhists, and many 'convert' Buddhists in Britain have grown up with no Christian background. Buddhist organizations may also attract new followers by encouraging self-reliance, explaining specific methods of practice, and offering personal spiritual guidance from experienced practitioners, in a context where neither theistic belief nor creedal assent are expected.

However, these are still general features, and only tentative suggestions can be offered about Buddhism's specific appeal in Britain. Batchelor's (1994: xiii) conclusion that contemporary Western Buddhists may still romanticize about Nirvana, treat Buddhism as an academic discipline or ignore elements they see as 'alien features of Asian culture' certainly rings true in a British context. The lure of the mysterious East, a scholarly and reserved approach, with personal (rather than institutional) choices about what to retain or discard, all appear characteristic of a British attitude towards spiritual practice in a materialistic age. It is hardly surprising that British Buddhists have tended to be middle-class and well educated, though the emphasis of new Buddhist movements on urban centres may be encouraging a wider membership.

The social structure of British Buddhist organizations may also appeal to people who wish to engage with religious practice in different ways. In all seven large traditions, the casual visitor may become a regular attender, a committed member and perhaps a group leader or even a teacher, while still involved in family life and secular work. If they wish to become ordained, there are often innovative liminal roles which allow them to live as community members and so test their readiness before making a lifetime commitment.

It seems likely that traditional forms of Buddhism will continue to attract followers in the future, adapting in different ways to British spiritual and social needs. Their monks and nuns will continue as celibate renunciates, teachers and exemplars, though with perhaps 500 of them in all (half of these in the NKT), they form rather less than 1 per cent of the convert Buddhist community. The newer forms of self-consciously Western Buddhism may become less controversial as they begin to engage with the wider Buddhist community, and the role of FWBO Order members (a little over 1 per cent of the convert Buddhist community) could be crucial here. Buddhist ideas will probably continue to percolate into British culture, partly due to a positive media image, and sometimes interwoven with New Age and other philosophies.

Some aspects of Buddhism in Britain might be compared to the situation in Chinese Buddhism, where different traditions borrowed from each other, with fuzzy boundaries between them. Other aspects are more like Japanese Buddhism, where different traditions 'had harder edges than in other Buddhist lands, and became more like separate sects' (Harvey, 1990: 163). There is no simple polarity here between traditional organizations and new Buddhist movements, and Buddhism in Britain may well come to follow either the Chinese or the Japanese model. Only when the majority of British Buddhists find a common English vocabulary for Buddhist teaching and practice, a group of wholly Western teachers and full independence from Asian Buddhist organizations, will a genuinely British Buddhism emerge. Even in a period of such rapid change, this seems many years away.

Meanwhile, there is considerable scope for further research on Buddhism in Britain, including the Tibetan Gelug school, the Community of Interbeing and 20 or more smaller traditions. Relatively little is known about the social and religious background of Buddhist converts, their relationship to Asian Buddhist communities and the significance of unaffiliated Buddhists and those for whom Buddhism forms only part of their spiritual practice.

* * *

Although we have already presented many conclusions in summarizing each dimension of each tradition, an overall picture still remains elusive. The interaction between dimensions, the differences between traditions, varying levels of commitment and differing attitudes towards adaptation and authority, all combine to produce a complex matrix of teaching and practice and organizational development, where common features seem increasingly difficult to trace.

Perhaps a philosophical analogy may help here. Ludwig Wittgenstein (1889–1951) (1967: 31–2) suggested that various types of language use had no essential common feature, but were instead 'related to one another in many different ways', and different forms of 'games' revealed 'a complicated network of similarities overlapping and criss-crossing', which he famously characterized as 'family resemblances'. Family members often look alike, not because they share a *single* defining feature, but because they each have *some* of the 'family resemblances' which allow both relatives and others to recognize them. This analogy may help us construct a list of common features or tendencies in British Buddhism, still using the dimensional model and reflecting the relative importance of each dimension. These 'family resemblances' may be listed here as:

- traditional silent meditation
- largely traditional devotional activities
- traditional teachings
- some emphasis on textual study
- a programme of retreats and courses
- ancient and contemporary narratives
- a common ethical code for all members
- an important teacher–pupil relationship
- mostly Western teachers
- increased lay participation

Each of these ten characteristics has a different emphasis in each Buddhist organization. Traditional silent meditation is a central part of the practice in six of the seven traditions. The Forest Sangha's Theravāda meditation, the SRM's Zen meditation, and Karma Kagyu's Tibetan meditation all appear unaltered from their respective Asian 'parent' schools, and both Samatha Trust and NKT meditation are only a little adapted in their structure. Even the FWBO, which draws on both Theravāda and Tibetan traditions, still uses traditional silent meditation as its central practice.

The exception here is SGI-UK which concentrates instead on chanting, and indeed all seven traditions use chanting and often other traditional devotional activities as an important aspect of their practice. The Samatha Trust, SGI-UK and Karma Kagyu seem wholly traditional here, chanting in the language of their respective parent schools. The Forest Sangha chant in English as well as Pali and the FWBO, SRM and NKT wholly in English, the last two using their own adapted musical style. Further activities include bowing and making offerings (in all seven traditions) and deity visualization in the Tibetan traditions and amongst ordained WBO members.

Six of the seven organizations use traditional teachings drawn directly from their Asian parent school, usually with little or no adaptation. Different teachings may perhaps be emphasized for a British audience, with the Forest Sangha downplaying cosmology and rebirth, for example, and the order and method of presenting teachings may be tailored to those at different levels of spiritual practice, particularly in the Tibetan traditions. The FWBO still uses traditional teachings from several schools, but has consciously combined them into a new body of Buddhist teaching seen as particularly appropriate in a modern Western society such as Britain.

Most traditions have some emphasis on formal textual study. SGI-UK and the NKT both have organized study programmes followed by committed members, concentrating exclusively on the writings of Nichiren and President Ikeda (SGI) and Geshe Kelsang (NKT). Forest Sangha monastics regularly study the *Vinaya* together on rains retreats, and some lay groups study Pali texts in translation. Samatha Trust groups often study texts together, usually but not exclusively from the Pali canon, and both Theravāda traditions include a few scholars and students of Pali. FWBO members are encouraged to study specific texts and Sangharakshita's commentaries in both classes and ordination courses. The SRM and Karma Kagyu traditions have little or no formal study, though of course individual monastics and lay people here and elsewhere may study texts on their own.

All seven organizations offer courses for their members, some of which are open to the public. Six organizations offer meditation retreats, ranging from introductory weekends to longer retreats for experienced meditators. Tibetan retreats are sometimes focussed on particular Buddhas or bodhisattvas, and Samye Ling runs both a 1-year and a 4-year retreat. SGI-UK runs training courses for their members, who are also invited for working weeks at Taplow Court. Some course programmes extend beyond conventional Buddhist practice: Samye Ling runs therapeutic courses and both SGI-UK and the FWBO sponsor cultural events.

Each tradition values the Buddha's life story, though further narratives are also often seen as important. The Theravāda traditions focus mainly on stories from the Pali canon, while the Japanese and Tibetan traditions may add the narratives of both bodhisattvas and later teachers in their particular school. These narratives often extend to include stories of contemporary figures such as Ajahn Chah, Rev. Master Jiyu, President Ikeda, Akong Rinpoche, Geshe Kelsang and Sangharakshita. All these figures are seen as important exemplars in their tradition, though with roles ranging from a spiritual friend to a founder and inspirational leader. The new Buddhist movements of SGI-UK, the NKT and FWBO have further important contemporary narratives used to explain or reinterpret their Asian roots.

Six traditions have formal ethical codes, usually based on the Five Precepts and often seen as guidelines rather than fixed rules. Apart from monastic celibacy, these codes are usually common to all members, with only minor differences between monastic and lay practice. All SRM members follow Zen's Ten Great Precepts; all Karma Kagyu practitioners follow the Five Golden Rules, using them as root vows in their monastic code, and all NKT followers aim to avoid the ten non-virtuous actions, which are elaborated in their ordination vows. In the FWBO the Ten Precepts undertaken at ordination build on the Five Precepts followed by all members, with an emphasis throughout on seeing them as 'Positive Precepts' rather than moral prohibitions. In the two lay movements, Samatha Trust members all follow the Five Precepts, and although SGI-UK has no formal ethical code, chanting is said to lead naturally to compassionate and altruistic behaviour, and this applies equally to all members. Only the Forest Sangha has different ethical codes for different groups: lay people follow the Five Precepts, *anagārikas* take the Eight Precepts, nuns take the Ten Precepts (different from those in the SRM and FWBO) and have their own innovative monastic code, while monks follow the full 227 *Vinaya* rules.

Almost all these organizations have some form of teacher–pupil relationship between leaders and members, though its significance and character are widely varied. Samatha Trust members learn to meditate under the direct supervision of a teacher, and this 'reporting' relationship continues for experienced practitioners and even for teachers themselves. The master–disciple relationship is crucial for OBC monks and nuns, leading to the 'Dharma transmission' which recognizes the disciple's commitment, and lay people also often look to Rev. Master Daishin and other senior monastics as teachers, though usually in a more general sense. FWBO members frequently rely on the 'Kalyana Mitra' relationship for spiritual guidance, and WBO members also establish a close relationship with their preceptor at ordination. Both Tibetan traditions rely on the role of the guru or spiritual guide. In the Karma Kagyu tradition this involves a personal relationship with a senior teacher, seen as essential to learn meditation and devotional practices. NKT members are usually taught by a more junior local teacher, though direct spiritual guidance from Geshe Kelsang – normally through his books rather than personal contact – is also seen as highly important. Similarly in SGI-UK, members may approach a local leader for advice, but usually regard President Ikeda as their spiritual leader, his advice again usually given in his writings rather than in person, except for senior members. No such personal teaching relationship exists in the Forest Sangha, though many would look to Ajahn Sumedho as their teacher, and both monastics and lay people may ask advice from monks and nuns when they need it.

Six traditions have mostly Western teachers, though some have highly influential Asian teachers as well. The Forest Sangha, Samatha Trust, SRM and FWBO have only Western teachers (though they have been influenced by Ajahn Chah, Nai Boonman, Keidō Chisan and Sangharakshita's teachers in India). Most SGI-UK teachers are also Western, though there are some Japanese local leaders, a Japanese vice general director and the highly influential figure of President Ikeda. Geshe Kelsang is the only remaining Tibetan in the NKT, although he is still regarded as the main spiritual guide, and all other teachers are Westerners. In the Karma Kagyu tradition, however, Western teachers are only gradually being recognized, and almost all senior teachers remain Tibetans.

Perhaps the most striking feature of British Buddhism – and of Western Buddhism as a whole – is the widespread and deepening involvement of lay people. As we have seen, only 2 per cent of the convert British Buddhist community is ordained, either as monks or nuns or as FWBO Order members, and both SGI-UK and the Samatha Trust are entirely lay organizations with their own leaders and teachers. The FWBO sees the distinction between monastics and lay people as irrelevant, with ordination reflecting deeper commitment rather than a change of lifestyle, and their centres, single-sex communities and Right Livelihood businesses provide a spiritual, social and economic context for members' lives.

New ways of involving lay people have also been devised in monastic traditions. Both the Karma Kagyu and NKT include small numbers of lay teachers, but their unique contribution here is the establishment of new Buddhist communities – notably at Samye Ling and Manjushri Centre – with a monastic core but a large majority of committed lay people, who are fully involved with the monks and nuns in communal life. While the Forest Sangha may appear conservative, the *upāsikā* movement and the liminal *anagārika* role provide new opportunities for lay people to develop their own practice, support the monastic *saṅgha* and prepare for ordination. The innovative roles of lay minister and postulant have a somewhat similar function in the SRM tradition, where lay people are encouraged to stay at Throssel Hole and considerable effort is put into supporting the lay community. Both the Theravāda and Zen monks also visit local lay groups regularly to support and encourage their practice.

These ten characteristics seem to be the most important 'family resemblances' or common features of British Buddhism. Each of them is wholly or partly present in at least five of the traditions, with largely traditional devotional activities, traditional teachings, course programmes, ancient and contemporary narratives and increased lay participation wholly or partly present in all seven. Each tradition has a different pattern here, and none shows all ten features in full – with no common ethical code in the Forest Sangha, no formal textual study in the SRM, mainly Tibetan rather than Western teachers in the Karma Kagyu tradition and so on.

These 'family resemblances' challenge the prevalent idea of a polarization between the more traditional organizations and the three large new Buddhist movements. The NKT, FWBO and SGI-UK have all joined the Network of Buddhist Organisations (NBO), but are still regarded with some suspicion, and each appears relatively isolated from other Buddhist movements. Their rapid growth through proselytizing, charismatic leadership and enthusiasm, their separation from their Asian roots and the new narratives developed to explain this separation, have all been used to emphasize the differences between them and traditional movements. However, the NKT and FWBO show almost as many of these ten common features as the Forest Sangha or Karma Kagyu and so could claim to be equally typical of British Buddhism. While still showing most of the features, SGI-UK appears as rather less typical, with no meditation or ethical code. As part of an international organization, it may reflect the position of SGI-USA, which stands apart from other traditions, as it 'fits awkwardly in the convert camp and follows its own unique developmental trajectory' (Seager, 2002: 113).

Returning to Wittgenstein's analogy, the traditions of Buddhism in Britain might be compared to family members who have lived in different countries for many years and now find themselves together in one place. This is not a family reunion, as most of them have rarely met before. Many will see their family resemblances immediately, while others struggle or even fail to recognize each other. One or two will claim that they alone have the true family characteristics or that a single characteristic – such as chanting or taking refuge – marks out the genuine Buddhist. The tendency to make this kind of exclusive claim may itself be a common feature of some Buddhist movements, though it is a family resemblance which other British Buddhists may wish not to recognize.

* * *

The experiential dimension seems to have no distinctive common feature which could be included here, mainly due to the wide variety of personal experience.

Ninian Smart concluded his *Dimensions of the Sacred* by underlining the ebb and flow of different aspects of spirituality: while the ritual dimension is no longer used to 'bend the powers of the world', the experiential dimension 'grows in importance as men and women search their inner lives for greater meaning' (Smart, 1996: 298). Wherever Buddhism spreads, its teaching and practice eventually combine with the local spiritual background – or the way local people search their inner lives – to produce something both ancient and new. How and when this might happen in Britain is still far from clear. No dominant British Buddhism has yet emerged, though there are many who would already call themselves British Buddhists. While they no longer recite the Psalms and do not live in the shadow of the Himālaya, they may still call upon the spirit of compassion and lift up their eyes to the hills.

BIBLIOGRAPHY

The bibliography is in three sections, listing first the authors of published works, then the titles of anonymous works, and finally the names of interviewees and personal correspondents.

Authors

Abhaya (1996) *Living the Skilful Life: An Introduction to Buddhist Ethics*, Birmingham: Windhorse Publications.

Akong Tulku Rinpoche (1994) *Taming the Tiger: Tibetan Teachings for Improving Daily Life*, London: Rider.

Allwright, Pat (1998) *Basics of Buddhism: Key Principles and How to Practise*, Taplow, Berkshire: Taplow Press.

Almond, Philip C. (1988) *The British Discovery of Buddhism*, Cambridge: Cambridge University Press.

Amaro, Ajahn (1994) 'The Four-Fold Assembly', *Forest Sangha Newsletter*, 28: 15–16.

—— (1999) 'The Open Day', *Forest Sangha Newsletter*, 50: 6.

Anando, Ajahn (1992) 'The First Bhikkhu Ordination at Chithurst', in Sumedho, Ajahn (ed.) (1992) *Cittaviveka: Teachings from the Silent Mind*, Great Gaddesden, Hertfordshire: Amaravati Publications (first published 1983).

Austin, Jack (1972) 'British Sangha', *Middle Way*, 47(2): 90–1.

Awakened Heart Sangha (2000) 'Discovering the Heart of Buddhism' (n.p.).

Barker, Eileen (1999) 'New Religious Movements: Their Incidence and Significance', in Wilson, Bryan and Cresswell, Jamie (eds) (1999) *New Religious Movements: Challenge and Response*, London: Routledge.

Barwick, Sandra (1988) 'Valley where Buddha is Laird', *Independent* (16 July): 13.

Batchelor, Stephen (1994) *The Awakening of the West: The Encounter of Buddhism and Western Culture*, London: Aquarian Press.

Baumann, Martin (1995) 'Creating a European Path to Nirvana: Historical and Contemporary Developments of Buddhism in Europe', *Journal of Contemporary Religion*, 10(1): 55–70.

—— (2000) 'Work as Dharma Practice: Right Livelihood Cooperatives of the FWBO', in Queen, Christopher S. (ed.) (2000) *Engaged Buddhism in the West*, Boston, MA: Wisdom Publications.

Baumann, Martin (2002) 'Buddhism in Europe: Past, Present, Prospects', in Prebish, Charles S. and Baumann, Martin (eds) (2002) *Westward Dharma: Buddhism Beyond Asia*, Berkeley, CA: University of California Press.

Belither, James (1997) *Modern Day Kadampas: The History and Development of the New Kadampa Tradition*, Ulverston: Conishead Priory.

Bell, Sandra (1991) 'Buddhism in Britain – Development and Adaptation', unpublished PhD thesis, University of Durham.

—— (2000) 'A Survey of Engaged Buddhism in Britain', in Queen, Christopher S. (ed.) (2000) *Engaged Buddhism in the West*, Boston, MA: Wisdom Publications.

Bishop, Peter (1993) *Dreams of Power: Tibetan Buddhism and the Western Imagination*, London: Athlone Press.

Blofield, John (1987) 'A Farewell Letter', *Middle Way*, 62(3): 151–5.

Bluck, Robert (2002) 'The Path of the Householder: Buddhist Lay Disciples in the Pali Canon', *Buddhist Studies Review*, 19(1): 1–18.

—— (2004) 'Buddhism and Ethnicity in Britain: The 2001 Census Data', *Journal of Global Buddhism* (www.globalbuddhism.org/5/bluck04.htm).

—— (2005) 'The Dimensions of Buddhism in Britain', unpublished PhD thesis, University of Sunderland.

Bocking, Brian (1994) 'Of Priests, Protests and Protestant Buddhists: The Case of Soka Gakkai International', in Clarke, Peter B. and Somers, Jeffrey (eds) (1994) *Japanese New Religions in the West*, Sandgate, Folkestone: Japan Library.

Boonman, Nai (2004) *From One to Nine* (n.p.).

Brandon, David (1976) *Zen in the Art of Helping*, London: Routledge.

Brear, Douglas (1975) 'Early Assumptions in Western Buddhist Studies', *Religion*, 5(2): 136–59.

Brown, Andrew (1996) 'Battle of the Buddhists', *Independent* (15 July): 2.

Buddhist Publishing Group (2003) 'Golden Buddha Centre' (n.p.).

Bunting, Madeleine (1996a) 'Smear campaign sparks safety fears over Dalai Lama's UK visit', *Guardian* (6 July): 1.

—— (1996b) 'Shadow boxing on the path to Nirvana', *Guardian* (6 July): 26.

—— (1996c) 'Sect disrobes British monk', *Guardian* (15 August): 9.

—— (1997) 'The Dark Side of Enlightenment', *Guardian* (27 October): 2.

Candasiri, Ajahn (1993) 'Seasoned in the Dhamma', *Forest Sangha Newsletter*, 23: 13–14.

Carmichael, Kay (1986) 'Tibet in Scotland', *New Society* (25 April): 14–15.

Causton, Richard (1995) *The Buddha in Daily Life: An Introduction to the Buddhism of Nichiren Daishonin*, London: Rider (first published as *Nichiren Shoshu Buddhism*, 1988).

Church, Alison M. (1982) 'Buddhist Groups in Britain', unpublished MA thesis, University of Manchester.

Clausen, Christopher (1975) 'Victorian Buddhism and the Origins of Comparative Religion', *Religion*, 5(1): 1–15.

Coleman, James William (2001) *The New Buddhism: The Western Transformation of an Ancient Tradition*, New York: Oxford University Press.

Cox, Basil (1978) 'Car Stickers', *Middle Way*, 53(2): 95.

Cresswell, Jamie (1994) 'The Dharma as Eternal Master', *Roots and Branches: Journal of the Network of Buddhist Organisations* (Autumn): 6–8.

Cush, Denise (1990) *Buddhists in Britain Today*, London: Hodder and Stoughton.

—— (1996) 'British Buddhism and the New Age', *Journal of Contemporary Religion*, 11(2): 195–208.

Davids, T.W. Rhys (1882) *Buddhism*, London: SPCK (first published 1877).

Davie, Grace (1994) *Religion in Britain since 1945: Believing without Belonging*, Oxford: Blackwell.

Denison, Paul (2001) 'History of the Samatha Trust', in *Phra Buddha Dhammacakra* (2001) Bankok: Phra Buddha Dhammacakra Creation Committee.

Denison, Simon (1989) 'Looking in on a World of Ordered Tranquillity', *Independent* (19 July): 19.

de Silva, Padmal (1993) 'Buddhism and Counselling', *British Journal of Guidance and Counselling*, 21(1): 30–4.

Eaton, R., G. Cien and A. Darvies (1975) 'An Appeal for Unity', *Middle Way*, 50(1): 42.

Eden, Philip (1997) 'The Temple at Amaravati', *Middle Way*, 71(4): 266–9.

—— (1999) 'Consecration of the Temple at Amaravati', *Middle Way*, 74(2): 67–8.

Ellis, Ieuan (1988) 'The Intellectual Challenge to "Official Religion" ', in Thomas, Terence (ed.) (1988) *The British: Their Religious Beliefs and Practices 1800–1986*, London: Routledge.

FWBO (1998) *The FWBO Files: A Response*, Birmingham: FWBO.

Gampopa, Jé (1995) *Gems of Dharma, Gems of Freedom* (trans. Ken and Katia Holmes), Forres, Scotland: Altea Publishing.

Goswell, Marilyn (1988) 'Motivational Factors in the Life of a Religious Community, and Related Changes in the Experience of Self', unpublished PhD thesis, University of Bath.

Green, Deirdre (1989) 'Buddhism in Britain: Skilful Means or Selling Out?', in Badham, Paul (ed.) (1989) *Religion, State and Society in Modern Britain*, Lampeter: Edwin Mellen Press.

Grimwood, Cordelia and Howes, Cliff (1983) 'Eastern Promise: The Social Worker, Client and Buddhist Ideas', *Social Work Today*, (13 September): 10–12.

Gross, Rita M. (1994) 'Buddhism', in Holm, Jean and Bowker, John (eds) (1994) *Women in Religion*, London: Pinter.

Guhyapati (1998) 'Family Matters', *Dharma Life*, 9: 60–1.

Hackney, Paul (1972) 'British Sangha', *Middle Way*, 46(4): 181–2.

Harris, Elizabeth (1997) 'Face to Faith: When East meets West', *Guardian* (15 November): 21.

Harris, Jose (1994) *Private Lives, Public Spirit: Britain 1870–1914*, London: Penguin.

Harvey, Peter (1990) *An Introduction to Buddhism: Teachings, History and Practices*, Cambridge: Cambridge University Press.

—— (2000) *An Introduction to Buddhist Ethics*, Cambridge: Cambridge University Press.

—— (n.d.) 'Introduction to Samatha Meditation' (n.p.).

—— (n.d.) 'The Thirty-two Marks of a Great Man' (n.p.).

Hodge, Stephen (1999) *Tibetan Buddhism*, London: Piatkus.

Hollenbeck, Rev. Oswin (2000) 'Conclave 2000: Continuing the Transmission', *Journal of the Order of Buddhist Contemplatives*, 15(5): 39–46.

Holmes, Ken (1982) 'A Garuda in the Glen: Fifteen Years of Kagyu Samye Ling', *Middle Way*, 57(2): 90–3.

—— (1989) 'Kagyu Samye Ling', *Middle Way*, 63(4): 219–23.

Holmes, Ken (1995) 'Foreword', in Gampopa, Jé (1995) *Gems of Dharma, Gems of Freedom* (trans. Ken and Katia Holmes), Forres, Scotland: Altea Publishing.

Humphreys, Christmas (1934) 'A Buddhist Funeral Service', *Buddhism in England*, 9(1): 19–21.

—— (1935) 'The Tenth Anniversary of the Buddhist Lodge, London', *Buddhism in England*, 9(5): 160–1.

—— (1943) 'The Price of Success of the Buddhist Society, London', *Middle Way*, 18(2): 28.

—— (1953) 'World Buddhism', *Middle Way*, 27(4): 113–16.

—— (1955) 'Our Thirtieth Anniversary Celebrations', *Middle Way*, 29(4): 171–6, 183.

—— (1956) 'Buddhism in the West', *Middle Way*, 31(1): 6–10.

—— (1958) 'Zen comes West', *Middle Way*, 32(4): 126–30.

—— (1964) 'Forty Years of Buddhism in England', *Middle Way*, 39(3): 97–9.

—— (1966) 'A Buddhist Conference in London', *Middle Way*, 41(2): 80–4.

—— (1968) *Sixty Years of Buddhism in Britain*, London: Buddhist Society.

Jamyang Buddhist Centre (2001) 'Venerable Denmo Locho Rinpoche' (n.p.).

Jones, Diana (1996) 'Upasika News', *Forest Sangha Newsletter*, 37: 14–15.

Kagyu Samye Ling (2004) *Course Programme* (n.p.).

Kappel, Joseph (1991) 'Another Going Forth', *Forest Sangha Newsletter*, 17: 4–5.

Kay, David N. (2004) *Tibetan and Zen Buddhism in Britain: Transplantation, Development and Adaptation*, London: RoutledgeCurzon.

Kelsang Gyatso, Geshe (1992) *Introduction to Buddhism*, London: Tharpa Publications.

—— (1997) *Heart Jewel: The Essential Practices of Kadampa Buddhism*, London: Tharpa Publications (first published 1991).

—— (2001) *Transform Your Life*, London: Tharpa Publications.

—— (2003) *The New Meditation Handbook*, Ulverston: Tharpa Publications.

Kennett, Rev. Master Jiyu (1973a) *Selling Water by the River: A Manual of Zen Training*, London: George Allen & Unwin.

—— (1973b) [untitled address] *Throssel Hole Priory Newsletter*, 1(1): 2–5.

—— (1977) *How to Grow a Lotus Blossom: or How a Zen Buddhist Prepares for Death*, Mount Shasta, CA: Shasta Abbey Press.

—— (1978a) 'On the Zen Teaching of So-called "Emptiness" ', *Journal of Throssel Hole Priory*, 5(6): 8–11.

—— (1978b) 'A Note from Rōshi Kennett', *Journal of Throssel Hole Priory*, 5(6): 20.

—— (1981) 'Do Women have the Buddha Nature?', in *Women in Buddhism* (n.p.).

—— (1983) 'Perfect Faith', *Journal of Throssel Hole Priory*, 10(4): 25–8.

—— (1986) 'The Great Heresies', *Journal of the Order of Buddhist Contemplatives*, 1(1): 2–9.

—— (1993) *How to Grow a Lotus Blossom: or How a Zen Buddhist Prepares for Death* (2nd ed.), Mount Shasta, CA: Shasta Abbey Press.

—— (1999) *Zen is Eternal Life* (4th ed.), Mount Shasta, CA: Shasta Abbey Press (first published as *Selling Water by the River*, 1973).

—— (2000) *Roar of the Tigress: The Oral Teachings of Rev. Master Jiyu-Kennett*, Mount Shasta, CA: Shasta Abbey Press.

—— (2002) *The Wild, White Goose: The Dairy of a Female Zen Priest* (2nd ed.), Mount Shasta, CA: Shasta Abbey Press (first published 1977–78 (2 vols)).

Kennett, Rev. Master Jiyu *et al.* (1996) *Serene Reflection Meditation* (6th ed.), Mount Shasta, CA: Shasta Abbey Press.

Keown, Damien (2003) *A Dictionary of Buddhism*, Oxford: Oxford University Press.

Khantipalo (2002) *Noble Friendship: Travels of a Buddhist Monk*, Birmingham: Windhorse Publications.

Kitigawa, Joseph M. and Strong, John S. (1985) 'Friedrich Max Müller and the comparative Study of Religion', in Smart *et al.* (eds) (1985) *Nineteenth Century Religious Thought in the West* (vol. 3), Cambridge: Cambridge University Press.

Kulananda (1992) 'Protestant Buddhism', *Religion*, 22: 101–7.

—— (1997a) 'The True Face of Buddhism', *Guardian* (29 October): 18.

—— (1997b) *Western Buddhism*, London: HarperCollins.

Levine, Norma (1993) 'The Incredible Monks', *Observer Magazine* (15 August): 32–3.

Lopez, Donald S. (1998) *Prisoners of Shangri-La: Tibetan Buddhism and the West*, Chicago: University of Chicago Press.

Loveard, Keith (1973) 'Tibetan Meditation Centre', *Middle Way*, 48(2): 88–9.

Macaulay, Sean (1986) 'Alice Goes to the Land of the Buddha', *The Times* (31 December): 11.

McNab, Usha *et al.* (1996) *The Suttanta on the Marks*, Llangunllo, Powys: Samatha Trust.

MacPhillamy, Rev Master Daizui (1978) 'A Note on Transmission and Priestly Rank', *Journal of Throssel Hole Priory* (July): 9–14.

—— (1997a) 'How the O.B.C. Works', *Journal of Throssel Hole Buddhist Abbey*, 24(1): 16–23.

—— (1997b) 'What Seems Important Now', *Journal of Throssel Hole Buddhist Abbey*, 24(2): 4–20.

—— (2000) 'Introduction', in Kennett, Rev. Master Jiyu (ed.) (2000) *Roar of the Tigress: The Oral Teachings of Rev. Master Jiyu-Kennett*, Mount Shasta, CA: Shasta Abbey Press.

—— (2001) 'The Eightfold Path', Order of Buddhist Contemplatives.

—— (2003) *Buddhism from Within*, Mount Shasta, CA: Shasta Abbey Press.

Marwick, Arthur (1996) *British Society since 1945* (3rd ed.), London: Penguin.

Medhina (1994) 'Dhamma School opens in Brighton', *Middle Way*, 69(3): 209.

Mellor, Philip A. (1989) 'The Cultural Translation of Buddhism: Problems of Theory and Method Arising in the Study of Buddhism in England', unpublished PhD thesis, University of Manchester.

—— (1991) 'Protestant Buddhism? The Cultural Translation of Buddhism in England', *Religion*, 21: 73–92.

Mitchison, Amanda (1988) 'Budding Buddhas', *New Society* (22 January): 8–9.

Morgan, Rev. Master Daishin (1983a) 'Choosing Your Way', *Journal of Throssel Hole Priory*, 10(1): 5–9.

—— (1983b) 'Why are Training and Enlightenment Differentiated since the Truth is Universal?', *Journal of Throssel Hole Priory*, 10(3): 3–8.

—— (1984) 'Respect', *Journal of Throssel Hole Priory*, 11(3–4): 4–10.

—— (1986) 'Avalokiteshwara Bodhisattva', *Journal of Throssel Hole Priory*, 13(3): 12–17.

—— (1991) 'The Lay Ministry', *Journal of Throssel Hole Priory*, 18(3): 24–7.

—— (1994a) 'Sōtō Zen Buddhism in Britain', in Clarke, Peter B. and Somers, Jeffrey (eds) (1994) *Japanese New Religions in the West*, Sandgate, Folkestone: Japan Library.

Morgan, Rev. Master Daishin (1994b) 'The Giving and Receiving of Dharma', *Root and Branches: Journal of the Network of Buddhist Organisations*, 1: 9–12.

—— (1996a) 'Physical Postures for Meditation', in Kennett, Rev. Master Jiyu *et al.* (eds) (1996) *Serene Reflection Meditation* (6th ed.), Mount Shasta, CA: Shasta Abbey Press.

—— (1996b) 'The Mind of Meditation', in Kennett, Rev. Master Jiyu *et al.* (1996) *Serene Reflection Meditation* (6th ed.), Mount Shasta, CA: Shasta Abbey Press.

—— (1997) 'The Precepts of the Buddhas', in *Receiving the Buddhist Precepts* (1997) Carrshield, Hexham: Throssel Hole Buddhist Abbey.

Nydahl, Ole and Aronoff, Carol (1989) *Practical Buddhism: The Kagyu Path*, Nevada City, CA: Blue Dolphin Publishing.

Oliver, Ian (1979) *Buddhism in Britain*, London: Rider.

Pamutto (1994) 'Lay Practice: Buddhism comes to Essex', *Forest Sangha Newsletter*, 30: 15–17.

Prebish, Charles S. and Baumann, Martin (eds) (2002) *Westward Dharma: Buddhism Beyond Asia*, Berkeley, CA: University of California Press.

Puttick, Elizabeth (1992) 'Why has Bodhidharma left for the West? The Growth and Appeal of Buddhism in Britain', *Religion Today*, 8(2): 5–10.

Queen, Christopher S. (ed.) (2000) *Engaged Buddhism in the West*, Boston, MA: Wisdom Publications.

Quirke, Thomas (1992) 'Zen and the Spiritual Heart of Scotland', *Times Saturday Review* (8 Feburary): 14–15.

Rahula, Walpola (1975) 'The Problem of the Prospect of the Sangha in the West', *Middle Way*, 49(4): 170–80.

Rawlinson, Andrew (1997) *The Book of Enlightened Masters: Western Teachers in Eastern Traditions*, Chicago, IL: Open Court.

Robins, M.H. (1961) ' "Precious Protector" ', *Middle Way*, 35(4): 125–6.

—— (1966) 'The Royal Opening of the Buddhapadipa Vihara at East Sheen', *Middle Way*, 41(3): 132.

Rowlands, Mark (ed.) (1982) *Abhidhamma Papers*, Manchester: Samatha Trust.

Samatha Association (n.d.) *Chanting Book*, Llangunllo, Powys: Samatha Trust.

Sangharakshita (1959) 'Ordination and Initiation in the Three Yānas', *Middle Way*, 34(3): 94–104.

—— (1965a) 'Sangha and laity', *The Buddhist*, 9(2): 29–30.

—— (1965b) 'Buddhism in England', *The Buddhist*, 9(6): 141–3.

—— (1967) *The Three Jewels: An Introduction to Buddhism*, London: Rider.

—— (1984) *The Ten Pillars of Buddhism*, Glasgow: Windhorse.

—— (1985) *The Eternal Legacy: An Introduction to the Canonical Literature of Buddhism*, London: Tharpa Publications.

—— (1988a) *The History of My Going for Refuge*, Glasgow: Windhorse.

—— (1988b) *The Religion of Art*, Glasgow: Windhorse.

—— (1990a) *New Currents in Western Buddhism: The Inner Meaning of the Friends of the Western Buddhist Order*, Glasgow: Windhorse.

—— (1990b) *My Relation to the Order*, Glasgow: Windhorse.

—— (1992a) *The FWBO and 'Protestant Buddhism': An Affirmation and a Protest*, Glasgow: Windhorse.

—— (1992b) *Buddhism and the West: The Integration of Buddhism into Western Society*, Glasgow: Windhorse.

—— (1993) *Forty-Three Years Ago: Reflections on my Bhikkhu Ordination*, Glasgow: Windhorse.
—— (1996a) *Extending the Hand of Fellowship: The Relation of the Western Buddhist Order to the Rest of the Buddhist World*, Birmingham: Windhorse.
—— (1996b) *Buddhism for Today – and Tomorrow*, Birmingham: Windhorse.
—— (1999) 'Wisdom Within Words', *Dharma Life*, 10: 28–32.
Sayers, Elizabeth (1981) 'The Barking Buddhists', *Middle Way*, 56(3): 139–42.
Schomberg, Rev. Kōshin (1997) 'Rev. Master Jiyu-Kennett's Liturgical Legacy', *Journal of the Order of Buddhist Contemplatives*, 11(4): 113–16.
Scott, David (1995) 'Modern British Buddhism: Patterns and Directions' (Seminar Paper for the Buddhist Forum), London: School of Oriental and African Studies.
Seager, Richard (2002) 'American Buddhism in the Making', in Prebish, Charles S. and Baumann, Martin (eds) (2002) *Westward Dharma: Buddhism Beyond Asia*, Berkeley, CA: University of California Press.
SGI (1996) *Sōka Gakkai International*, Tokyo: SGI.
SGI-UK (1993) *The Art of Living: An Introduction to the Buddhism of Nichiren Daishonin*, Taplow, Berkshire: SGI-UK.
SGI-UK (n.d.) *Introducing SGI-UK*, Taplow, Berkshire: SGI-UK.
Sharkey, Alex (1998) 'The Lamas of Lambeth', *Weekend Guardian* (25 July): 30.
Sharp, George (1984) 'The English Sangha Trust', *Middle Way*, 59(2): 100–1.
—— (1999) 'A Personal View', *Forest Sangha Newsletter*, 50: 7.
Shaw, Sarah (1991) 'The Samatha Trust', *Middle Way*, 66(1): 58.
Shukman, Henry (1999) 'Friends of the Western Buddhist Order: Friends, Foes and Files', *Tricycle*, 8(4): 66–8, 112–18.
Side, Dominique (1996) 'An Interview with Ajahn Sumedho', *View*, 5: 4–9.
Smart, Ninian (1996) *Dimensions of the Sacred: An Anatomy of the World's Beliefs*, London: HarperCollins.
—— (1997) *Reflections in the Mirror of Religion*, London: Macmillan.
Snelling, John (1987) *The Buddhist Handbook*, London: Century Hutchinson.
Sogyal Rinpoche (1979) 'Tibetan Buddhism for the West', *Middle Way*, 53(4): 197–8, 200.
Stevens, Rev. Teigan (1980) 'Training in the World', *Journal of the Throssel Hole Priory*, 7(7–9): 2–6.
Stevenson, John (1984) *British Society 1914–45*. London: Penguin.
Subhuti (1985) *An Old Net for New Monsters*, Glasgow: Windhorse.
—— (1986) 'Heirs of the Dharma', *Golden Drum*, 2: 3.
—— (1988) *Buddhism for Today: A Portrait of a New Buddhist Movement*, Glasgow: Windhorse (first published in 1983).
—— (1994) *Sangharakshita: A New Voice in the Buddhist Tradition*, Birmingham: Windhorse.
—— (1995a) *Bringing Buddhism to the West: A Life of Sangharakshita*, Birmingham: Windhorse.
—— (1995b) *Women, Men and Angels*, Birmingham: Windhorse.
—— (2000) 'Marriage in the Western Buddhist Order', *Madhyamaka*, 3: 6–17.
Sucitto, Ajahn (1991) 'Introduction', in Sumedho, Ajahn (ed.) (1991) *The Way It Is*, Great Gaddesden, Hertfordshire: Amaravati Publications.
—— (1992a) 'How the Buddha Came to Sussex', in Sumedho, Ajahn (ed.) (1992) *Cittaviveka: Teachings from the Silent Mind*, Great Gaddesden, Hertfordshire: Amaravati Publications (first published 1983).

Sucitto, Ajahn (1992b) 'Introduction', in Sumedho, Ajahn (ed.) (1992) *Cittaviveka: Teachings from the Silent Mind*, Great Gaddesden, Hertfordshire: Amaravati Publications (first published 1983).

—— (1994) 'Obituary: Greg Klein (Ajahn Anando)', *Forest Sangha Newsletter*, 29: 8–9.

—— (1995) 'Jugglers Wanted', *Forest Sangha Newsletter*, 31: 3.

—— (1996) 'Editor's Introduction', in Sumedho, Ajahn (ed.) (1996) *The Mind and the Way: Buddhist Reflections on Life*, London: Rider.

—— (1998a) *Buddhist Meditation: The Foundations*, Great Gaddesden, Hertfordshire: Amaravati Publications.

—— (1998b) 'Editorial: The Four-fold Assembly', *Forest Sangha Newsletter*, 43: 3–4.

—— (2005) 'Meditation Hall', *Resurgence*, 230: 34–5.

Sumedho, Ajahn (1991) *The Way It Is*, Great Gaddesden, Hertfordshire: Amaravati Publications.

—— (1992a) *Cittaviveka: Teachings from the Silent Mind*, Great Gaddesden, Hertfordshire: Amaravati Publications (first published 1983).

—— (1992b) *The Four Noble Truths*. Great Gaddesden, Hertfordshire: Amaravati Publications.

—— (1995) 'A Temple Arises', *Forest Sangha Newsletter*, 33: 1–3.

—— (1996) *The Mind and the Way: Buddhist Reflections on Life*, London: Rider.

Sutcliffe, Sylvia and Sutcliffe, Barry (1995) *Committed to Buddhism: A Buddhist Community*, Norwich: Religious and Moral Education Press.

Thomas, Terence (ed.) (1988) *The British: Their Religious Beliefs and Practices 1800–1986*, London: Routledge.

Tiradhammo Bhikkhu (1985) 'The Practice of the Vinaya Discipline', *Middle Way*, 60(1): 11–15.

Titmuss, Christopher (1999) *The Power of Meditation*, London: Apple Press.

Trungpa, Chögyam (1987) *Cutting Through Spiritual Materialism*, Boston, MA: Shambala (first published 1973).

—— (1996) *Meditation in Action*, Boston, MA: Shambala (first published 1969).

Tweed, Thomas A. (1999) 'Night-Stand Buddhists and Other Creatures: Sympathizers, Adherents, and the Study of Religion', in Williams, D.R. and Queen, C.S. (eds) (1999) *American Buddhism: Methods and Findings in Recent Scholarship*, Richmond, Surrey: Curzon Press.

Vajraketu (1997) 'Marketing Values', *Dharma Life*, 6: 24–7.

Viradhammo, Ajahn (1996) 'Amaravati', *Forest Sangha Newsletter*, 38: 16–17.

Vishvapani (1997) 'Face to Faith: Buddhism Distorted', *Guardian* (8 November): 21.

Walshe, Maurice (1963) 'Inauguration of the Hampstead Buddhist Vihara', *Middle Way*, 37(4): 172.

—— (1967) 'Annual General Meeting of the Buddhist Sangha Association' *The Buddhist*, 11(2): 8–13.

—— (1978) 'An English Sangha' *Middle Way*, 53(3): 167–8.

—— (1979) 'Hampstead Buddhist Vihara Closes', *Middle Way*, 54(2): 135.

—— (1992) 'Morality in Buddhism', *Middle Way*, 66(4): 254–5.

Waterhouse, Helen (1997) *Buddhism in Bath: Adaptation and Authority*, Leeds: Community Religions Project Monograph Series, University of Leeds.

—— (2001) 'Representing Western Buddhism: A United Kingdom Focus', in Beckerlegge, Gwilym (ed.) (2001) *From Sacred Text to Internet*, Aldershot: Ashgate.

Watson, Burton (1993) *The Lotus Sutra*, New York: Columbia University Press.

Wheeler, Roger (1984a) 'Achaan Sumedho Interviewed', *Middle Way*, 59(1): 39–44.
—— (1984b) 'Achaan Sumedho Interviewed', *Middle Way*, 59(2): 81–3.
—— (1985) 'Achaan Sumedho Interviewed', *Middle Way*, 59(4): 237–43.
Wigmore, Nigel (1985) 'Eavesdropping on Another World', *Guardian* (15 May): 10.
Williams, Paul (1989) *Mahāyāna Buddhism: The Doctrinal Foundations*, London: Routledge.
—— (1996) 'Dorje Shugden', *Middle Way*, 71(2): 130–2.
Wilson, Bryan (2000) 'The British Movement and its Members', in Machacek, David and Wilson, Bryan (eds) (2000) *Global Citizens: The Sōka Gakkai Movement in the World*, Oxford: Oxford University Press.
Wilson, Bryan and Cresswell, Jamie (eds) (1999) *New Religious Movements: Challenge and Response*, London: Routledge.
Wilson, Bryan and Dobbelaere, Karl (1994) *A Time to Chant: The Sōka Gakkai Buddhists in Britain*, Oxford: Clarendon Press.
Wittgenstein, Ludwig (1967) *Philosophical Investigations* (3rd ed.), Oxford: Blackwell (first published in 1953).
Yeshe Losal, Lama (1997) 'The Refuge Tree', *Middle Way*, 72(3): 167–70.
—— (1998) 'The Refuge Tree', *Middle Way*, 72(4): 231–3.
—— (2001) *Living Dharma*, Eskdalemuir: Dzalendara Publishing.
—— (n.d.) 'The Five Golden Rules' in 'Kagyu Samye Ling' (n.p).

Other works

25 Years of Samye' Ling: a Celebration (1993) Eskdalemuir: Samye Ling Tibetan Centre.
Abhidhamma Adventures (1996) Llangunllo, Powys: Samatha Trust.
'Amaravati Sangha News' (1988) *Middle Way*, 63(3): 172–4.
'Amaravati Sangha News' (1992) *Middle Way*, 67(3): 188–90.
'Amaravati Sangha Newsletter' (1988) *Middle Way*, 62(4): 279–80.
'Announcement' (1983) *Journal of Throssel Hole Priory*, 10(1): 4.
'The Buddha comes to Sussex' (1979) *Everyman*, BBC1 (7 October).
'Buddha Day at Amaravati' (1986) *Middle Way*, 61(2): 121–3.
'Buddhism: The New Kadampa Tradition' (n.d.).
'Buddhism, Sex and the Spiritual Life' (1987) *Golden Drum*, 6: 4–14.
'Buddhism in Birmingham' (1972) *Middle Way*, 47(2): 88–9.
'Buddhism in Britain: Conference Report' (1987) *Middle Way*, 62(3): 183–6.
'Buddhism in the West' (1937) *Buddhism in England*, 12(2): 33.
Buddhist Directory (1981) (2nd ed.) London: Buddhist Society.
Buddhist Directory (1991) (5th ed.) London: Buddhist Society.
Buddhist Directory (1994) (6th ed.) London: Buddhist Society.
Buddhist Directory (1997) R.B. Parsons (ed.) (7th ed.) London: Buddhist Society.
Buddhist Directory (2000) R.B. Parsons (ed.) (8th ed.) London: Buddhist Society.
Buddhist Directory (2003) Martin Murray and R.B. Parsons (eds) (9th ed.) London: Buddhist Society.
Buddhist Meditation (n.d.) Llangunllo, Powys: Samatha Trust.
'Buddhist News' (1961) *Middle Way*, 36(3): 130.
'Buddhists and their teaching come to tiny Chithurst' (1979) *East Hampshire Post* (19 July): 24.
'The Buddhist Society, London, and its New Headquarters' (1943) *Middle Way*, 18(2): 25.

Buddhist Writings on Meditation and Daily Practice (1998) (trans. Rev. Hubert Nearman), Mount Shasta, CA: Shasta Abbey Press.

Bylaws of the Order of Buddhist Contemplatives (2002) (n.p.).

Chanting Book (1994) Great Gaddesden, Hertfordshire: Amaravati Publications.

'Chenrezig Prayers' (1979) Eskdalemuir: Kagyu Samye Ling.

'Chithurst' (1989) *Middle Way*, 64(3): 187–8.

'Chithurst Newsletter' (1982) *Middle Way*, 56(4): 199–200.

'Chithurst Newsletter' (1983a) *Middle Way*, 57(4): 222–3.

'Chithurst Newsletter' (1983b) *Middle Way*, 58(2): 125–6.

'Chithurst Newsletter' (1983c) *Middle Way*, 58(3): 182–4.

'Combining Technology and Nature on Holy Island' (1996) *Architects' Journal* (18 April): 32–8.

'The Conferring of the Charter of Throssel Hole Buddhist Abbey' (1997) *Journal of Throssel Hole Buddhist Abbey*, 24(1): 12–14.

Directory of Kadampa Buddhist Centres and Branches (2003) (n.p.).

Discipline and Conventions of Theravada Buddhist Renunciate Communities: A Guide for the Western Sangha (n.d.). Belsay, Northumberland: River Publications.

'Disclaimer' (1979) *Journal of Throssel Hole Priory*, 6(1–3): 15–16.

'Edinburgh' (1990) *Middle Way*, 65(2): 123.

'Editorial' (1928) *Buddhism in England*, 3(3): 50.

'Editorial' (1983) *Middle Way*, 58(3): 141–2.

'Editorial' (1987) *Middle Way*, 62(2): 77–9.

'Editorial' (1989) *Forest Sangha Newsletter*, 7: 7.

'Empowerment' (1992) *Full Moon*, 5: 2.

'The False and the True' (1940) *Buddhism in England*, 14(6): 149.

'Friends of the Western Buddhist Order' (1980) *Middle Way*, 55(3): 145.

'Friends of the Western Buddhist Order' (1997) *Middle Way*, 72(1): 61–2.

'From the Nuns' Community' (1998) *Forest Sangha Newsletter*, 43: 17–18.

'FWBO' (1987) *Middle Way*, 62(2): 144.

The FWBO Files (1998) (www.ex-cult.org/fwbo/fwbofiles).

FWBO Puja Book (1995) Birmingham: Windhorse.

'FWBO Report' (1992) *Middle Way*, 67(1): 66–7.

'FWBO Report' (1993) *Middle Way*, 68(2): 114.

'FWBO Report' (1996) *Middle Way*, 71(3): 206.

'Groups Weekend: Nov 23–25 1990' (1991) *Journal of Throssel Hole Priory*, 18(1): 24–9.

A Handbook of Devas (n.d.) Llangunllo, Powys: Samatha Trust.

'A Healthy Constitution' (1992) *Full Moon*, 7: 36.

'Heruka Buddhist Centre' (1991) *Middle Way*, 66(3): 184.

'His Holiness Penor Rinpoche' (2003) London: Palyul Centre.

'Jamyang Meditation Centre' (1990) *Middle Way*, 65(3): 179.

'Jamyang Meditation Centre' (1994) *Middle Way*, 69(1): 53–4.

'Jamyang Meditation Centre' (1996) *Middle Way*, 71(1): 69–71.

'Kagyu Ling' (1976) *Middle Way*, 50(4): 192.

'Karma Kagyu Samye–Ling Tibetan Centre' (1979) *Middle Way*, 53(4): 236–7.

'Lama Zopa Rinpoche' (1995) *Middle Way*, 70(1): 24.

'Learning to Meditate' (n.d.) London: Budacom.

The Liturgy of the Order of Buddhist Contemplatives for the Laity (1990) (2nd ed.) Mount Shasta, CA: Shasta Abbey Press.

'London Buddhist Centre' (2001).

'Manjushri Institute' (1978) *Middle Way*, 53(3): 171.

'Manjushri Institute' (1986) *Middle Way*, 61(3): 207–8.

'Manjushri Institute' (1987) *Middle Way*, 62(2): 134.

'Manjushri Institute' (1988) *Middle Way*, 63(3): 182–3.

'Meditation: Its Place in Western Buddhism' (1965) *Middle Way*, 40(3): 97.

'Method and Inspiration' (1996) *Samatha*, 2: 11–12.

'The Network of Buddhist Organisations (UK)' (1994) *Journal of Throssel Hole Priory*, 21(2): 34–5.

'The New Meditation Hall' (1988) *Journal of Throssel Hole Priory*, 15(2): 30–4.

'News from the Dechen Community' (1996) *Middle Way*, 71(2): 138–9.

'Nichiren Shoshu' (1987) *Middle Way*, 62(1): 70.

'On Becoming a Buddhist' (1929) *Buddhism in England*, 4(3): 50.

One Year After: Reflections on a Meditation Week (1972) (n.p.).

Opening the Doors to the Deathless (1999) Great Gaddesden, Hertfordshire: Amaravati Publications.

'Over the Moon' (1992) *Full Moon*, 7: 46.

Oxford English Dictionary (1989) (2nd ed.) Oxford: Clarendon Press.

'Padmaloka Notebook' (1986) *Golden Drum*, 2: 26.

'Practice' (2002) *Samatha*, 8: 9–18.

'Priory News' (1979) *Journal of Throssel Hole Priory*, 6(11–12): 18–20.

Religions in the UK (1993) Paul Welter (ed.) Derby: University of Derby.

Religions in the UK (1997) Paul Welter (ed.) (2nd ed.) Derby: University of Derby.

Religions in the UK (2001) Paul Weller (ed.) (3rd ed.) Derby: University of Derby.

'Roman Catholic anti-Buddhism Propaganda' (1928) *Buddhism in England*, 3(5): 115–17.

Roots and Branches: Journal of the Network of Buddhist Organisations (1994) (Autumn).

Rules of the Order of Buddhist Contemplatives (2000) (n.p.).

'Sakya Thinley Rinchen Ling' (1989) *Middle Way*, 64(3): 189–90.

'The Samatha Trust' (1991) *Middle Way*, 65(4): 263.

'The Sangha in the West' (1944) *Middle Way*, 18(6): 123.

'The Sixty-two Centres of the NKT Mandala' (1992) *Full Moon*, 7: 42–5.

'The Size of the Society' (1983) *Middle Way*, 58(1): 54–5.

'Soto Zen Meditation Groups' (1974) *Throssel Hole Priory Newsletter*, 1(4): 5.

'Staying at Amaravati: Information for Guests' (n.d.) Amaravati Buddhist Monastery.

'Sukhavati is . . .' (1978) *Middle Way*, 53(3): 148–9.

Thirty-Two Marks: The Search (1995) Llangunllo, Powys: Samatha Trust.

'Throssel Hole Priory: 1972–1992' (1992) *Journal of Throssel Hole Priory*, 19(3): 17–19.

'To Our Readers' (1983) *Journal of Throssel Hole Priory*, 10(2): 2–3.

The Universal Monarch (1987) Llangunllo, Powys: Samatha Trust.

'The Upasika Training' (1997) (n.p.).

'The Ven. Sthavira Sangharakshita: A Statement' (1967) *The Buddhist*, 11(2): 13.

The Vows and Commitments of Kadampa Buddhism (2002) Ulverston: Tharpa Publications.

'Weekend Meditation Retreats' (2003) (NKT publicity leaflet).

'Wesak Celebration' (1984) *Middle Way*, 59(4): 54.

'Working Visits at Manjushri Buddhist Centre' (n.d.) (NKT publicity leaflet).

www.ex-cult.org/fwbo/fwbofiles [FWBO Files website].

www.forestsangha.org [Forest Sangha website].

www.fwbo.org.uk [FWBO website].
www.interbeing.org.uk [Community of Interbeing website]
www.manjushri.org.uk [Manjushri Mahayana Buddhist Centre website].
www.OBCon.org [OBC website].
www.quaker.org.uk [Society of Friends website]
www.samatha.org. [Samatha Trust website]
www.samye.org.uk [Samye Ling website].
www.sgi.org [Sōka Gakkai International website].
www.statistics.gov.uk/census2001 [UK 2001 Census data website].
'Zen Ordination at Chithurst' (1984) *Middle Way*, 59(3): 195.

Interviews and personal communications

Ariyasilo, Ajahn (2002) Interview with Robert Bluck, Amaravati Monastery.
Belither, James (2004) Interview with Robert Bluck, Manjushri Buddhist Centre.
Candasiri, Ajahn (2002) Interview with Robert Bluck, Amaravati Monastery.
Cresswell, Jamie (2004) Personal communication.
Curry, Julia (2004) Interview with Robert Bluck, via email.
Dechi, Ani (2002) Interview with Robert Bluck, Samye Ling.
Dharmaghosha (2002) Interview with Robert Bluck, Newcastle Buddhist Centre.
Duff, David (2002) Interview with Robert Bluck, Taplow Court.
Harvey, Peter (2003) Interview with Robert Bluck, Durham.
—— (2004) Personal communication.
Hunter, Anne (2002) Interview with Robert Bluck, Taplow Court.
Jenkins, Sue (2004) Interview with Robert Bluck, Manjushri Buddhist Centre.
Jutindharo, Ajahn (2002) Interview with Robert Bluck Amaravati Monastery.
Kunzang, Gelongma (2002) Interview with Robert Bluck, Samye Ling.
Lamzang, Karma (2002) Interview with Robert Bluck, Samye Ling.
McGowan, Rev. Master Raymond (2004) Interview with Robert Bluck, Throssel Hole.
McKenzie, Annick (2002) Interview with Robert Bluck, Taplow Court.
Morgan, Rev. Master Daishin (2004) Interview with Robert Bluck, Throssel Hole.
Namgyal, Kelsang (2004) Interview with Robert Bluck, Manjushri Buddhist Centre.
Pagpa, Kelsang (2004) Interview with Robert Bluck, Manjushri Buddhist Centre.
Prasad, Kadam Ganesh (2004) Interview with Robert Bluck, Compassion Buddhist Centre, Newcastle.
Punnyo, Ven (2001) Interview with Robert Bluck, Harnham Monastery.
Rose, Ian (2004) Interview with Robert Bluck, by telephone.
Samuels, Robert (2002) Interview with Robert Bluck, Taplow Court.
Sanghadevi (2002) Interview with Robert Bluck, Madhyamaloka Centre.
Sawhney, Sharmila (2002) Interview with Robert Bluck, Taplow Court.
Shanks, John (2002) Interview with Robert Bluck, Samye Ling.
Stanier, Pamela (2003) Interview with Robert Bluck, by email.
Sumedho, Ajahn (2002) Interview with Robert Bluck, Leicester Buddhist Summer School.
Suvaco, Ven (2002) Interview with Robert Bluck, Amaravati Monastery.
Vajragupta (2002) Interview with Robert Bluck, Madhyamaloka Centre.
Vipassi, Ajahn (2000) Personal communication.
Vishvapani (2002) Interview with Robert Bluck, Madhyamaloka Centre.

—— (2004) Personal communication.

Voiels, Veronica (2003) Interview with Robert Bluck, Manchester Samatha Centre.

Watson, Rev. Berwyn (2004) Interview with Robert Bluck, Throssel Hole.

Whitmore, Indra (2002) Interview with Robert Bluck, Taplow Court.

Yeshe Losal, Lama (2004) Interview with Robert Bluck, Samye Ling.

INDEX